ALSO BY EDWARD COUNTRYMAN

A People in Revolution: The American Revolution and
Political Society in New York, 1760–1790

Americans: A Collision of Histories

Shane (with Evonne von Heussen–Countryman)

The Empire State (coauthor)

How Did American Slavery Begin? (editor)

What Did the Constitution Mean to Early Americans? (editor)

The American Revolution

The
AMERICAN
REVOLUTION

Revised Edition

———◆◆◆———

Edward Countryman

ᵼ HILL AND WANG

A division of Farrar, Straus and Giroux

New York

Hill and Wang
A division of Farrar, Straus and Giroux
18 West 18th Street, New York 10011

Library of Congress Control Number: 2002111966
ISBN-13: 978-0-8090-2562-6
ISBN-10: 0-8090-2562-0

Designed by Jonathan D. Lippincott

www.fsgbooks.com

7   9   11   13   14   12   10   8

Still
for Alfred Young
with admiration and with thanks
that go beyond writing history

Contents

Acknowledgments to
the Revised Edition

I owe the contents of both versions of this book to the many historians who have demonstrated how large and transforming an event the American Revolution was. The first edition thanks the people who influenced my thinking as of 1985. The changes in the revised edition are directly in response to criticisms from Michael McGiffert, Fredrika Teute, Robert Gross, James Axtell, and the members of a demanding colloquium at the Institute of Early American History and Culture in 1994. I also am in debt to Michael Zuckerman, Philip Deloria, and Sylvia Frey for comments on the final version of the revised argument, as I presented it at an Institute of Early American History and Culture conference in 1995. In larger terms I owe a great deal to David Weber and the Western historians I have gotten to know through being his colleague. I owe many thanks to my other colleagues at Southern Methodist University, particularly to Kenneth Hamilton, Thomas J. Knock, and John Mears. Imaginary and real maps figure strongly in my thinking, and I cannot look now at a map of colonial and revolutionary America without being reminded of all those historians' influence. My debt to Alfred Young remains enormous.

When I met Evonne von Heussen–Countryman my knowledge of her fields (psychology and medicine) and hers of mine were equally minimal. Her eagerness then to learn about what I did led to many questions about the American Revolution while we were walking on the South Devon Coast Path. She still knows far more than I do about matters of the human mind and body. Like Sam Countryman, whose questions I acknowledged in the first edition, she played a major role in my launching this book. She played an even larger one in my revising it.

Acknowledgments to the First Edition

I could not have written this book by myself. My greatest debt is to the community of historians who have explored the Revolution during the past two decades. I have borrowed from almost all of them, and I hope I have not done violence to their work. Writing under the aegis of Arthur Wang and Eric Foner has been a pleasure. I am grateful to them for inviting me to do the book and for endless good advice, from first plans to final draft. I tried out my earliest sketch on friends scattered across America and Europe, and I appreciate the time and the effort they took in their replies. Among them are Hugh Bell, William Dusinberre, Richard Gildrie, Robert Gross, George Kirsch, Bruce Laurie, Callum MacDonald, Mary Beth Norton, and Mary Ryan. The book bears the marks of a summer of research at the American Antiquarian Society, and I want to acknowledge the award of a Samuel Foster Haven Fellowship that made the trip possible. The University of Warwick gave me a term off to write. A pamphlet-length version of my argument appeared in 1983 under the title *The People's American Revolution* in the series published by the British Association for American Studies. Donald Ratcliffe, who edited the pamphlet, may recognize his influence here as well.

Evonne von Heussen has been marvelously supportive

throughout the project. So have her sparkling daughters, Karon and Kirstein. In a way, Sam Countryman got the book started, by asking his father to tell him about the Revolution while we were hiking in New Hampshire. Since the beginning, all four have reminded me that books are not the same as life.

E.C.

Preface

Two decades ago publisher Arthur W. Wang and editor Eric Foner invited me to write *The American Revolution*. At the time, my goal was to write a synthesis of current scholarship on the Revolution and argue that the events of American independence were as much about internal conflict and change as about independence from Britain. Nobody was arguing seriously in 1983 that the Revolution merely separated the "political bonds" that had connected "one people" to "another," while leaving that people unchanged. There were wide, deep gulfs between the American colonies and the American Republic.

Even at best, explaining an event that occurred centuries ago is an exercise in weaving roughly. Any historian must approach a subject in a spirit of humility, aware that something will be missed, inevitably. Important figures like George Washington or the Mohawk leader and British officer Thayendanegea (Joseph Brant), who left mountains of evidence, still can surprise us. When we turn to an historical episode that involved intense pain, creative debate, decades of tumult, and millions of people, an "ultimate" or "definitive" explanation is impossible.

Nonetheless, there seemed no doubt that the American Revolution was revolutionary. It belongs within a general category that includes the English Revolution of the 1640s, the French

and Haitian revolutions of the 1790s, and twentieth-century revolutions in places as diverse as China, Mexico, Russia, and Iran.
The main issue for debate about the American events was what
counted most for fundamental understanding. Was it the ways
that the revolutionary era's different kinds of people experienced
change and conflicted with one another, a position that historians of the American Revolution have called "neo-progressive"?
That stance harks back to the work of Carl Becker, who suggested in 1909 that the Revolution was a struggle among white
colonials over "who should rule at home," to Charles A. Beard,
who ventured an "economic interpretation" of the Constitution
in 1915, and to J. Franklin Jameson, who saw the Revolution as a
"social movement." In recent years this neo-progressive position
has been most strongly identified with Alfred F. Young and Gary
B. Nash, but it has broadened to include feminist and race-
aware perspectives. Most recently of all, such historians as Saul
Cornell, Woody Holton, and Marjoleine Kars have revived it.
Or was the central problem how an emergent people created
the United States around a shared, if contentious, political
language, a position historians have called "neo-Whig"? The
nineteenth-century historian George Bancroft saw it that way,
and in modern times the point has been developed by Bernard
Bailyn, Edmund S. Morgan, J.G.A. Pocock, and Gordon S.
Wood, among others.

   In fact, posing the question in any either/or way ignores the
complexity and the irrationality of much human action. Hope,
unspoken desire, identity, belonging, emulation, memory, fear,
anger, resentment, envy: all of these emotions and more can
bear on a difficult choice. Counting up assets to determine
somebody's relative wealth, looking for how the person identified with one group or another, or finding echoes of the books a
person had read in what s/he wrote only begins the task of understanding what motivated the person to do something, particularly in an extraordinary time.

   When *The American Revolution* was published in 1985, I was

in a very opportune position. The debate was losing steam. If the contentious questions were not resolved, the debaters, at least, were exhausted. For two decades monographs, journal articles, and collections of essays about one new topic or another had poured forth. The flow virtually stopped in the mid-1980s, and writers turned their attention elsewhere. During the late 1980s and early 1990s the *William and Mary Quarterly*, which is the premier journal for early American specialists, published hardly any fresh research on the Revolution. Early in the next decade, however, discussion resumed anew, as two of the foremost historians showed.

One is Gordon S. Wood. His *The Creation of the American Republic, 1776–1787*, published in 1969, showed how an English-derived "Whig science of politics" yielded, after years of impassioned discussion that turned on both large ideas and personal interests, to a native-grown "American science of politics." In 1993 Wood brought out *The Radicalism of the American Revolution*, which expanded the theme of transformation. He broadened his time frame, beginning the book in the mid-eighteenth century and ending it in the age of Andrew Jackson. He also broadened his organizing concepts, starting with monarchy, turning to republicanism, and finishing with democracy. For him, the large story of the Revolution was how the first had yielded to the second, and the second to the last.

In the same year Alfred F. Young assembled an anthology of original essays, following on his earlier collection, *The American Revolution: Explorations in the History of American Radicalism* (1976). The earlier book had been the central text for the idea that experience and conflict, rather than values and agreement, counted most during the destruction of British rule and the emergence of the republic. Now the subject had changed: Like Wood, Young's contributors were interested in the Revolution's larger consequences. The new book was titled *Beyond the American Revolution*.

Other issues also were opening up for new debate. One was

the role of Great Britain. I asserted in 1985 that without the administrative and fiscal policy changes that Britain began to institute in 1763, there might have been discontent in the colonies,
but there would have been no Revolution, no independence, no
republic as we know it. Britain fought a long, expensive, difficult, and ultimately futile war to prevent the Revolution from
succeeding. Losing was a profound humiliation. Still, for some
historians, including me, it had seemed possible to tell the story
of the Revolution in terms of events and developments only
within America itself.

That needs correcting. One reason is the problem of identity.
Almost until independence, white colonials' quarrel with the
British government turned on being British while dwelling outside the "realm" of England, Scotland, and Wales. The problem
of belonging to Britain did not affect just them. Black people
were enslaved in the colonies because of a commerce in human
beings and in plantation goods that the British government fos-
tered. That commerce had brought prosperity to Bristol and Liverpool, and to New York and Newport. It paid for fashionable
town houses both in London and Charles Town and for country
houses both in Gloucestershire and along the Potomac. Most
Indians east of the Mississippi understood that their own survival depended at least partly on their relations with London
rather than with New York, Philadelphia, or Williamsburg alone.
The British connection was everywhere, and an account of the
Revolution that more or less ignored it was inadequate.

Not surprisingly, writers picked up on that problem. Historian Marc Egnal divided the male colonial elite into two groups.
One group, the "expansionists," had a westward-facing continental vision and were the emergent patriot leaders. The other
group looked eastward, toward Britain, and most would become
either tepid patriots or outright loyalists. Writer Theodore
Draper, who has studied many revolutions, asked in his book *A
Struggle for Power* whether the American Revolution was most of
all a conflict that pitted elites in the American colonies against

elites in the British metropolis. Historian Fred Anderson stretched the Revolution's beginnings back to the Seven Years War between Britain and France, in a globe-spanning account of that great struggle. Focusing tightly on the Albany Congress of 1754, historian Timothy Shannon demonstrated how that meeting's proposals laid bare both British and colonial conceptions of what being British *and* colonial meant.

As Anderson and Shannon particularly realized, the effects of European colonization reached very deep into the American interior. It makes no sense to think of eighteenth-century North America as virgin land or empty space. The best current metaphor is historian Richard White's notion of a "Middle Ground," where Europeans and Native Americans met, mingled, fought, and for a very long time coexisted. He and others are proving that well before the Revolution, territory west of the Appalachians, north of the Rio Grande, and east of California was strongly influenced by what was happening on the Atlantic coast and in Europe. Shock waves of commerce, politics, culture, disease, and war reverberated across most of the continent. Any new account of the Revolution would have to include what people of the interior did and experienced, and how Atlantic coast independence changed the matrix of power and commerce far beyond the Mississippi River.

As of 1763 the British claim to dominion extended from the Atlantic shore to the Mississippi River and from the Florida and Louisiana boundaries to far north of the Great Lakes and the St. Lawrence. One way or another, everybody within that area "belonged" to Britain, and British power could reach every group and every person within it. As of 1783 a new American power was shaping itself over much of that same enormous territory. It did not yet possess Florida or Louisiana; it never would acquire Canada, but like British power before 1776, American power could reach every group and every person within an enormous domain. The story of the Revolution needs to be told in continent-spanning terms. Those terms include understanding the changing lines on maps that defined both the property rights of individuals and groups and the jurisdiction of legal authorities.

From the Treaty of Paris of 1763 until the Treaty of Paris of 1783, Britain maintained that everybody in eastern North America "belonged" to it. *Belonging* can imply membership, participation among fellows for the sake of a common goal; the idea of citizenship expresses that sense perfectly. But *belonging* also can mean being possessed, in the way that an object belongs to its owner. For a human being, belonging in this way implies some combination of accepting one's subordination while also claiming the protection of somebody more powerful in a dangerous world.

Theoretically, that is the sense in which subjects belonged to a king, wives and children belonged to husbands and fathers, and slaves belonged to masters. For adult white males who chose the American side, the Revolution brought a shift from subjection to citizenship. For everybody else, including Native Americans who had been Britain's allies but not citizens or subjects, the problem was more complex. It would not be resolved when the Revolution supposedly ended, with the adoption of the federal Constitution. As ongoing litigation between Indian nations and state and federal governments shows, it is not resolved yet. In our own time slavery and the legal doctrine of *feme covert* have gone, but echoes of both persist.

Belonging is a legal concept, but it is also a psychological one. Belonging and identity are not synonymous but belonging is a matter of identity. In Western society at least, identity tends to mean the complete individuality of people whose foremost possession is themselves. Yet even the most rugged individualism grows out of belonging, or having belonged, to something larger: a family, a town, a congregation, a group, a profession, a sex, a race, a class, a nation. In intellectual terms, identity has become an extremely lively and very compelling topic. People do change their identities, but it is not easy. Writing this, I thought for a

moment about my own experience. I have lived for long periods
in New Zealand and in Britain, but no matter how fond I became of these countries I never considered taking their citizenship, whatever else I might change. Being American is
fundamental to who I am. Perhaps being British seemed equally
fundamental to almost all white colonials in 1763. How and at
what price did people give up their Britishness?

One possible explanation is that those British people were already Americans without knowing it: They just had to come to
terms with their own situation. That explanation may fit the an-
glophobe Thomas Jefferson, but it flies in the face of the experience of George Washington and Benjamin Franklin. Both craved
the approval of London and its representatives, well into their
adult lives. The idea that people were American before independence cannot explain the large number of loyalists during
the Revolution. It cannot explain the colonials' reluctance to become independent even after war broke out in 1775. Nor can it
deal with the problem that arose with independence: how to belong to America if a person was not white, male, and adult, with
at least the prospect of owning property.

One major challenge to the idea that the American Revolution really was revolutionary is that it did not destroy slavery, as
the Revolution in France supposedly did. The challenge is
wrong-headed, and not just because slavery did not actually end
in France's American possessions until 1848. In 1760 slavery was
a fact of life in many parts of the world. In the Americas it could
be found from Buenos Aires to Quebec. Brazil, the West Indies,
the Carolina/Georgia lowlands, and the Chesapeake were all
slave societies, where everything else depended on the claim
of one sort of people to own the bodies, labor power, future,
and progeny of another. To British policy-makers, the sugar-
producing West Indies counted far more strongly in both economic and political terms than the mainland, so much more that
when the mainland war seemed lost, defending the islands became the goal of British strategy. Slavery and the wealth that

slaves produced but others enjoyed were facts of life everywhere.

By 1790 the long global destruction of slavery was under way,
and that destruction began in revolutionary America—in Vermont in 1777, in Pennsylvania in 1780, and in Massachusetts in
1783. Virginian George Washington moved from unquestioning
acceptance of slavery to wanting to free himself from his slaves
and finally to freeing his entire slave force. He was not the only
southern planter who set his slaves free. There were far more
slave owners, including Thomas Jefferson, who worried a great
deal while doing relatively little.

Much more was involved than the stricken consciences of a
growing number of whites. Slaves made the most of the revolutionary moment, finding their freedom not only in America but
also in Canada, Britain, and Sierra Leone. Speaking in 1851, the
former slave Frederick Douglass would call the United States
Constitution a "glorious liberty document." But the Revolution
also led to the Cotton Kingdom, spreading from the Atlantic
coast to Texas. More than a quarter of all the slaves imported
from Africa to North America came after independence. Both
the partial demolition of slavery and the emergence of "the
South" with its "peculiar institution" were part of the Revolution.

Where and among whom did the Revolution happen? No
one can strip the people of Boston and Concord, New York City
and Saratoga, Philadelphia and Valley Forge, Williamsburg and
Yorktown, or Charles Town and Guilford Court House of their
major parts in the story. Nor can anyone deny the importance of
the Revolution's truly remarkable group of leaders: George
Washington, John Adams, Samuel Adams, Thomas Jefferson,
Thomas Paine, James Madison, Alexander Hamilton, and others. Except for Benjamin Franklin, whose scientific and literary
contributions had brought him fame already, these men emerged
onto the world stage from provincial obscurity. Part of their
eventual sense of new belonging was to the American Republic.

Another part was belonging to one another as fellow Men Who Accomplished the Founding.

They were not alone in transforming their sense of who they were in the world. "Remember the Ladies," wrote Abigail Smith Adams to her husband John in 1776. "Why should I not have liberty whilst you strive for liberty?" asked Mary Hay Burn of her husband, also named John, the same year. "Born free in Africa, a slave in America, he purchased Liberty, professed Christianity, lived reputably, and died hopefully," reads the epitaph of Amos Fortune in Jaffrey, New Hampshire, dated 1801. "But Brothers, did you remember that the difference is about our land," asked the Cherokee Old Tassel of North Carolina emissaries in 1776. "Both Buildings and Rulers are the Work of Our Hands" boasted the house carpenters of Philadelphia as they celebrated the Constitution on July 4, 1788.

Whatever the redheaded Virginian slave owner Thomas Jefferson wrote in 1776 about all men being created equal, Americans carried many of the inequalities that had gone with being British into the new era. At least part of the problem of forming new identities was how to reconcile undoubted differences among themselves with the idea that in some sense they were, or ought to be, equal. Americans were quick to produce new inequalities as well, which leads to the third problem about the Revolution that needs posing now. That problem is the relationship between the events of the independence period and the expanding, democratic, capitalist, ruthlessly developing, winners-and-losers, rich-people-and-poor-people America of today to which the Revolution led.

One possibility is to deny that the relationship presents any problem at all. In this view colonial America already was dynamic and capitalist, full of people pursuing their own happiness, waiting only to embark on the economic development that the nineteenth century brought. Like Canada and New Zealand, but unlike Kenya or Tanzania or India, the United States was a "neo-Europe."

But it is hard to imagine that the British government would have tolerated Derbyshire-born Samuel Slater's outright theft of British cotton-spinning technology in 1791 for the benefit of a Rhode Island firm, or Francis Cabot Lowell's spying on the latest textile machines in 1811 for the benefit of his cotton mill in Massachusetts. It is difficult to imagine the Erie Canal, if Britain had been able to protect Iroquois land rights across what is now central and western New York. It is not easy to imagine British administrators conceiving the new states and the land grid that Jefferson conjured up as a way of distributing and capitalizing the northwest territory land that Indians had regarded as entirely their own. It is possible to imagine Alabama and Mississippi becoming the cotton kingdom under British auspices, but it is not so easy to imagine British rule contributing to an industrializing New England to rival industrialized Lancashire or to the emergence of New York as a financial center to compete with London.

Unless we appreciate these issues of space, identity, power, economics, and contradiction, we cannot appreciate what all the people of the revolutionary era lived through. We cannot understand what they lost or what they achieved. Washington Irving's fable of Rip Van Winkle suggests by its device of a long, long sleep how great a difference the American Revolution made. Rip awakens into a transformed world that makes no sense to him at all. But transformation can never create perfection. As Rip came to appreciate, many of the old problems were gone, abandoned like outmoded science, but other problems persisted, and new ones had been raised that still remain unanswered. To paraphrase another great American writer, William Faulkner, issues of the Revolution are not past, even now.

The American Revolution

One

MONARCHY, SUBJECTS, AND EMPIRE:

THE BRITISH REGIME IN AMERICA

I

An accurate map of colonial America early in 1775 would show much more than the thirteen rebellious colonies. It would also show the British provinces that refused independence, from Barbados to Nova Scotia. It would show Guadeloupe, Martinique, St. Pierre, and Miquelon, the sugar and fishing islands that France still controlled, the newly "British" places called Quebec, Montreal, Detroit, and Vincennes, and the Spanish-run towns of St. Louis and New Orleans. The map would show real Spanish settlements stretching in an enormous arc from the east coast of Florida to the central coast of California. Surrounding the settlements were enormous areas where Native people rather than whites named places and ordered the course of events. East of the Mississippi these included Iroquois country, the Ohio River Valley, the lands of the Creek, Cherokee, Choctaw, and Chickasaw, and what long had been called the *pays d'en haut* (upper country) between Lake Michigan and the Mississippi River. Enslaved Africans and their American-born progeny put no names on maps, but black people were everywhere, and their marks were upon the land in Massachusetts and New York as well as in Maryland, South Carolina, and Louisiana.

The ideal map would be animated, showing people moving

across enormous distances. Some were Natives, refugees head-
ing west. Their migration pushed other Indians farther west,
driving people like the Lakota Sioux from the forest onto the
open plains. On the plains the Sioux, as well as the Cheyenne,
Arapaho, Comanche, Kiowa, Pawnee, and Apache, felt pressure
not just from the east but also from Spaniards in Texas, New
Mexico, and California. Some Native people knew that Russians
were beginning to establish themselves along the Pacific shore,
in camps and small settlements that stretched southward from
Alaska.

Europeans kept crossing the North Atlantic in large numbers, until the very moment that war broke out between Britain
and the Atlantic coast colonies. Many departed from ports in
Scotland and the north of England. They entered America at
Halifax or New York or Philadelphia and made their way to the
march lands that separated white-run and Native areas all the
way from the Champlain Valley to the Georgia interior. Once
settled, whether as legal landowners, as tenants, or simply as
squatters, they tried to establish small-scale farms. Among them
was the Scotsman John Commons, or Cummins, who came to
northern New York about 1774 and who could not make up his
mind between King and Congress two years later.

Other Europeans, primarily city folk, circulated around an
enormous ring of Atlantic ports: within the British Isles, along
the edge of continental Europe, on the coast of Africa, and on
the western Atlantic shore from the Rio de la Plata to the St.
Lawrence. Among the wanderers were seafarers as well as the
land-bound sojourners who plied their trade in one port or another before moving on and finally settling. Young Benjamin
Franklin, who started in Boston, escaped to Philadelphia in 1723,
and worked for a while in London, is a perfect example. So is
Thomas Paine, who left behind a failed career and two mar-
riages in England in 1774 to try his fortune in Philadelphia. So is
Olaudah Equiano, whose autobiography tells of being enslaved
as a child in Africa, seeing the Caribbean and the North Ameri-

can mainland, and taking part in naval battles off the French coastline and at the mouth of the St. Lawrence. He died free and a famous author in England.

Until the war of independence brought an end to commerce, very large numbers of people were crossing against their own will, with hardly any prospect of going back. Some were Britons who had been sentenced by a court of law to "transportation" to America rather than to prison or the gallows. In the eighteenth century these involuntary immigrants outnumbered Britons who migrated freely. Far more of the forced immigrants, however, were Africans. Some had been captured in warfare, like Ibrahima, an African prince who ended up in Mississippi. Or, they were kidnapped, then trekked across the difficult African interior to such ports as Luanda, Elmina, and Cape Coast, where they were kept in disease-ridden jails like criminals or in holding pens like beasts, then were loaded onto ships that were even more foul. The vessel's home port might be London or Bristol, but it also might be Newport or Norfolk. If the new slaves survived their capture and journey, they might end up anywhere in the Americas. Wherever they arrived, their lives henceforth would not be their own. Very few experienced either the travels or the opportunities that fate granted to Equiano, although Ibrahima did win recognition for what he had been and finally gained his freedom. He died on his way back home.

"Colonial America" included every part of the western hemisphere that felt the impact of Europeans. Even if we leave aside the Pacific Coast, Central America, and South America, colonial America was huge. It was densely organized. It teemed with all different sorts of people who were connected to one another, to Europe, to Africa, and even to Asia in many ways.

The map would have to show one particular complexity in great detail: Simply put, what was where? On modern maps the lines are clearly inscribed. The United States, Canada, and Mexico meet but do not overlap. Cities, counties, states, and provinces have definite boundaries. Many of those boundaries, such as the irregular shapes of New York or Virginia or Texas, and even the rectangles called Colorado and Wyoming, are so familiar that they have become second nature to Americans today, despite the obvious point that nature never draws either long straight lines or right angles, let alone in succession. Within jurisdictions the lines that mark out separate parcels of property are carefully surveyed and filed in public registers, so that buying and selling can go on with minimal difficulty.

In late colonial America the boundaries between jurisdictions and property were nothing like so neat. Until France withdrew in 1763, governors in Montreal and their counterparts in Philadelphia and Williamsburg exchanged endless correspondence about their respective kings' "undoubted right" to the country between the Ohio River and the Great Lakes, including the site of Pittsburgh. The Six Iroquois Nations had their own perspective on the Ohio Valley, regarding themselves as guardians of and spokesmen for the Indians there—although those Indians thought otherwise. Citing a treaty of 1670, Spain claimed that Florida's northern boundary ran between modern Savannah and Charleston, while a British charter of 1665 drew the boundary of "Carolina" straight across the Florida peninsula. Letters and assertions could not make anyone withdraw from disputed territory. These were problems that would be settled by unrest or even war and ratified, eventually, by court cases and diplomacy.

Within British America, provincial boundaries were anything but certain. Virginia's southern line had been established in principle by the charter that James I granted in 1606. But well into the eighteenth century, a person dwelling south of the James River (or, as Carolinians would have seen it, north of Albemarle Sound) might face demands from both Virginia and North Carolina to pay taxes, perform militia or jury or road service, and give obedience to the laws. In practical terms Virginia's northern boundary ran along the Potomac River, which separated it from Maryland. But in theory that boundary extended northwestward with no limit at all. Maryland, Delaware, Pennsylvania, New Jersey, and Connecticut all were hemmed in, whether by the terms of their charters or by the presence of their neighbors. But their actual boundaries remained uncertain.

New York's familiar outline was not shown on any colonial-era document. Colonel Guy Johnson drew a map in 1771 that showed the Six Iroquois Nations west of the "line of property" that they and his uncle, Sir William Johnson, had worked out at Fort Stanwix three years earlier. New York seemed to end at that line, with no claim beyond it to either property or jurisdiction, other than ambiguous statements from the Iroquois that New York officials construed as establishing the Indians' vassalage. Drawing a detailed map of the "province of New York" a few years later, British cartographer Claude-Joseph Sauthier showed the land of the Six Nations in the same terms. It was white space, devoid of either geographical or political markings—and also devoid, supposedly, of interest to New Yorkers.

Sauthier's real interest was the borderland where New York met New England. He included much detail to suggest that New York had good claim to all of what now is Vermont, and to parts of western Massachusetts and Connecticut. But New Hampshire also claimed the Green Mountains, and many people from Massachusetts and Connecticut were taking up "New Hampshire Grants," denying New York's authority. Meanwhile Massachusetts could argue that its royal charter gave it title to the Iroquois land between Seneca Lake and the Niagara River. Even Connecticut had a vague claim to the Wyoming Valley in east-central Pennsylvania.

Everywhere "jarring interests" competed for the political authority and the property rights that would come from drawing one set of lines rather than another on an authoritative map. Where Indians had the strength, and were able to make their own assertions about what belonged to whom and on what terms, they figured among those interests. Among the possible forms of landholding were collective tribal possession of land, townships whose "proprietors" held some town land in common; freehold individual farms; great tenanted estates like Rensselaerswyck in New York; the essentially feudal province of Pennsylvania; southern family holdings that were "entailed" to prevent inheritance from breaking them up; and lands where a squatter's ability to stay put either went uncontested or jarred against an absentee's claim, recorded far away.

All these variations existed within fields of force that emanated from provincial capitals and from port cities where legislators enacted laws, governors sometimes vetoed them, courts adjudicated their meaning, traders shipped and received goods, and artisans produced wares for both local and distant markets. Ultimately those fields of force centered on London—or so the British government claimed.

Seen from the air, the Atlantic coast states today still look like Europe, with its hodgepodge of fields, forests, lanes, and hedges. For good reason: As in Europe, the human landscape here emerged out of one local conflict after another. Today most of that legally defined landscape is frozen; it changes only as legitimate "heirs and assigns" combine, sell, and divide property passed to them by bequeathal and sale. Only a few lines, particularly Native claims to sovereign rights that are immune to state authority, remain in fundamental contention, for the federal courts to resolve.

In colonial America, however, the same landscape was alive with political contention. No court, whether in the colonies or in England, was in a position to resolve authoritatively most of the issues at stake. After the world-shaking conflict between France and England ended in 1763, strife continued within "British America" among individuals, groups, and jurisdictions, often disputing in the most fundamental terms about how to understand and use the land. Like Europe's hodgepodge, the Atlantic coast landscape had been inscribed upon the earth by a prerevolutionary ancien régime, one that was very different from the enlightened, rational "new order of the ages" that the leaders of the American Revolution believed they produced.

II

The phrase ancien régime, or "old order," was employed analytically in 1856 by the French thinker Alexis de Tocqueville to describe what his own country had left behind after 1789. Two decades earlier Tocqueville had described democracy in America in very incisive and not entirely laudatory terms. Entranced, during the travels in 1831–32 that led to his American book, with the novelty and seemingly endless possibility that he saw, Tocqueville did not realize that America too bore the burden of the deeper European past, as well as the complications that came from being outside Europe and with including many people who were not European at all. The tangle of overlapping boundaries that a good map would have shown in 1763 or 1776 was part of the burden of colonial American history. What other weighty dreams or nightmares rested upon the shoulders of the living?

Lines of political authority were at least as tangled as lines of property. Historians make a conventional distinction among chartered colonies (those that operated under a formal grant of both property and authority from the Crown), proprietary colonies (essentially feudal domains, with property and power concentrated in one great family), and royal colonies (those ruled directly under the Crown). Among the chartered colonies, Connecticut and Rhode Island were so completely self-contained, even electing their own governors, that little change was required for them to adapt to republican independence. For many purposes they already enjoyed it. Elsewhere adaptation was more difficult.

Virginia was founded by a chartered commercial company, but the charter was voided in 1624. Thereafter the province was royal. Massachusetts started off as a chartered colony in 1629, lost its charter in 1684, and gained a new one in 1692. Under its first charter it ruled itself, entirely. Under the second the king appointed its governor, which made the colony technically royal. But unlike other royal colonies, the Massachusetts governor's council was nominated by the assembly (on behalf of the electorate) rather than by the governor (in the name of the Crown). New York never had a charter. Surrendered by the Dutch in 1664, it began its English-dominated history as a proprietary colony. The proprietor was James, duke of York, the brother of the childless Charles II. When James became king upon Charles's death, New York became a royal colony, with no charter or proprietary rights. New Jersey, Maryland, and the two Carolinas began under proprietors, became royal, and then straddled the two forms, with the Crown naming the chief officials but proprietors retaining title to much of the land. Pennsylvania remained proprietary throughout its colonial history, despite strong efforts in the early 1760s to vacate the power of the Penn family and subject the province directly to the Crown. The two prime movers were Benjamin Franklin, who understood how to shift position and later became a revolutionary hero, and his friend Joseph Galloway, who did not understand. Galloway was written out of official history in 1774 when the First Continental Congress "expunged" from its records his proposals for reconciliation.

Variations on these fugal themes of Crown, grandees, power, land, and colonial people abound. British administration of the American colonies had no system, no rationality, and the lack of rationality is precisely the point. At the heart of modernity is the idea that people and groups can control their own situations entirely. The boast is overly ambitious, but it has underpinned half a millennium of Western civilization. Like its French counterpart, the American Revolution cut straight through many of the old questions that set the agenda of the ancien régime, both in terms of political power and in terms of the weight of the past.

At the Revolution's beginning most people lived within a ram-shackle framework bequeathed from the past that was difficult to change. At its end many newly self-defined Americans be-lieved that they could remake the world for the sake of their own pursuits of happiness. In many ways they were correct, though they did not reckon the cost, which other people in their world would pay.

Structurally, the colonial political order was a mess. Official positions often seemed to exist only for the sake of providing employment for politically appropriate persons. Once in office, a person would inevitably be caught between what authority com-manded and what local conditions told him to do. Authority did not always have the louder voice. In 1743 George Clinton, a rear admiral and son of the earl of Lincoln, arrived in New York with a commission to govern in the king's name. His combination of naval rank, blood that ran deepest blue, and strong political con-nections ought to have given him extraordinary power. But Clin-ton's decade-long governorship was a disaster: for himself, for royal revenues, and for the Crown that he represented. Within days of his arrival in 1753 his successor, Sir Danvers Osborne, hanged himself, not just because of the personal tragedy of his young wife's death but also because of what he was supposed to govern. In Virginia governor upon governor took the other tack, simply accepting that what the province's House of Burgesses wanted also was what would make him rich and respected. Though none realized it, Britain's governors, the lieutenant-governors who often acted in their stead, and colonial politicians were caught in a very deep problem: the nature of the British state.

For political purposes, England had swallowed Wales during the Middle Ages, though Welsh language and identity never have been lost. In 1603 James VI of Scotland acquired the title James I of England, ruling each place as a separate kingdom. In 1707 the parliament in Edinburgh was suppressed, creating the "United Kingdom" of England, Wales, and Scotland, to be called

Great Britain when taken together. By itself, the new "British" monarchy was not absolute, and wearers of the crown were not able to do whatever they desired. Queen Anne, who reigned at the time of the union (from 1702 to 1714), and the monarchs who followed her would be bound by Parliament, which could give consent but also withhold it. In eighteenth-century "Whig" theory, Parliament's ability to restrain the Crown was the very essence of British liberty, which was envied all across Europe. Even George III never thought of himself as anything but British liberty's guardian.

That same liberty was celebrated by Britons everywhere: within the "realm" of England, Scotland, and Wales; in the still-separate kingdom of Ireland, which had its own parliament in Dublin; and in "dominions" that included the Channel Islands (Guernsey, Jersey, Alderney), the Isle of Man, and the colonies across the Atlantic Ocean. But despite praise from figures as diverse as Montesquieu, Mozart, and Benjamin Franklin, British liberty was profoundly ambiguous. Part of the crisis between Britain and its colonies was the growing realization that liberty meant different things to Britons "at home" and to those in the colonies.

The rule of many polities by one Crown on varying terms is known as *composite monarchy*. It is not far from the modern concept of the British Commonwealth of Nations, in which Canada, Australia, New Zealand, Papua New Guinea, Jamaica, Barbados, and Britain itself share one sovereign but act on their own for all effective purposes. Composite monarchy expresses the idea that James I could also be James VI if he should journey from London to Edinburgh. Similar situations had existed all over medieval and early modern Europe. One king might reign over both Poland and Lithuania, and another over both Sweden and Pomerania. A "Hall of the Realms" in Madrid celebrated the many separate kingdoms ruled by Spain's monarchs. Under the single Spanish king, his subjects in Naples, Barcelona, Madrid, and Mexico City had varying privileges.

Local privileges varied under the British Crown, too. Since 1494 Poyning's Law rendered the Irish parliament subordinate to its British counterpart in Westminster. The Dublin body remained a parliament, however, existing of its own right, not a local council created by a statute for the sake of convenience or efficiency. Despite the abolition of the Scottish parliament, Scottish and English law operated on different principles, as they do today. The House of Keys on the Isle of Man was independent of the House of Commons in Westminster, as it also remains to this day.

Within the United Kingdom English peers sat of right in the House of Lords, but Scottish peers elected delegates to represent them. The universities of Oxford and Cambridge enjoyed the privilege, or "liberty," of sending their own members to the House of Commons, but universities in Scotland did not. A "rotten borough" like Old Sarum, which had virtually no inhabitants, could elect a member of Parliament while a bustling, growing town like Sheffield or Leeds went without representation. All of these peculiarities had their American counterparts. A peer who lived in America, such as George Washington's patron Lord Fairfax, enjoyed respect but no special political rights. The College of William and Mary had its own delegate to the House of Burgesses, but Harvard and Yale had none in their provinces' assemblies. Several of New York's quasi-feudal manors elected their own assemblymen, but not all manors had that privilege.

Colonials enjoyed some liberties that were denied to their fellows "at home." One was the ownership of slaves, which colonial statutes allowed but which metropolitan British law did not recognize. Another was growing tobacco, which was forbidden to British farmers. Conversely, Britons enjoyed some privileges that were denied to colonials. The English, Welsh, and Scots enjoyed a common market. They could trade freely among themselves, unhindered by internal taxes or customs barriers. They also could trade directly with foreign countries. No such freedom existed, however, between separate colonies, between the colonies and places that were not British, or even between the colonies and Britain. Colonial statutes were subject to veto by both provincial governors and the Crown, whereas during the reign of Queen Anne "royal assent" became a mere formality for acts of Parliament.

When it came to internal matters, however, the Virginia Burgesses or the Massachusetts Assembly seemed to colonials to be equal to Britain's House of Commons. Those bodies, and their counterparts elsewhere, followed the rules and precedents of the House of Commons. Unlike local councils in Britain, they did not owe their power to a parliamentary statute. They stemmed solely from the Crown, either directly in a charter grant or indirectly through the initial summons by a governor or a proprietor. The colonial legislatures did accept that in some respects Parliament was their superior, but so did the parliament in Dublin. The fabric of British liberty was woven with uneven threads in an elaborate pattern. As law dictionaries said, British liberties were privileges that went with the particular kind of Briton a person was and with the particular community to which that Briton belonged. Equality, whether of condition or of rights, had nothing to do with the glorious condition of being British and free.

The eighteenth century saw a growing trend within Britain to assert that the King- (or Queen-) in-Parliament was totally powerful. Once Parliament consented, in this view, there were no more limits upon the British monarch than there were upon the French monarch Louis XIV, who could boast, "*L'État, c'est moi*" (The state is myself), or the Spanish kings whose decrees began "*Yo, el Rey*" (I, the King). The great legal theorist Sir William Blackstone made that point explicit in 1765. Eighteenth-century monarchs, particularly George II and his grandson George III, were actively involved in Parliamentary affairs. The Crown's favor largely determined who would fill ministerial offices and receive great favors. Today the Crown is an office of ceremony, and the power once held by George III can be exercised instead by a strong-willed prime minister who can dominate the House of Commons, likewise setting the agenda and handing out favors. Hence the combined power of Parliament and Crown remains absolute.

III

John Winthrop, founding governor of Massachusetts, explained the theory of uneven conditions and rights as early as 1630. Preaching a shipboard sermon to his fellow Puritans, he declared that inequality was God's will, so that the rich and the powerful could take care of the poor and the weak in a difficult, dangerous world. For their part, the poor and weak could show gratitude and deference. If one accepted the idea that the inequality of human beings resulted from divine will, the theory made sense. It accounted for the differences between women and men, commoners and nobles, country people and townsfolk, the poor and the wealthy, the ignorant and the educated, children and adults. Monarchy, the fount of all honor in the world, was explainable; so was its complete opposite, slavery, which meant complete dishonor. Monarchy, slavery, and all the degrees of freedom and respect that lay in between were ordained by a God whose purposes could not be known.

Winthrop's theory fitted well with the unevenness of a monarchy that ruled its acknowledged subjects in one way in one dominion and in another way elsewhere. In practical terms, that pattern of protection, reciprocity, and loyalty could, for example, explain the British monarch's relations with Indians. These people were neither British (as white Virginians and Pennsylvanians claimed to be) nor slaves stripped of all rights. Reciprocity, not subjection, was the key. Through his agents a monarch could provide gifts of weapons, blankets, pots, alcohol, and protection against land-hungry settlers. In return, Indians could give wartime strength and border security. Linked to such reciprocity was the metaphor of fatherhood, which Indians could interpret to mean benevolence even if Europeans were employing it to mean authority.

The Crown asserted its paramount position in 1756 by commissioning Colonel (later Sir) William Johnson and John Stuart to oversee all Indian affairs. The two superintendents cooperated with provincial politicians and were influenced by what those politicians had to say and to offer. Johnson even remained a member of the provincial council of New York. But like royal governors, the Indian superintendents acted on the monarch's behalf and took their orders from Westminster. Through them, in theory, the Mohawk and Delaware and Cherokee and Creek would enjoy their own distinct situations, their own "liberties and immunities." Like the lines of jurisdiction and property drawn on colonial maps, the relationships among Indians, colonial authorities, and the Crown were real but also alive with ambiguity and mutual misunderstanding.

IV

Reality did not measure up to theory, of course. Some royal officials understood what the Crown's interests required, but they generally found themselves in trouble with the locals for carrying it out. Cadwallader Colden, a physician who left Scotland in 1710 and settled in New York in 1717, served the Crown loyally in New York and finished his six-decade American career as a deeply unpopular lieutenant-governor (1761–76). He was matched both in his loyalty and his unpopularity by Boston-born, Harvard-educated Thomas Hutchinson, who had the extremely unhappy task of governing Massachusetts from 1769 to 1774. Benjamin Franklin's son William proved equally loyal as the final royal governor of New Jersey.

At the opposite extreme, other emissaries proved entirely venal, using their positions to line their own pockets with fees for granting land to others, and to make grants to themselves. Two separate aristocrats who governed New York, Lord Cornbury (1701–08) and the earl of Dunmore (1770–71), became notorious for their land policies. Cornbury's replacement stripped him of the immunity that went with being governor, whereupon the locals threw him in jail. When Dunmore was transferred to Virginia, he disgraced himself in a drunken public tirade. Benning and John Wentworth, the father and son who governed New Hampshire in succession from 1741 to 1775, caused no such local outrage. But they did profit enormously by allowing the tall, straight white pines reserved for the Royal Navy to be sold on the private market. They also granted large amounts of land west of the Connecticut River, fully aware that good title could not be guaranteed because New York also claimed the region.

Virginians had perhaps the best continuing relations with the succession of gentlemen, knights, and peers whom Britain sent over. The governor's palace in Williamsburg was fit for a viceroy, though the power symbolized in its Georgian architecture was matched in the capitol building that stood a few minutes' walk away, where the provincial elite gathered in the House of Burgesses. Governors from Sir William Berkeley in the mid-seventeenth century to Francis Fauquier, who patronized the young Thomas Jefferson, to Baron de Botetourt, who had to deal with Virginians during the difficult late 1760s, learned how to cultivate rather than alienate the planter class. The arrangement had its rewards on both sides. But throughout the revolutionary period those very planters offered what appeared to be a strong lead both to their own people and to other provinces/states.

Whether British or American-born, people like the Wentworths, Sir William Johnson, Cadwallader Colden, colonial agents Benjamin Franklin and Thomas Pownall, and merchants from Boston to Charles Town all learned to play the game of Anglo-American politics. On both sides of the ocean friendship, alliance, influence, and sometimes outright bribes could open the doors of powerful people; conflicting friendships, stronger alliances, and even bigger bribes could keep those same doors closed. A really skillful player like Johnson could climb from obscure birth to wealth and respect. Born to a middling Irish Catholic family in 1715, he realized how much better his chances would be if he became Anglican, so he converted. He migrated to New York and allied himself with Captain Peter Warren, who commanded the navy's duty ship in the harbor and who speculated heavily in New York land. In 1738 Johnson settled in the Mohawk Valley to act as Warren's land agent. He learned the Mohawk language and Iroquois customs. He quickly began acquiring land himself and understood that he would do well to distance himself from the Albany merchants and politicians who traditionally handled Indian affairs on behalf of the province and, in theory, the Crown.

Johnson had a "good" Seven Years War, rising to a generalship, gaining credit for a victory over the French at Lake George, being made Indian superintendent, and acquiring a hereditary baronetcy. He also maintained his ties to Warren, who returned to England as a knighted admiral and became a member of Parliament. In effect, Johnson became a marcher lord, standing at the edge of contested royal dominions, much as Englishmen with the title *marquess* had stood along the border with medieval Wales. After the war the baronet turned his fortified holding into a gentleman's estate, where he personally owned the courthouse, the jail, and the church and where he appointed the judges, the sheriff, and the minister. He also decreed who would represent the Mohawk Valley in the provincial assembly. He recruited loyal tenants from Highland Scotland, continued to deal with Indians, and dealt directly with officials in London. He was a great lord in everything except formal title.

Johnson served London well, and the Crown rewarded him heavily. But Johnson also could serve himself and his local allies. Official policy after 1763 was to keep colonial settlements from expanding into Indian country, beyond the crest of the Appalachian Mountains. Enforcing that limit was part of Johnson's responsibility. No one expected that the limit would last forever. In fact it lasted only until 1768, when Johnson negotiated a treaty at Fort Stanwix (modern Rome, New York) with the Iroquois Confederacy. The Six Nations' own land remained immune from wholesale settlement, secured by the "line of property" that appears on Guy Johnson's and Claude-Joseph Sauthier's maps. But the treaty opened up settlement in far western Pennsylvania, the Ohio country, and Kentucky, despite the outrage of Shawnee, Delaware, Mingo Iroquois, and Cherokee who believed that one way or another the land was theirs. Apart from the Iroquois, they began to talk among themselves about unity, whatever their tribal differences and their historic rivalries.

V

All the people of British America lived within a single economic web of manufacturing and trading. The web had been established by the Acts of Trade and Navigation that Parliament had passed piecemeal after the Stuart monarchy's restoration in 1660. Colonials used the term *empire* to describe their relationship with England. They thought of empire in terms of shared glory, rather than in the modern sense of an underdeveloped periphery that is subordinate to a self-defined metropolis or core. In theory, at least, the relationship was reciprocal and equal, but in fact it was not equal at all, whether between Britons and colonials or among colonials of different sorts. People in the colonies had economic as well as religious and cultural reasons both to differ from metropolitan Britons and to conflict with them.

To British policy-makers, the ideal colony was one that produced raw materials that could not be grown or goods that could not be made within the realm, shipped this valuable produce "home" for finishing and possible sale elsewhere, and in turn consumed finished British goods. Colonial products could be taxed at British ports, lessening the tax burden on the realm and guaranteeing to the monarchy an income over which Parliament had no say. Reshipped elsewhere in Europe, those finished goods would benefit British merchants; selling them to the colonial market would benefit not just merchants but manufacturers. Requiring that all colonial trade be carried in British vessels with British crews meant prosperity for shipyards, ropewalks, sail lofts, and the foundries where anchors, stays, and blocks and tackle were produced. It also guaranteed the existence of a fleet and of the skilled seafarers to man it in wartime.

West Indies sugar and Chesapeake tobacco were also "enumerated," which prevented their sale outside the realm and dominions. Britain's own woodlands were close to exhaustion. Pitch and tar from southern yellow pines, tall, straight white pine masts from northern New England, and oak timbers lessened dependence on the Baltic countries, which were the main alternative source. So colonial naval stores were enumerated as well. But Britons consumed little rice, so South Carolina and Georgia rice could be sold direct to southern Europe, helping to pay for citrus fruit, oil, and wine. Legally, at least, colonials could not carry the manufacture of iron beyond the first stage of smelting the ore into "pig" or bar iron, so that they would not dent Britain's monopoly on finished wares. The pig iron could become finished metal goods in the endless workshops of the English Midlands "Black Country." Even fully finished colonial products could meet British needs. From the northern Chesapeake to north of Boston, colonial shipwrights were constructing vessels. Officially these qualified as British, and many did end up registered in British ports, adding to the merchant navy's enormous carrying capacity.

But other sectors of the colonial economy did not mesh so well with Britain's. The wheat that was grown in the Virginia and Maryland piedmont, in the northern Chesapeake, and in Pennsylvania, New Jersey, and New York was a rival to the British crop. It found markets elsewhere. Some American wheat went to the West Indies, where it helped to feed sugar-producing slaves. Other American grain found its market in western Europe, including Britain's arch-rival France, even in time of war. Whether they knew it or not, the farmers who grew the wheat, the millers who ground it into flour, the woodcutters and blacksmiths who provided staves and hoops for barrels to ship it, and the merchants who consigned it had a different relationship with metropolitan Britain than did tobacco planters. When George Washington abandoned tobacco for wheat production at Mount Vernon early in the 1760s, he was taking a step on his own long journey from being British, though provincial, to being not British at all.

The same problem held for New England fishermen. British vessels as well as colonial ones harvested cod and haddock on the Grand Banks and St. George's Bank. So, like Carolina rice, New England salt cod was sold to southern Europe and to the West Indies. Of the exported rice and fish, the European markets got the best and the "refuse" went to the Caribbean. The Yankee commercial fleet did have the protection of British men-of-war against piracy and wartime enemies. Its vessels might well carry forest products or southern staples to Britain. But they were also likely to take their cargoes of grain and dried fish directly to Bordeaux or Oporto or Cadiz or even to Marseilles and Naples.

The southern mainland colonies had only one really significant urban place, Charles Town (Charleston after 1783), in South Carolina. In the colonial era Charles Town was not a city in legal terms, or even an incorporated town. It was just a place with a name. Yet in 1770 its roughly nine thousand people experienced dense urban life. They included political officials who either enforced the will of the king or represented the desires of Carolinians, and major and minor merchants who shipped rice and brought in slaves and consumer goods. They included free white artisans whose handmade saddles and harnesses and candlesticks and silver competed with British offerings. The town's people also included numerous slaves, serving in the townhouses of the rich, in artisans' workshops, and at all sorts of degrading and menial labor.

The next major town to the north was Baltimore, Maryland. Like Charles Town, it had about nine thousand people in 1770. Baltimore was a wheat port, the northernmost and by far the largest in the arc of milling and shipping towns that extended from Richmond, Virginia, westward beyond the Blue Ridge, and curved back toward the upper Chesapeake. The production of wheat was more complex than that of tobacco. It had to be milled into flour, bolted for consistency, and often baked into long-lasting biscuit. Both flour and biscuit needed barrels, which required staves and hoops. Making staves required sawmills, and making hoops required smelters and forges. Sawmills, smelters, and forges sent their output to Baltimore's prosperous shipyards as well.

Shipping required pools of capital to finance voyages and insurance partnerships. It required bills of exchange and relationships of trust with faceless partners across long distances. It also meant the possibility of clashes among shippers and insurers, on the one side, and the seafarers who manned the vessels, the artisans who built and rigged them, and other working men whose economy was local rather than imperial. None of those clashes even touched on the fundamental conflict between masters and their slaves who were in the shipyards and the blacksmith shops.

Variations on that same complex urban pattern held in all the northern ports. Great merchants had their British correspondents, who often were family members or in-laws. A "protested" bill of exchange could mean a firm's collapse and a family's disgrace. A traveling artisan could find work on both sides of the ocean. Yet London, Bristol, and Liverpool, on the one hand, and Boston, New York, and Philadelphia, on the other, were rivals. British policy-makers were quicker to understand this than colonials.

When young Benjamin Franklin left Boston for Philadelphia, he found a town that was only a few decades old. Its main business was exporting wheat and receiving goods from Britain and from the other colonies. But the city contained greater possibilities for complexity than Charles Town. By the time of independence its cultural apparatus included newspapers, the College of Philadelphia, a hospital, and the "junto" of artisans that Franklin helped organize before he retired from printing to lead the life of a gentleman scientist and politician. It sold pig iron from New Jersey foundries to England and quasi-legal finished iron products on the local market. Its artisans brewed beer, baked bread, made household furniture, stitched clothing, and built ships. Many of their products competed with imports from Britain. Some gentry, like the lawyer John Dickinson, affected the life of country gentlemen at seats outside the city. Others, like Franklin, lived well in Philadelphia's heart, uninterested in country life.

Be they gentry or of the middling sort, Philadelphians paid attention to Franklin's adages about how to prosper in urban commercial life. They built up capital and cultivated the personal habits that favored investing it rather than consuming it. Philadelphia's streets were full of seafarers, townspeople, migrants passing through, Indians, slaves, and in some years soldiers. Philadelphians spoke English, Welsh, German, and many Indian tongues. They worshiped as Quakers, Presbyterians, Anglicans, Moravians, and—because Pennsylvania was open—Catholics and Jews. Some, like Franklin himself, did not worship formally. All these people needed information, and Franklin understood the importance of information in his commercial world. He found his own way to wealth and fame through his newspaper, his publishing business, and the connections that later gained him the office of British postmaster general in America. His Philadelphia prospered because it was growing into something more complex.

Not everybody in the city prospered. Beneath Philadelphia's

gentry and its middling sort on the social scale were poor white
working people: day laborers, longshoremen, cooks, and seam-
stresses. Some were free, while others were indentured servants
who had come from Britain under bondage, to serve out the cost
of their passage. Beneath them all were the slaves, amounting to
perhaps seven percent of Philadelphia's population.

In many respects New York and Boston were similar to
Philadelphia, but they were not identical. By 1774 Philadelphia
was British America's largest city, with perhaps 30,000 people.
New York had about 25,000. Both Philadelphia and New York
were growing, but since 1750 Boston had stagnated at about
15,000. During the French and Indian War New York flourished
mightily as the main point of entry for British troops and supplies. It shipped Hudson Valley and New Jersey produce as well
as iron. It shipped forest products in large quantities: staves,
shingles, pot and pearl ashes, and timbers. It was the headquar-
ters of the royal army and navy. But after 1763 its transatlantic
sector suffered equally mightily, and poverty became a real problem. Slaves constituted about twenty percent of its population,
the largest proportion north of the plantation zone. As the slaves
well knew, in 1741 an abortive conspiracy of slaves and sympathetic whites had led to punishments as extreme as slow roast-
ing, for the sake of imposing the maximum possible pain.

Boston, for its part, was in economic and social trouble. It
did not export grain. Its shipbuilding industry was moving
to outports like Salem, Massachusetts, and Portsmouth, New
Hampshire. Its population of genuinely poor people was getting
larger and seemed increasingly permanent. Bostonians like the
cobblers Ebenezer Mackintosh (who would lead the Stamp Act
riots in 1765) and George Robert Twelves Hewes (who took part
in the destruction of the tea in 1773) lived near the edge of
poverty. Losing the struggle for a livelihood meant the poorhouse
or the humiliation of outrelief. Yet Boston also supported Harvard College, which was already more than a seminary for
Puritan ministers. Well-off Bostonians purchased highly crafted

silver goods from Paul Revere. Some, including Revere himself, commissioned portraits from the talented John Singleton Copley. Copley painted many Bostonians of note, including the politician Samuel Adams and the prosperous merchant Elizabeth Murray Smith Inman, who traded on her own throughout her adult life and bequeathed a sizable sum for the benefit of other women who wanted to enter business.

VI

George Washington, Sir William Johnson, Benjamin Franklin, and Paul Revere dominate our images of late-colonial British America. All four of them left behind a great deal of evidence about how they lived and what they thought. Except for Revere, all were members of a provincial elite, displaying themselves constantly to their associates and their inferiors as men fit to rule. Both Johnson Hall in the Mohawk Valley and Washington's Mount Vernon proclaimed the strength, the wealth, and perhaps the wisdom of the men who owned them. So did what those men wore, what they ate and how they ate it, the drink they imbibed, what they read, what they could talk about, whom they knew, and the ways they danced and played.

Both Johnson and Franklin walked the British public stage as well, though the parvenu Franklin found himself excluded from the brightest London limelights. The young George Washington wanted respect and acceptance from metropolitan Britons, as he showed by fawning on Major General Edward Braddock in 1756. But he remained an outsider until he could star on a stage of his own. John Singleton Copley, like the equally talented Philadelphia painter Benjamin West, went to London to develop his skills and to add to his lucrative business in portraits the much more prestigious genre of history painting.

Johnson, Franklin, Washington, Revere, Copley, and West all were caught up in what historian Richard Bushman has called "the refinement of America." Paul Revere had no thoughts of going to London, or even entering the top levels of colonial life, and his house in Boston did not display wealth or power. Still, it did show Revere's liking for comfort and his good taste, as did the silverware he made. Artisans like Revere as well as town professionals like the lawyer John Adams; merchants like the De Lanceys of New York and the Shippens of Philadelphia; landowners like the Connecticut Valley "river gods," self-risen men on the model of Franklin; and southern planters from the Carrolls of Maryland to the Pinckneys of South Carolina shared the recognition that the world had good things and rich ideas to offer.

They were emulating what they believed to be the best English taste. Washington's order books show endless evidence of his desire to keep up. Franklin's first portrait, painted by Robert Feke about 1746, two years before Franklin retired from printing, presents an awkward provincial, ill at ease in his black suit and wig. His relaxed, comfortable London portrait of 1767, however, has him wearing a full wig, a brightly colored coat, and an equally bright waistcoat. He posed while reading, to show that he no longer printed books but rather consumed them. Elizabeth Murray Smith Inman posed for Copley wearing a sumptuous silk dress, and the strength in her face shows that she had earned the money to pay for it herself. Samuel Adams sat for Copley in a plain brown suit, pointing at a copy of the Massachusetts charter. His costume and pose placed Adams in a long line of stern representatives of republican virtue that reached back to ancient Rome, but he was still a gentleman. Revere chose his workman's leather waistcoat, but he wore it over a fine white shirt. He sits reflecting on the political meaning of a silver teapot he has made, with his tools in front of him.

The expression of refinement implied celebrating what a hardworking individual could achieve. White colonials had no monopoly on it. The Mohawk Thayendanegea (Joseph Brant) dined at the table of Sir William Johnson, who was his brother-in-law. Brant wrote excellent English, lived in a European-style house, worshiped in Anglican churches, belonged to a lodge of Freemasons, traveled to London, met the king, and had portraits done by George Romney and Gilbert Stuart. Yet he was a "man of two worlds," who could conduct Indian diplomacy according to the traditional formulas. Johnson, who spoke Mohawk and could wear Indian costume and conform to Indian etiquette, straddled boundaries as well. Refinement and provincial envy of the good things and the bright ideas of the British metropolis were not the only elements in colonial culture.

In the cities an ethos flourished among ordinary working people that was very different from the notion of individual self-improvement. That ethos could be found all around the Atlantic basin in the mid-eighteenth century, in places as diverse as Boston, New York, Bogotá, London, and Paris. It celebrated people joining together to cope with their common plight, rather than individuals making the most of themselves. It involved seafarers, working townsfolk who never would know gentility, ordinary farmers, and even slaves. We should not romanticize: Slaves made the dreadful Atlantic crossing in ships that hardworking shipwrights constructed. They were manacled by irons that hardworking blacksmiths forged. The vessels were navigated by hardworking sailors. Nonetheless, the sense of shared oppression and of having the means to deal with it was real.

In the great circle of Atlantic port cities, there was a widespread "corporatist" belief that during times of stress profits in distant markets were less important than the well-being of a community's members. Members of the upper crust shared that belief and could impose market regulations, price controls, and embargoes in order to protect the supply of necessities for all. It was a way of preserving their power, demonstrating that they could take care of people who were "poore, weake, and in subjeccion," as John Winthrop's 1630 sermon advised.

If the elite failed, the crowd could act. Popular uprisings for the sake of market controls during times of economic dearth, or to keep out pestilence while an epidemic raged, or to prevent seafarers from being impressed into the harsh, dangerous life of the royal navy all took place in eighteenth-century colonial cities, just as they did across the Atlantic. Many crowds were socially mixed, including middle-class men and even gentry in addition to working people and the "sailors, Negroes, and boys" who would receive the blame if a crowd got out of hand. Other crowds were drawn strictly from the "lower sort," who defended their own interests by either forcing the elite to act or by securing their needs directly. Either sort of crowd rising was likely to include disguise and costume, though it was rare for anybody actually to be fooled as to the identities of the participants.

These uprisings drew on European traditions of ritual upheaval and misrule. One was Carnival, the one moment in the tedious year when the world could be turned upside down. During the celebration and revelry a commoner might be a king, a peasant might be a lord, a woman might be a man, and, in some American places, a slave might be a master. Another was "rough music" or, as the French called it, *charivari*. Taken strictly, this was ritual harassment of a newly married couple on their wedding night with "a serenade of pots, tuneless horns, bells, and drums." More loosely it was a way for the community to intrude on somebody's supposedly private business. "Riding Skimmington" was a particular form of shaming, perhaps of a nagging wife, but more generally of a cuckold or a faithless husband. Again by extension it could be used against anybody who violated a community's norms. The person being shamed might be ducked in a pond, ridden on a rail, paraded past the gallows, or given a painful coat of tar and feathers.

Crowds drew on historical memory as well, particularly in Boston. Every November 5 colonial Bostonians celebrated Pope's Day. It marked the discovery and punishment of the Gunpowder Plot, led by the Roman Catholic Guy Fawkes, who planned to destroy Parliament with explosives. Fawkes and his fellow conspirators were burned at the stake, and during the Boston commemoration effigies of him, the Pope, and the Devil would suffer the same fate on a public bonfire. During the day crowds of Bostonians would parade with their own effigies, competing (and perhaps brawling) for the honor of having them burned. Most of the paraders were working men, drawn respectively from the town's north and south ends. The English still celebrate Guy Fawkes Day, though its origins are all but forgotten. For eighteenth-century English and Bostonians alike, however, it was a way to remember that being English meant being Protestant and free. Beneath the patriotic surface it also commemorated the seventeenth-century English Revolution that had overthrown and beheaded Charles I, abolished the House of Lords, and tried for a time to build an English republic.

The urban crowds that participated in these traditions played a very important part in the resistance to British policies that was the first stage of the Revolution. But people who lived in the countryside also knew about collective violence. Often they practiced it for goals that were more fundamental and nonnegotiable than lowering the price of bread, beer, and firewood, stopping a naval press gang, or castigating the pope.

The Stono Rebellion in South Carolina in 1739 and the abortive slave conspiracy that terrified white New Yorkers in 1741 pitted slaves against masters. Although Indians were unlikely to go to war against passing traders, people who wanted to move onto the Indians' land could become another matter. For their part, the settlers were likely to regard all Indians as hostile, even Christian ones who lived in houses and wore European clothes. Many great landed estates rested on doubtful titles or straddled uncertain boundaries, as in North Carolina, New Jersey, the Hudson Valley, and the Green Mountains. Small farmers were unlikely to accept permanent tenant status on such estates. They wanted to own their land, and the ownership and use of land could not be compromised. If land risings broke out, as they did in all those places, landowners and political authorities would use militia and even British troops to put them down and would order the death penalty for captured leaders.

"Mobs, a sort of them at least, are constitutional," said Lieutenant-Governor Thomas Hutchinson of Massachusetts in 1768. For him to say so was remarkable, because during Boston's Stamp Act upheaval three years earlier, his own house had been thoroughly sacked. What Hutchinson most likely had in mind was that colonial-era governments had very few agencies to enforce laws. For the most part they relied on mobs instead, meaning the mixed mobs whose members might also form a sheriff's posse, a militia unit, or a volunteer fire company. Whether "constitutional" or not, colonial mobs were a fact of life.

VII

After 1763 what held it all together was belonging to Great Britain, not just in terms of power, authority, war, commerce, and most white colonials' culture, but in terms of who colonials thought they were. They thought they were British. The very notion of British identity, as opposed to English, Welsh, or Scottish, was an eighteenth-century invention that possessed enormous power. Being Protestant formed a major part of being British.

Though most Britons associated Catholicism with arbitrary power, oppressive church structures, and poverty, even Catholic Britons, such as the dukes of Norfolk and many of the Carrolls of Maryland, were loyal to the Crown. Catholic parents who were rich enough to want education for their sons had to send them to France rather than to England or even to Massachusetts or Virginia, for no Catholic could enter Oxford or Cambridge or Harvard or William and Mary, or qualify for the bar at the Inns of Court in London.

Anglicanism was the official church in the southern colonies, but "toleration" was the law. Catholics faced no outright official persecution if they minded their own business and heard mass in private. Non-Anglican Protestants were guaranteed toleration and public worship, and they created a rich cultural life, based in Scotland on the Kirk and the Scottish universities and in England on Quaker meetings, dissenting chapels, and academies. North of Maryland non-Anglican Protestants were entirely free to gain higher education and enter public life.

This degree of religious toleration allowed colonials to share in a sense of being free and powerful. Like Britons "at home," they displayed no great love for George I, whose first language was German and who was much more interested in his German electorate of Hanover than in Britain. Britons showed little more regard for George II, even though he was the last British monarch to lead an army into battle. But the accession of George III in 1760 sparked an outburst of delight on both sides of the Atlantic. Colonials could not witness the elaborate ceremonial of the new king's coronation, but they could read newspaper accounts avidly. New Yorkers erected an equestrian statue of the king in 1763 to mark his accession.

When George III became king, the Seven Years War was ending in British victory. The war had begun in western Pennsylvania, when a youthful George Washington blundered into a firefight with French troops. It ended with the enormous but expensive triumph of General Wolfe over General Montcalm at Quebec City in 1759. There was debate in London about whether Britain should demand Canada or the Caribbean sugar islands of Guadeloupe and Martinique as its victory prize. Proponents of taking the islands reasoned that leaving Canada for France would hem in the northern colonies economically and thereby prevent them from becoming more like Britain and therefore a rival to it.

Benjamin Franklin opened the issue of the future of British America as early as 1751, when he circulated his *Observations Concerning the Increase of Mankind* among his friends in the

American Philosophical Society. Franklin had noticed that the American population was doubling every two decades, partly from immigration but more importantly from natural increase. More people meant more wealth and more power, and Franklin drew an optimistic inference: The numbers suggested that the American population would outstrip metropolitan Britain. When that happened "the greatest number of Englishmen will be on this side of the water." Franklin concluded that Britain should not hold back colonial development. The pamphlet was published in 1755, one year after Franklin's highly publicized plan for colonial political and military union. When he published the pamphlet Franklin could not see that to some policy-makers in London he was predicting not a great "accession of power" and an inexhaustible market for British manufactures, but rather a threat from the colonies to Britain itself.

To white colonials, it seemed more and more that humiliations abounded. During the previous conflict with France (King George's War, 1744–48), New Englanders had captured the great French fortress of Louisbourg on the Gulf of St. Lawrence—and they did it virtually on their own. They saw this venture as an important contribution to the war effort, but British diplomats used the fortress as a pawn and in the peace treaty traded it back to France. Colonel George Washington, commander of the Virginia militia, found himself ranked below the lowest British regular captain. British officers and soldiers scorned their New England counterparts for supposed cowardice and amateurism. The New Englanders, for their part, were appalled by the British class system, with its rigid separation between officers and ordinary soldiers, and the ferocity of army discipline. Civilians in places like New York City, Albany, and Philadelphia, who saw British troops firsthand in large numbers, drew the same conclusion.

British commanders in chief, particularly generals Edward Braddock, James Abercrombie, and Lord Loudon, tried to dominate colonials by sheer bluster. The office of commander in chief was supposedly superior to any other colonial post. To some colonials, it seemed to threaten a governor-generalship or vice-royalty. The appointment of William Johnson and John Stuart as Indian superintendents in 1756 meant the loss of colonial governments' power to deal with Indians and to acquire their land. Indians who had sided with the British in the war came to recognize afterward how little they might count in both war and diplomacy. Indians who had sided with France, for their part, needed now to deal with enemies of long standing. Postwar commander in chief Sir Jeffrey Amherst, appointed in 1759, wanted Indians of all sorts to accept that they simply were subjects, that their task was to obey, and that the presents that long had lubricated English diplomacy with them would dwindle and eventually cease. Yet most Indians who were in close contact with Europeans now saw Britain as their best ally against their land-hungry neighbors.

Slaves had no reason to love the British, but their main problems were much closer to their own lives. To virtually all white colonials, being British remained the best possible way to be a human being. Like the British at home, they were riven among themselves, by the hurly-burly of politics, by religion, and by ethnicity and social class. Their disputes would figure powerfully in the crisis with Britain that was about to begin, and even more powerfully in the war of independence and the subsequent peace. But not until after the war actually broke out did more than a tiny number of them begin thinking that rather than being Britons in America, they were not Britons at all.

Two

BRITISH CHALLENGE, ELITE RESPONSE

George Grenville was an unlikely man to begin a revolution. When he became the king's prime minister in 1763, he inherited a financial mess and his immediate goal was to straighten it out. Britain had spent itself close to bankruptcy defeating France in the Seven Years, or French and Indian, War. Now it stood supreme from America to India. Someone had to pay, and in Grenville's view the North American colonies had delayed paying long enough. It was time for them to assume at least the costs of their own administration and defense. So, with the approval of young King George III, Grenville launched Parliament on a program of imperial reform. Grenville, and perhaps the king as well, also had a deeper thought. Drawing on a strand of British official thought that reached back at least to midcentury, the reforms would be "great and necessary measures" that would guarantee Britain's primacy in the face of what was starting to look like danger from the colonies.

Daniel Dulany was equally unlikely for the role. A wealthy Marylander, he knew that the British Empire had been good to him. In 1776, when choices became final, he would choose that empire rather than America. But as he studied Grenville's reforms in 1765, Dulany felt himself not only aggrieved but insulted. He saw through the hollow arguments that Parliament's propagandists were making, and he decided to say so publicly. The pamphlet he wrote bore a windy eighteenth-century title: *Considerations on the Propriety of Imposing Taxes in the British Colonies, for the Purpose of Raising a Revenue, by Act of Parliament.* Learned, somewhat pedantic, and intense, it was written for men of Dulany's kind. But the colonies had many men like Dulany, men who were very privileged and who saw in Grenville's program the worst threat their privileges had ever faced. Such men could tell both themselves and their world that their cause *was* their world's, and they could do it with conviction.

Neither Grenville nor Dulany began the Revolution, of course. Grenville's importance lies in his temporary mastery of Parliament at a time when Britain's rulers had every reason to change the way they ran their empire. Dulany's lies in the way he expressed the first response of a large sector of the American elite. Understanding them and what they stood for is not the same as understanding the Revolution. But we cannot make sense of the Revolution unless we realize why and how Britain's rulers challenged American autonomy, and why and how America's leaders responded.

The main story is easy to follow. In 1764, 1765, 1767, and 1773, the British government forced the issue of the extent of its power over the American colonies. On each occasion, the fundamental problem was whether Parliament could tax the colonies or whether only their own assemblies had that right. Parliament's first attempt was ambiguous, and so was the American response. But on the other three occasions the result was naked confrontation, both in words, as heated debate raged in meetings and the press, and in deeds. Twice Parliament backed down, repealing its Stamp Act of 1765 after a winter of protest had rendered it unworkable, and its Townshend duties of 1767 after an extended boycott of British commerce by American merchants. The third occasion came in 1773, when Bostonians dumped East India Company tea into their harbor rather than allow it to be unloaded and have parliamentary duties paid on it. They thought Britain would back down yet again. When the British did not and insisted that Boston pay for the tea, the final rupture began.

Beneath the taxation issue, other problems festered and sometimes broke into the open. The presence of British troops and sailors proved a major irritant, first in New York City and, after 1768, in Boston. Customs men seemed to be everywhere, picking on one technicality after another to obtain condemnations on cargoes and ships. The colonial court system presented problem after problem. Should judges hold their posts for life, or only for as long as the Crown wanted? Should some offenses be tried in courts of vice-admiralty, where no jury ever sat? Who would have the final decision if a case went to appeal? How far could a court go in assisting and protecting British officials? Could a servant of the Crown expect a fair trial in an American courtroom? Problems like these became utterly entangled, and so did endless local questions. Lurking behind all the specific issues were two deep questions. First, what did it mean to be British and enjoy British liberty if a person did not dwell within the United Kingdom of England, Wales, and Scotland? Second, was there real strength in the idea (or fear) that the balance of power, productivity, and wealth would tilt from Britain to the North American provinces? Without realizing how metropolitan Britons might dread such a development, Benjamin Franklin predicted in 1751 that there would be a peaceful transit of power. As if to confirm the point, the poet Philip Freneau spoke of America's "rising glory" when he graduated from the College of New Jersey (Princeton) in 1772. Unraveling these issues proved impossible until the question of independence cut through the knot and forced all colonials to decide which side they were on.

I

The end of the Seven Years War in 1763 marked more than the defeat of France. It ensured Britain's preeminence in Europe's trade with Africa and Asia. It gave Britain access to the riches of the Spanish Empire. It confirmed that London was the financial heart of the Western world. Perhaps the greatest sign of Britain's strength was that over the next fifty years it was able to lose the American colonies, undergo industrialization, fight the wars of the French Revolution, and still remain the world's foremost power.

But if Britain was victorious in 1763, it was also exhausted. The struggle with France had lasted half a century. It had been fought at sea and on battlefields in Europe, America, and Asia. The fleets and the armies had been expensive. Moreover, like any victorious imperial statesman, Grenville knew that troops and ships would have to remain on station to safeguard what had been won. The problem was how to pay for them.

The prime minister looked westward for an answer. The colonists in North America were Britons overseas, and no Britons had gained more than they from France's defeat. Ever since they had won their first footholds in the New World, the colonists had lived with warfare. They had fought the Dutch, the Spanish, the French, and, always, the Indians. Their goal, like that of Britain itself, had been mastery. In immediate terms they wanted control of the seaboard, the fur trade, and the vast rich lands of the interior. Now they had achieved that, all of it. In larger terms, some of them already saw a vision of their own potential strength. One sign had been the New England expedition of 1745 that captured the mighty French fortress of Louisbourg in Nova Scotia without help. Another came in 1754, when Benjamin Franklin proposed a plan of colonial unity to a congress in Albany, New York. A third, not long after, was the skill with which young Colonel George Washington saved himself and the Virginia militiamen he led from the disastrous defeat that the British general Edward Braddock suffered in western Pennsylvania.

Whatever their vision of the future, colonials of all sorts knew how high a price they had paid for Britain's victory. Frontier people had lived with terror and had dealt in it themselves. Disease and battle had devoured men who went off to fight. Tax bills had soared. The colonists believed they had done their part.

But George Grenville saw it differently. From his point of view, the colonials had won great gains at little cost. He knew that only rarely had the separate provinces managed to cooperate in the war effort. One colony might commit men and resources; another would hold back. Colonial ships supposedly carrying prisoners for exchange had in fact carried goods to sell. Fur traders in Albany had dealt with their French counterparts in Montreal. Sugar and molasses from the French and Spanish Caribbean had flowed freely to the distilleries and the refineries of New York and Boston.

Grenville also knew how difficult a task Britain's colonial administrators faced. Governors could not obtain their salaries unless they violated their instructions. Customs men could not convince American juries to convict smugglers. The White Pine Act, the Iron Act, the Hat Act, and the Molasses Act could not be enforced. Other powerful Britons held a similar view. Grenville's parliamentary colleague Charles Townshend recalled how he had had to deal with the land riots that plagued New Jersey at midcentury and how he had decided then that the Americans could not rule themselves. Powerful officials of the Anglican Church cursed New England for its Puritanism and Virginia for its insistence that parsons were merely the servants of planters.

Grenville had every reason to think he could do something about these problems in a way that everyone would accept. He knew perfectly well how the absolute monarchies in France and Spain would have handled them, but the French and Spanish way was not the British. Grenville was the king's servant, but only because he could command the support of the Commons as well as the Crown. Parliament was the safeguard of all Britons. Only with its consent could the king raise taxes or pass laws. No Briton need fear that an arbitrary monarchy would ever confiscate his property—Parliament existed to prevent that. It was a sacred British belief that the king could do no wrong. It was an equally sacred belief that Parliament could do no harm to the British Constitution. Ultimately, Parliament and its ways *were* the Constitution, so close was the tie between them. When the Boston lawyer and pamphleteer James Otis tried to work out a way of separating them, all he got for his effort was more disturbance in his own already unstable mind.

The costs of the war, the looseness of the empire, the certainty that Parliament was the right institution to legislate a remedy; these formed the background to Grenville's decision to change the way the colonies were run. The immediate goal was modest: The colonists simply had to pay the costs of their own administration. Grenville proposed three steps to achieve that goal. He took two of them in the Revenue Act, or "Sugar Act," of 1764. First, the notorious inefficiency of the Navigation System had to be brought to an end. Wholesale smuggling and haphazard enforcement would stop. If colonial juries would not bring in convictions, let offenders be tried in courts of vice-admiralty. The first of these began sitting in Halifax, Nova Scotia, in 1764. In 1768 others were established in Boston, Philadelphia, and Charles Town. These were special courts originally intended to deal with the technicalities of maritime law, where a trained judge, appointed to serve at the Crown's pleasure, would have the only say. If there were not enough petty officials to enforce the law, more would be appointed. If they faced damage suits when they could not make their charges stick, the courts would protect them with certificates of "probable cause." If the customs service was still not up to the job, the royal navy would help. Customs men and sailors alike would have the incentive of gaining one-third the value of every ship and cargo on which they secured a condemnation. It made no difference that this was the same principle on which the navy operated against wartime enemies. Smugglers, after all, were the enemies of the imperial system.

The second step that the Sugar Act took built on practices that the Navigation System had long established. Sugar was the foremost American product, and in 1733 the Molasses Act had been passed to restrict British commerce to the produce of the British sugar islands. The act allowed sugar and molasses from places such as Jamaica and Barbados to be traded freely within the empire. But it imposed a prohibitive duty on the produce of the French and Spanish islands and of Brazil. On molasses, it was sixpence per gallon. The purpose of that duty had not been to raise revenue but rather to secure British markets for British planters. Many of those planters lived as absentees in England, and some sat in Parliament. They had a way of seeing that the British government protected their interests.

But the tax on foreign molasses had rarely been collected in the colonies. Grenville's plan was to reduce it to threepence a gallon and to enforce the new rate rigorously. There would be new duties on other goods as well, including some on the inter-colonial trade. Elaborate paperwork would have to accompany every cargo to guarantee that there was no fraud. The purpose was not to protect producers elsewhere in the empire; it was to raise revenue. The act's preamble said so. Despite some pamphlets written in protest and some resolutions by a few provincial assemblies, the act took effect. British officials enforced it as well as they could until war finally broke out a decade later.

Grenville's third step was more sweeping. The Sugar Act imposed duties to be collected at colonial ports, but the real goal was to reach into the heart of the American economy. The result was the Stamp Act. Grenville signaled his intention to introduce it as early as March 1764, but Parliament did not pass it until more than a year later. It was to take effect on November 1, 1765.

Using stamps to raise revenue was nothing new. Colonial assemblies occasionally had imposed stamp duties, and the British people were used to them; to this day, the British government has some in effect. The principle was simple. Before one could legally possess an object or carry out an action listed in the act, one had to buy the appropriate stamp from an official distributor. The act of 1765 imposed a host of stamp duties. All documents bearing on court cases, or on church matters, or on admission to public office would have to be stamped. So would bills of lading, letters of marque, deeds, other documents in land transactions, liquor licenses, wills, probate orders, bail bonds, and articles of apprenticeship. Passports and notarizations, dice and playing cards, newspapers and pamphlets, almanacs and calendars, all would have to have stamps. There would also have to be a separate stamp for each sheet of a legal document and for each advertisement in a publication, and on publications that were not in English the duty would be doubled. The act set up sliding scales: The larger a land transaction or a book, the greater the duty. In the view of policy-makers, the Stamp Act would be virtually self-enforcing, without any need for elaborate bureaucracy. Appointing a stamp distributor for each province would be enough.

The Stamp Act specified that these duties were payable in sterling. Americans would not be able to use the foreign coins, the paper currency, the bills of exchange, or the direct barter to which they were accustomed. The act would be enforced in the vice-admiralty courts, which in 1765 meant going to Halifax for the trial. A successful prosecution under the act would mean confiscation of the goods or the land involved, with one-third of the booty each for the local stamp distributor, the provincial governor, and whoever had informed. The revenues raised would remain in the colonies, paying the salaries of officials and the costs of troops. But neither troops nor officials would be subject to colonial control.

The Stamp Act differed in important ways from all previous imperial legislation. One was its pervasiveness. Any colonist who bought or sold land, became an apprentice, went to church, married, read a newspaper, drank in a tavern, gambled, took public office, shipped goods elsewhere, or went to court would feel its effects. A second was its mode of collection: The taxes would be constantly evident, not paid once at a port of entry and then hidden in the overall price. A third was its requirement that payment be in sterling, with the threat of forfeiture if payment was not made. For people who rarely saw hard British coin, that threat was real. The act was part of a general assault on provincial paper money. Since 1752 the New England colonies had been forbidden to make their money legal tender, and in 1764 that prohibition was extended to all the colonies. The Stamp Act managed to offend everyone. The rich, the poor, producers, consumers, the powerful, the powerless, people of commerce, people of the fields, old people making their wills, young people planning to marry, pious people going to church, ribald people going to the tavern, all of them would feel it. Can there be any wonder that the colonists did not like it?

The movement that nullified the Stamp Act and forced its repeal was the first great drama of the Revolution. How that movement came about, who made it up, and how taking part in it changed the Americans themselves will be central problems discussed in this chapter and the next. The movement itself changed the issues. Colonial writers attacked the rationales that British spokesmen offered. They forced inconsistencies into the open; they made Parliament search for new ways to achieve its goals. Direct colonial action made whole policies unworkable. Despite the number of times the British backed down, colonial resistance stiffened England's determination to finally resolve the issue its way. The Sugar Act and the Stamp Act were simply the first expressions of a larger British policy aimed at establishing new, firmer control over the colonies. It makes sense to look at that policy as a whole, rather than to take incidents one by one.

The central issue was Parliament's power to legislate for the colonies and to tax them. In strict theory, the two were not the same. Legislation meant requiring people to do some things and forbidding them to do others. Legally, it was an act of sovereign power. In British usage *sovereign power* meant the king, the House of Lords, and the House of Commons acting together as the King-in-Parliament. But taxes were another matter. Britons regarded them as the free gift of the people for the king's use. Legally, a tax was an act not of the government but rather of the people, through their representatives. That is why only the Commons, which represented the people, could initiate money bills and amend them. The House of Lords could do no more than say yea or nay to whatever the House of Commons produced.

Some aspects of the new British policy were clearly acts of government. The Proclamation Line that was intended to keep whites and Indians apart and thus prevent frontier warfare was one. So, too, was the decision to establish an American Board of Customs Commissioners and site it in Boston, and the decision in 1768 to deploy troops there for the commissioners' protection. So, too, was the decision in 1774 to organize a government on French lines for the conquered province of Quebec. Some of these actions, certainly, were statesmanlike. The Proclamation Line may have represented the last real hope that the western Indians would be able to preserve their way of life. By recognizing the French customs and the Roman Catholic faith of the *habitants*, the Quebec Act may have kept Canada from undergoing the agony that has tortured Ireland. Almost everyone in the colonies recognized that sometimes such acts were necessary and that the King-in-Parliament was the best means for carrying them out. By itself, none of these acts would have caused more than debate and mild protest before 1760. The Quebec Act probably would have led to more than most. It offended the land hunger of Virginians by taking the Mississippi Valley out of their control, and it offended the anti-Catholicism of New Englanders by recognizing popery virtually next door. But the colonists would have had little ground to attack the principle that Parliament could pass such an act if it chose.

These acts caused more than simple debate because they became closely bound to the problem of taxation. Parliament itself made the confusion worse at a number of points. The first came in the spring of 1766, in the form of the Declaratory Act.

Parliament enacted this law as a gesture to its own self-image. The Stamp Act had proven unworkable in the colonies, and opposition to it was rising even in Britain. For reasons that had nothing to do with America, Grenville had lost both the king's confidence and his hold over the Commons and had stepped down. His loss of power was part of a larger problem of maintaining stable ministries that King George faced until Frederick, Lord North emerged as prime minister in 1770. Central in the ministry that followed Grenville was William Pitt, the architect of Britain's defeat of France and a man who believed that the Stamp Act was a prime piece of foolishness. Pitt's French policies and his attitude toward the Stamp Act made him a hero to all Americans, but he also believed in Parliament's supremacy. The Declaratory Act asserted that Parliament had power "to make laws and statutes . . . to bind the colonies and people of *America* . . . in all cases whatsoever." It seemed straightforward, but it was a masterpiece of doublespeak. An Englishman could take "all cases whatsoever" to include taxation. A colonial could take it that "laws and statutes" and taxation were not the same thing. But however one read it, it appeared at the time to be little more than a blustering afterthought, a gesture to Parliament's wounded pride at having had to repeal the Stamp Act.

It became clear in the following year, 1767, that it was more. At the same time when it had passed the Stamp Act, Parliament had also passed a Mutiny Act (also known as a Quartering Act) to provide for the care of British troops stationed in the colonies. This law required that each colonial assembly appropriate money to house the troops and supply their needs. New York's assembly refused to comply. Parliament's response was stern. It passed an act that forbade the assembly to do anything at all until it voted the money the Mutiny Act required. The assembly finally did what Parliament wanted, but people all over America saw the New York Restraining Act as disgraceful. Moreover, the supply of the troops stationed in New York City would remain a political sore spot into the next decade.

A second problem with more general implications also broke out in 1767. It seemed to some British officials that the Americans had rejected the Stamp Act solely because of *where* the tax would be collected. They would accept an "external" tax, collected at the ports, but they would not accept an "internal" one, collected where they did business. Britons did have reasons for their confusion. One was the long submission of the colonists to the Navigation System, which used punitive taxes as a means of directing colonial trade where Britain wanted it to go. Another was that despite some murmuring and halfhearted protest, they also submitted to the Sugar Act, which was explicitly intended to raise revenue. A third was ambiguity in some of their protests against the Stamp Act. According to one widely circulated report, Virginia Burgesses objected on the ground that they had always controlled their own "internal polity and taxation." Did that mean internal affairs and *all* taxation? Or would they accept a parliamentary tax if it was collected at the ports rather than within the province? Whatever the Virginians meant, Benjamin Franklin gave the impression in testimony before the House of Commons that an external tax would be acceptable.

The Burgesses' objection seems purely technical, but throughout the colonial years technical questions had led to lengthy debates, usually between governors and assemblies. Now the chancellor of the exchequer, Charles Townshend, made a blunder that allowed the British government to be brought in. Townshend found himself obliged to raise more money, for he had allowed a massive drop in Britain's taxation of its own land. The seeming American distinction between external taxes and internal ones offered the chancellor a solution.

He proposed that Parliament raise colonial revenue by taxing painters' colors, glass, lead, paper, and tea as they entered colonial ports. These were among the duties that the newly created American customs commissioners were given the task of collecting.

Townshend's program failed. Though the taxes remained on the law books until 1770, collecting them proved impossible. The result was that once again Parliament's pride and the problem of colonial revenue became intertwined. When Parliament did repeal the duties, it left the tax on tea in effect. This, like the Declaratory Act, was a gesture to Parliament's own self-image. Whether there was any point in levying taxes when those taxes could not be collected seemed immaterial. It was important to assert the principle that Parliament could do what it wanted, when it wanted, to whom it wanted.

In fact, once the other duties were repealed, the tea tax was more or less successfully collected, at least on tea that was legitimately imported rather than "honestly smuggled." In 1773, however, Parliament once again turned to the American colonies to resolve problems that had arisen elsewhere. Again it demonstrated that the Americans counted least as far as it was concerned. In 1733 the voices of West Indies sugar planters had rung loudest in the Commons, and the result had been the Molasses Act. In 1767 Townshend had risked setting off an American uproar in order to lower taxes for British landowners, and the result had been renewed resistance. Now it was the East India Company whose interests seemed most important; the result was the beginning of the final crisis.

Like the chartered companies that began American colonization, the East India Company tried to carry out both the private function of making a profit and the public task of governing a society. Like the colonization companies, it mixed these in a way that made it impossible to do either. Thanks to its ramshackle structure and to the ineptitude, or worse, of its servants, the company was failing either to return a profit to its shareholders or to consolidate Britain's hold on India. But the company's survival was important, both for British purposes of state and for the fortunes of the many well-placed investors who had money in it. Parliament decided to rescue it—the result was the Tea Act of 1773.

The act gave the East India Company two benefits. One was to allow it to market its tea directly to America, using its own agents there. Now it could bypass the network of auctions, wholesalers, and colonial merchants through which its tea previously had been sold. This was a straightforward rationalization of its business. It would give the company the same efficiency and economies of scale that global corporations seek in our own time. The other benefit was to free the company of the duty on tea that it imported to Britain and then reshipped to America. Only the Townshend tax of threepence a pound would remain. The combination, ministers foresaw, would make taxed tea sold by the company so cheap that it could undercut both tea that was traded legitimately by American merchants and tea that was smuggled in, usually by the same merchants. The consumer would benefit, for tea would drop in price. The company would benefit, for it would find the revenue in America that it could not raise in Britain or the East. The treasury would benefit, for taxes would be raised. Parliament's pride would benefit, for at last the colonies would have accepted a tax that Parliament had imposed. No one in London thought very much about the American merchants who might be crushed by the East India Company's newfound strength.

The Sugar Act, the Stamp Act, the Townshend taxes, the Tea Act—these were the major mileposts along the road to imperial crisis. Had Parliament not passed them, there certainly would have been no American Revolution. What lay behind them? Was it mere blundering and happenstance, as many historians have thought? Was it conspiracy, as rebellious Americans came to believe? Or was there a logic built into the imperial situation that was working itself out?

It was neither incompetence nor simple accident. The men who made British policy—Grenville, Townshend, Lord Hillsborough, Lord Shelburne, Lord North, King George—were as capable of both wisdom and folly as anyone else. They did their work, however, within a larger framework of British needs, and they made policy to suit those needs. Despite colonial fears, that framework was not held together by conspiracy. Rather, it rested on the realities of power and development within the empire. British landowners, West Indies sugar planters who actually lived in England, and the East India Company all had louder voices in Whitehall than the North Americans. So, too, did the royal governors and placemen who filled their correspondence with reports of colonial "disorder." British policy responded.

In the long run, British policy would lead to stagnation and underdevelopment for the North American economy, and this was no accident. The southern and Caribbean colonial economies suited British needs perfectly. The goods they produced had to be marketed in Britain. If they grew more produce than the metropolis needed, Britain would get the benefit of selling the surplus elsewhere in Europe. The wheat, corn, rye, and animals that northern farmers raised were less necessary to Britain itself, so it let them be marketed more freely. But the northern towns offered the possibility of complex urban economic development that would compete directly with Britain. Restraining that development was one thrust of eighteenth-century British colonial policy. The Hat Act and the Iron Act were not themselves serious restrictions, but they did point the way to further curbs on colonial industry. In 1764 Grenville's government followed the precedent those acts set when it forbade colonial assemblies to make their paper currencies legal tender. The Sugar Act, the Stamp Act, and the Townshend taxes were efforts to cream off what American development was producing. The Tea Act was a direct assault by the empire's foremost economic power on the merchants of the port towns.

Writer Theodore Draper suggests that British fear of American development was a central theme in the transatlantic "struggle for power." It *is* the case that during the very same years British domination over Ireland and India was leading to the long-term subordination of their economies to British needs. In those countries, local merchants and local trading networks were crushed as the British moved in. Local industry was stifled so British industry could prosper. Local agriculture was organized to produce staple crops for Britain to process, rather than mixed crops for local people to use. When Britain turned from "salutary neglect" to stricter control, it pointed its North American policy in the same direction.

The simple facts were these. The colonies were vibrant, dynamic, and only partly tied into the network of imperial control. Britain, more vibrant, more dynamic, was determined to organize the world for its own benefit. It had been willing to wage endless war with France and Spain for mastery. It had a government that was committed in both practical terms and in principle to the idea that power should be centralized in London. Now Britain was willing to do what was necessary in order to keep its colonies colonial. Given its situation, its rulers would have been foolish to do anything else. But given America's situation, its people would have been equally foolish not to resist.

II

Britain achieved something quite remarkable in 1765: It brought its subjects in America closer together than they had ever come before. The people who made up colonial America had little to unite them, other than in the vague sense that they all felt the power of Britain. Part of the history of the Revolution tells how some of them created a common political identity. But other parts tell how they developed many separate identities, not only as Carolinians or Pennsylvanians or New Yorkers but also as merchants, planters, artisans, and farmers, as black people, Indi-

ans, and women—and as loyalists. Most of all, the Revolution's
story tells how one coalition after another was built, what it
achieved, and what became of it. The coalitions that came together in 1765, 1767, and 1773 to oppose British policy were not
the same as the one that formed in 1776 to win independence.
Nor was any of these groups identical to the coalition of 1787–88
that established the United States.

We must take each of these alliances on its own terms. What
groups formed them? What did they share? In what ways did
they differ? What did each group seek? How did they come to
political consciousness? Asking such questions destroys the notion that we can simply speak of "Americans" or "colonists" or
even "revolutionaries." It also destroys the notion that we can
treat the Revolution as one group's exclusive property and then
measure everyone else by that group's standard. Asking these
questions enables us to understand much more clearly what the
Revolution was. It enables us to see much more readily the
changes that it brought to people's lives.

Throughout the era Americans who would have called themselves the "better sort" were important. Sometimes they acted
together. Sometimes they split apart. Sometimes they virtually
decided what would happen. Sometimes they reacted to events
thrust upon them. Sometimes these great planters, large northern landowners, well-to-do merchants, skilled lawyers, and
smooth politicians got all they wanted. Sometimes they did not.
But there is no understanding the Revolution without understanding what they did.

Like everyone else, the rulers of colonial America confronted
the crisis in terms of what they were. By the time of the Stamp
Act, they had established a lively tradition of open political debate. For decades they had been turning small problems into
large issues, honing their constitutional principles and their political rhetoric to a fine sharpness. How, with whom, and over
what they disputed varied, of course. New Englanders proclaimed how much they valued domestic peace, and proceeded

to assail one another. In New York, New Jersey, and Pennsylvania, public life was endlessly factious. Farther south slavery gave white rulers good reason to keep close together, but they never hesitated to open verbal fire on governors or on British officials. Ordinary people in all the colonies became used to the spectacle of the elite arguing loudly about its problems. They became used as well to the elite's insisting that whatever the argument was about, it made a difference to everyone. The most potent weapon colonial leaders held was their assertive language and their public style.

This tradition of debate and argument, in a press that was as free as any in the eighteenth-century world, helps to explain the sheer wordiness of the Revolution. Between the Stamp Act and the Constitution, American printers poured out political pamphlets, newspaper essays, broadsides, poems, sermons, songs, and doggerel. Town meetings, popular conventions, revolutionary committees, and regular assemblies passed endless declarations and resolutions. The "better sort" did not produce all this often-heated discourse. Watching ordinary people learn to think and especially to speak for themselves is one of the most exciting aspects of watching the Revolution develop. But except for Tom Paine and a few others, the major authors of the era either came from the upper class or hoped to join it. What they wrote tells us a great deal about how people of their kind confronted the crises and problems of their age. From 1763 to 1776, the problem was relations with Britain. Men who set out to write in opposition had two main tasks before them. One was to show what the real effects of British policy were. The other was to turn the crisis from a series of troubles and quandaries into a pattern that made sense.

Some elite writers saw the gathering problems in sharply material terms. One such was Governor Stephen Hopkins of Rhode Island, who published *Essay on the Trade of the Northern Colonies* in 1764. Unlike any other province except Connecticut, Rhode Island elected its own governor. Most colonial magis-

trates came to their posts from Britain, but Hopkins was a
Rhode Islander. He owed his high office to other colonials who
chose him to fill it, not to the favor of distant great men. Provi-
dence and Newport, which dominated Rhode Island's economy,
were trading towns, and Hopkins could see what George
Grenville's policies would mean for them. He understood the realities of power in the imperial framework as well. He wrote his
essay to show the real effects of the empire at work.

The governor's main argument was simple: The northern
colonies needed free trade, both with the non-British Caribbean
and with the Old World. Hopkins skipped lightly over the fact
that slaves formed one of the most valuable commodities in
which his people dealt. His major point was that, despite imperial theory, the restrictions that Britain imposed on colonial trade
did not serve the commonweal. They simply served the interests
of some, especially West Indies planters. Those privileged men
enjoyed high prices in a guaranteed market, because the northern ports could not get enough sugar and molasses. They also
enjoyed a ready, cheap supply of foodstuffs and manufactured
goods, because a constant glut in West Indies markets kept
prices there low. What counted was simply the ability to get
things done in London. These men had it, and the North Americans did not. In the short run, that fact would lead to stagnation
for the northern colonies. In the long run, it would create problems for Britain, because the colonies would not buy British
manufactures if they could not pay for them.

Hopkins came as close as any writer to speaking for the entire colonial merchant class, but in 1769 a Charles Town merchant, Henry Laurens, decided that the time had come to speak
for himself. By then Laurens and John Hancock of Boston were
the foremost victims of the "customs racketeering" that plagued
colonial administration in the late 1760s. The Sugar Act and the
Townshend taxes had established so many technicalities and formal requirements for colonial traders to meet that a clever customs man could fleece them almost at will. One trick was to

allow long-established ways of doing business to continue even though the law now forbade them, and then to crack down suddenly. Another was to make a minor technical violation the excuse for condemning a whole ship and cargo. Courts readily protected officials with certificates of "probable cause" even when the charge came to nothing.

Major merchants like Laurens and Hancock lost a great deal of property to customs men who operated this way. Boatmen taking small cargoes across provincial boundaries and seamen with small private ventures hidden in some corner on the ships they sailed became victims, too. In Laurens's case the hurt was especially galling, for the judge of the vice-admiralty court in Charles Town was his own nephew, Egerton Leigh. Indeed, for a time Leigh not only presided over the court where his uncle's ships were condemned but, as attorney general of South Carolina, also assisted in bringing the prosecutions. Laurens finally decided to let the world know what was going on, so he published his *Extracts from the Proceedings of the Court of Vice-Admiralty.* The pamphlet was not much more than a listing of the misfortunes its author had suffered at the court's hands. But the simple documentation filled a full forty-one pages, and Laurens went on to discuss the general injustices that were built into British customs procedure. By 1769 virtually anyone who had any reason to deal with the customs service knew such stories. Like Hopkins, Laurens was reflecting on the way that Americans lived as inferiors in the imperial world. Merely to point that fact out was to bring its rightfulness into question.

Many other writers, however, made their case differently. To understand what they were saying, we must confront the language they used. We might compare the problems to be found in reading them with the difficulties that someone from another age might have with writing from our own time. Such a reader would need to appreciate how figures like Darwin, Marx, Freud, and Einstein have shaped our mental world. They are not the only influences on us, of course: Judaism, Christianity, and Islam are only three of many others. But to a reader who did not understand what we mean by terms like *evolution, social class, personality,* and *relativity*, our language would be gibberish.

The eighteenth-century literate elite lived in a different mental world. They used terms that we also use, such as *liberty, virtue,* and *corruption*, but they did not necessarily mean what we mean by them. Their language, the reality that their language described, and the way their language shaped their thoughts and actions have been the subject of intensive investigation by historians, including Caroline Robbins, Bernard Bailyn, J.G.A. Pocock, and Gordon S. Wood. What they have found is central to how we now understand the Revolution.

The roots of eighteenth-century political language lay in three very different historical experiences. The first took place centuries earlier, in the Renaissance city-states of northern Italy. All over Europe the power of the Holy Roman Empire and of the papacy was waning. So were the ways of life and the patterns of belief on which that power had rested. In Spain, France, and England, the result was the emergence of energetic new monarchies ruling whole nations. But in places like Florence, Venice, and Milan, people turned instead to the idea of a republic, of a society where citizens ruled themselves. Breathing new life into traditions passed down from ancient Greece and Rome, they found in republicanism a better way of running their societies.

Yet their efforts failed again and again. Great Italian families like the Borgias and outside powers like France disrupted republican experiments repeatedly. It began to seem inevitable that a republic would fail and a despot would arise. Influential thinkers like Niccolò Machiavelli became preoccupied with the problem of why this was so. The result of their labors was a theory of politics and a theory of history. For the first time since the classical age, it became possible to see the world that people lived in as the product of human action rather than of divine will or mere chance. Their political theory held that a republic became possible only when its citizens thought of the whole, not of them-selves. Central to it was the notion that the good citizen was a man of virtue. The word *virtue* connoted not sexual morality but, rather, tough independence, physical strength, military courage, and public spirit. Virtue was impossible if a man owed his well-being to someone else. In consequence, thinkers concluded that a society of small producers was far more likely to generate a vir-tuous citizenry than one of masters and servants or landlords and tenants. Their republican theory of history told these same thinkers that even if men could establish such a society, it was unlikely to last long. The very energy of hardy republicans would lead to conquest, accumulation, and eventually to luxury and de-cay. For these theorists, republicanism offered the best possible way to live, the only way, in fact, to be fully human. Yet of ne-cessity, it seemed, every attempt to live by it was doomed to fail. The books that developed this line of thought, such as Machi-avelli's *Discourses on the First Ten Books of Livy*, became central texts for all political philosophy in the early modern world.

The second source lay in medieval England. There parlia-mentarians and jurists had developed a body of law that consis-tently emphasized the rights of the individual rather than the power of the ruler. In this common-law tradition, a man could be sure he was free if he knew that his person and his property were his own. English common law did not presume that such freedom was a natural or a human right, only that it was a right of English subjects. It did not presume that all English subjects were equal, for class, sex, and age all made great differences in the amount of freedom a person could enjoy. But it did assume that someone who enjoyed freedom had every reason to hang on to it; and its technicalities, precedents, and procedures offered means to defend this freedom when it was threatened. The most obvious was the need to convince a jury drawn from a defen-dant's neighbors, rather than a judge appointed by the king, be-fore a person could be convicted. What this had in common with the Italian tradition was the belief that liberty was good, that it could be enjoyed only in very specific social conditions, and that those conditions were easily lost. But for the Italian thinkers, liberty was a public right that allowed a citizen to take part in running society. For common-law jurists, it was private, the right of a subject to be sure of where he stood.

The third source lay in the upheavals that England went through in the seventeenth and eighteenth centuries. The Puritan Revolution of the 1640s, the Glorious Revolution of 1688, and the gradual settling down that Sir Robert Walpole imposed in the 1720s and 1730s offered endless material for discussion. English people had deposed two kings, sending one to the scaffold and the other into exile. They had lived for more than a decade without a king or a House of Lords. They hobbled the restored monarchy with the Bill of Rights and subordinated it to Parliament. Diggers, Levellers, the Family of Love, Fifth Monarchy Men, and their heirs produced a popular radicalism that made Oliver Cromwell's look tepid. In the midst of it all, a long series of writers speculated on the history and the meaning of British freedom. The French social theorist Montesquieu celebrated Britain's eighteenth-century settlements as the perfection of political wisdom. Even after the Revolution Mozart would invoke the notion of being free and English through the character Blonde in his opera *Die Entführung aus dem Serail* (*The Escape from the Seraglio*). Caught in a Turkish harem, she sings that "a heart born to freedom cannot let itself be enslaved." She is English, and all of educated Europe would have grasped the reference.

English thinkers, too, encouraged the world to believe that Britons were uniquely free. But from James Harrington and John Milton in the mid-seventeenth century to Richard Price and Catharine Macaulay in the late eighteenth, "real Whigs" or "commonwealthmen" or "country" thinkers stressed how constant was the danger that freedom would be lost. Writing together as "Cato," the popular pamphleteers John Trenchard and

Thomas Gordon insisted throughout Walpole's time that it virtually was lost. Even in England, Walpole's administration acquired the derisive nickname "old corruption." "Cato's" essays
were more commonly read and more frequently imitated by
colonials than any other English writings.

Drawing on all these traditions, American writers came to
see the political world in terms of an unending struggle between
liberty and its enemies. Sometimes they called the enemy of liberty power. By that, they usually meant a government's ability
and desire to make people do what it wanted. Sometimes they
called it oppression. By that, they meant the use of inordinate
strength to take away the property of free men and turn them
into cringing dependents. Sometimes they described it as corruption. This was not simple bribe taking or embezzlement. It
was their shorthand for all the social entanglements and all the
dependency that came with any way of life much more complex
than simple farming.

When Virginia's planters responded to the Stamp Act, they
brought their own experience and this language together.
Spurred by the anger of a young member named Patrick Henry,
they passed a series of resolutions against the act in June 1765.
Widely and not always accurately reported, these resolutions declared Virginia's opposition to the act on four separate grounds.
First, Virginia's founders had lost none of their English "Liberties, Privileges, Franchises and Immunities" when they emi-
grated. Second, two royal charters had confirmed their rights.
Third, the right to tax themselves by consent of their own representatives was "the distinguishing Characteristick" of their
"*British* freedom." Fourth, they had always controlled their own
"internal Polity and Taxation." As the Burgesses knew, the Stamp
Act challenged them in two ways. First, it threatened the property of all colonials, for if Parliament could take anything, it
could take everything. Second, it threatened the Burgesses' own
position as privileged men, for if Parliament could tax Virginians,

their own house would quickly fade to inconsequence. The Irish gentry had seen exactly that fate befall their Parliament in Dublin, and no Burgess wanted it to happen in Williamsburg.

Assemblies elsewhere followed the Virginians' lead. By the end of 1765, Rhode Island, Pennsylvania, Maryland, Connecticut, Massachusetts, South Carolina, New Jersey, and New York all had adopted similar resolves. In October a Stamp Act Congress with delegates from nine colonies gathered in New York City. The congress adopted fourteen resolutions against the act. Making all the points the Virginians had made, it went on to defend jury trials, to protest the act's burdens, and to assert that America already contributed enormously to Britain's well-being. It finished its work with petitions to Parliament and an address to the king. Clearly, the leaders of the colonies were alarmed.

Yet many problems remained. Political representation was a Briton's right, but Parliament said that *its* members represented the interests of all. The Burgesses asserted their control over "internal Polity and Taxation," but what did they mean by the phrase? If the colonials accepted that Parliament could legislate for them, how could they deny that it could tax them? What if Parliament passed a tax but called it a law? The Americans invoked the "ancient constitution," but Parliament itself was the heart of that Constitution. How, then, could Parliament violate it? These problems preoccupied many American writers through the decade of imperial strife. As they wrestled with them, writers destroyed not only the rationale for specific taxes and laws but also most of the rationale for the empire itself.

Daniel Dulany's historic moment came when he decided to address the first of these problems, Parliament's assertion that it stood for Britons everywhere. The claim was put strongly in the aftermath of the Sugar Act by ministerial spokesman Thomas Whately. In his pamphlet *The Regulations Lately Made concerning the Colonies and the Taxes Imposed upon Them, Considered*, Whately argued that whether or not a person could vote for a member of Parliament meant nothing. There were whole boroughs, like Leeds, Halifax, Birmingham, and Manchester, that sent no members at all. Not a single woman or child enjoyed the suffrage. Some important groups, like the merchants of London, had no immediate representation; others, like the universities at Oxford and Cambridge, did. Whately's point was that Parliament did not speak for particular interests; rather, its purpose was to determine the good of all. Like disenfranchised Britons, colonials all enjoyed "virtual" representation in the Commons. No British subject was "actually [represented], all are virtually represented in Parliament, for every Member sits . . . not as Representative of his own Constituents, but as one of that august Assembly by which all the Commons of *Great Britain* are represented."

Dulany had no trouble destroying Whately's logic. That there were English boroughs that had no members of their own did not mean that their people enjoyed no immediate representation. Every county in the realm had at least two members sitting for it, and a person did not have to stop living in Birmingham to vote for a member for Warwickshire. Even if he had no vote, he knew that the members for his county would have to pay the same taxes as himself and that they would know quickly if the burden became too great. But the only way a colonial could enjoy either a vote for Parliament or a seat in it was to move to Britain, and that meant that he would no longer be a colonial. Parliament might tax the colonies till they had nothing left, but its members would feel not the slightest pain. By the time Dulany had finished with Whately's argument, it lay in shreds. The British would not try to use it again.

John Dickinson succeeded Dulany as the foremost American pamphleteer. Though he was a wealthy lawyer from Philadelphia, Dickinson pretended in his writing to be a simple "Farmer in Pennsylvania." In December 1767 he began publishing a series of "Letters" in the *Pennsylvania Chronicle*. Other newspapers quickly picked them up, and by March 1768 all twelve had been collected in a single pamphlet. Like Daniel Dulany, Dickinson was a man led by both interest and temperament to a conservative view of the world. Unlike Dulany, Dickinson chose the American side at independence, but he spent so long making up his mind that many people believed he had become a Tory. His London legal education gave him close ties to Britain. His great fortune gave him much to lose. The world as it was had been good to him, and that showed in his choice of words. "This I call an innovation," he thundered in his second Letter. It was the strongest condemnation he could imagine.

In 1767 Dickinson found many "innovations" to worry about. One was the act suspending New York's assembly until it voted supplies for British troops stationed there, as Parliament required. By suspending the assembly, Parliament had posed the problem of the constitutional standing of the colonial legislatures. Assemblymen had long assumed that somehow they were both subordinate in the imperial system and the equals of Parliament in regard to their own societies. They opened their sessions with the same rituals; their members claimed the same immunities and privileges; they prefaced their statutes with the same legal formulas. But did they really amount to nothing more than local conveniences, comparable to an English borough council? Could Parliament suspend or change them at will? For Dickinson, the answer was clear: "The assembly of New-York either had, or had not, a right to refuse submission" to the Quartering Act. "If they had, and I imagine no American will say they had not, then the parliament had *no right* to compel them to execute it or to punish them for not executing it."

But Dickinson's great subject was the Townshend taxes. Charles Townshend had proposed them to Parliament with the firm belief that the distinction between an internal tax and an external one was silly. But he also thought that the Americans themselves had made it and that they ought to be prepared to live with the consequences. What, in fact, *did* the Virginia Burgesses mean in 1765 when they claimed control over their own "internal Polity and Taxation"? Were they conceding Townshend's point in advance? Or were they asserting the right to control all their internal affairs and all their taxation as well?

For Dickinson, a tax was a tax. Whatever its form, Parliament had no right to levy one on the colonies. No innovator, he fell back on a point the colonials had been making all along: "The parliament . . . possesses a legal authority to *regulate* the trade of Great-Britain, and all her colonies," but it had no right to tax the colonies in any way. Where and how a tax was collected made no difference. Parliament itself had announced that the purpose of the Sugar Act, the Stamp Act, and the Townshend taxes was to raise revenue, not to regulate trade. The British tradition that a tax was the free gift of the people either meant that the colonials taxed themselves or it meant nothing at all.

John Dickinson had the genuine conservative's acute awareness that one thing leads to another. "All artful rulers," he wrote, "who strive to extend their power . . . endeavor to give to their attempts as much semblance of legality as possible. Those who succeed them may . . . go a little further, for each new encroachment will be strengthened by a former . . . A free people therefore can never be too quick in observing, nor too firm in opposing the beginnings of *alteration* . . . respecting institutions formed for their security." For him, as for the Burgesses and for Daniel Dulany, the task before the colonists was simply to hold on to a good state of affairs. They had learned well the lessons that their heritage had taught them. They knew how easily their liberty could be lost.

Yet Dickinson kept stumbling over the problem of the subordinate position that the colonials occupied. On the surface, he offered no objection: "He, who considers these provinces as states distinct from the British Empire, has very slender notions of *justice* or of their *interests*. We are but parts of a *whole*; and therefore there must exist a power somewhere to preside, and preserve the connection . . . This power is lodged in the parliament." Yet the contradiction remained: "We are as much dependent on Great-Britain, as a perfectly free people can be on another." Was it really possible to be both dependent and free at the same time? Being dependent meant that the colonials never could be their own masters. The theory of the British Empire rested on the belief that all its parts were interdependent, that within it all conflicting interests were balanced. Its laws were "calculated to regulate trade, and preserve or promote a mutually beneficial intercourse." But as Dickinson could not help seeing, the reality was different. The colonies were underdeveloped, "a country of planters, farmers, and fishermen, not of manufacturers." What Americans needed, they had to buy. "Inexpressible . . . must be our distresses in evading the late acts, by the disuse" of British products. The cause lay in the imperial tie: "Great Britain had prohibited the manufacturing [of] iron and steel in these colonies . . . the *like* right she must have to prohibit any other manufactures among us." But why?

In 1774 Thomas Jefferson asked himself that question and decided that it had no answer, at least from the colonial point of view. Jefferson had been elected to Virginia's first revolutionary convention, and when illness kept him from attending, he drafted resolutions for it to consider. The convention took a less advanced stance than his, but his draft appeared in pamphlet form under the title *A Summary View of the Rights of British America*. What he wrote marked one of the major intellectual milestones on America's road away from Britain.

The question of what Parliament could and could not do to the colonies had vexed many a writer. It bothered the Boston politician and pamphleteer James Otis so much that it contributed to the loss of his sanity. But for Jefferson it did not exist. Parliament could do nothing. The first settlers had taken with them not the legal rights and obligations of Englishmen but the natural rights of emigrants. Once in America, they were free to establish "new societies, under such laws and regulations as to them [should] seem most likely to promote public happiness." Britain had asserted no "claim of superiority or dependence" then, and the emigrants had accepted none. Nor had Britain

borne the cost of settlement. The colonists' "own blood was spilt
. . . their own fortunes expended . . . for themselves they fought,
for themselves they conquered, and for themselves they have
right to" the land they had won. At most, Parliament had lent
them "assistance against an enemy," but accepting that aid had
never meant that the colonists "submitted themselves to her sovereignty." Parliament's claim to authority over the colonies was
no more than usurpation. The colonists had to live with the reality of dependency and subordination, but it never had been a
matter of right. The Navigation Acts, the Hat and Iron Acts,
even the act establishing an American post office were "void,"
for "the British parliament has no right to exercise authority
over us."

Jefferson's view of American history cut through all the intellectual tangles that had grown up around British policy. The
Stamp Act, the Townshend Acts, the New York Restraining Act,
the Tea Act, and now, in 1774, the laws passed to punish Boston
for the Tea Party offered good evidence that there was a concerted campaign to destroy American liberty. But in principle
they were no different from the acts that had gone before. To
Jefferson, Parliament had never possessed the right to pass any
of them. There was no need to worry about the difference between legislation and taxation, or between internal taxes and external ones. There was no need for elaborate explanations of
why the colonists did not enjoy representation in Parliament or
of what Parliament meant when it passed this law or that. There
was no reason at all why "160,000 electors in the island of Great
Britain should give law to four millions in the states of America,
every individual of whom is equal to every individual of them."

Not much was left when Jefferson finished his demolition of
the British theory of empire. All that still held it together was the
person of the king. Jefferson drafted the *Summary View* in
the form of suggestions for a "humble and dutiful" address to be
"presented to his majesty." To that extent, he bowed to the po-
lite formulas of his time. But for Jefferson, George III had little

about him of majesty. The king was "no more than the chief officer of the people, appointed by the laws, and circumscribed
with definite powers, to assist in working the great machine of
government." His power was for the people's "use, and conse-
quently subject to their superintendance." The empire was no
more than a network of separate republics, held together because they all shared the same constitutional monarch. Jefferson
was presenting a perfect statement of the notion of composite
monarchy, stripped of any notion that the monarch could be absolute either in the British realm or in the American dominions.
But he was colliding directly with the doctrine that the British
King-in-Parliament enjoyed absolute authority over all British
people and possessions.

Jefferson still thought that the network of separate republics
might last indefinitely. It was neither Americans' "wish, nor our
interest to separate." But no longer could the empire be based
on the subordination of one part of it to another. Colonials
would not cringe before the king: "Let those flatter who fear; it
is not an American art." Nor would they accept that Britons
could speak to him on Americans' behalf: "You have no ministers
for American affairs, because you have taken none from among
us." Nor would they grant any longer that their own economies
existed for the good of Britain rather than for the good of themselves: Let Parliament "not think to exclude us from going to
other markets to dispose of those commodities which they cannot use, or to supply those wants which they cannot supply."
Jefferson had stepped out of a world of hierarchy and subordination and into one of equality among men and among societies.
Only two things kept the step from being complete. One was
what little remained of Jefferson's acceptance that the king was
his sovereign. The Virginian would deal with that problem two
years later, when he wrote the Declaration of Independence.
The other was his own sovereignty, far greater than any the king
ever claimed, over the women in his life and over the slaves
whose labor gave him the time to think his soaring thoughts and

to write his elegant prose. That was a problem that Thomas Jefferson never would resolve.

III

Stephen Hopkins, Henry Laurens, the Burgesses of Virginia, Daniel Dulany, John Dickinson, and Thomas Jefferson: These were far from the only important writers on the imperial crisis. Some, like Martin Howard of Rhode Island, Samuel Seabury of New York, and Joseph Galloway of Pennsylvania, put the case against resistance. What they did took courage, for they suffered much more than the merely verbal wrath of their fellows for doing it. Others, like James Otis and John and Samuel Adams of Massachusetts, Alexander Hamilton of New York, and Richard Bland of Virginia, made powerful points on the colonial side. Men and some women who are much less well known turned out an array of pieces, short and long, that often tell a different story from the writings of the major pamphleteers. But the writers we have looked at show in sharp relief what happened to the colonial elite as they confronted the crisis.

Dulany and Dickinson illustrate the doubts and fears with which many of them had to deal. Dulany was far from the only man who was profoundly alarmed in the mid-1760s by Parliament and was even more alarmed in the mid-1770s by his fellow Americans. Dickinson was one of many who stood trembling on the edge in 1776, unable to make up his mind to live with what he had helped to start. Henry Laurens and the Virginia Burgesses show the wide range of arguments that the spokesmen for resistance used. For Laurens, the problems were hard and practical; for the Burgesses, they were matters of constitutionality and law. But for both, considerable self-interest was at stake. Laurens knew that he faced debtor's prison if the customs service continued much longer to have its way with his goods. Colonial assemblymen knew that they faced a future without power if Parliament could just sweep aside the way things had "always" been done.

Yet beneath the variations, there were parallel lines of development. One line led from doubt and uncertainty to militance. Tortured reasoning about laws and taxes and about internal taxes and external ones gave way to Jefferson's argument that Parliament could do nothing at all. Begging and petitioning gave way to the straightforward assertion of equality. Fawning on "the best of kings" yielded to boldly advising that "the name of George the third" not "be a blot in the page of history." A second development was the growing realization of what it meant to be unequal. Jefferson's assertion that colonials were as good as Britons was new. But it marked the resolution of a problem that had plagued every single one of his predecessors.

Most important, these writers moved ever closer to an awareness that, whatever needed doing, they could not do it alone. Dulany reasoned in abstruse legalities; Laurens described endless technical procedures; Dickinson flavored his prose with Latin quotations. But Jefferson wrote in clear, polished, highly readable English. The difference is not simply between three writers whose style was indifferent and one whose style was superb. It is that Jefferson understood that debate was one thing and resistance another. He saw that people outside his own class would have to be the real source of resistance; indeed, that for a decade now that was just what they had been. Debating fundamental issues is an important part of the process of any revolution. When people begin doing it, that is one sign that something has gone profoundly wrong in their lives. But intense as it was, the debate that Britain's policies provoked was only one of the elements that turned ordinary Americans from colonials to revolutionaries.

Three

RIOTS, RADICAL POLITICS,

AND RESISTANCE

Early Americans lived in a violent world. Colonizers from England, the Netherlands, Spain, France, and Portugal waged endless violent struggles for dominion. Whites throughout the hemisphere used violence to drive Indians from the land and more violence to make blacks labor upon it. Sea captains used the whip on their sailors. Rulers employed the organized violence of the state to keep "lesser" people in their place. That included deploying the regular army, mobilizing the militia, and publicly executing criminals, leaving their bodies to rot in full view. Seventeenth-century Puritan New Englanders used violence against witches and Quakers. Eighteenth-century Anglican Virginians used it against Baptists and Methodists. Drinking men in taverns settled their arguments with fists and knives. People in crowds threatened violence and sometimes turned to it to resolve problems that no one of them alone could handle.

These people were violent in a style that was normal and acceptable in their own early modern world, on both sides of the Atlantic. British colonials shared that style with Creoles in South America, with Britons who had stayed behind, and with people all over mainland Europe. That style was open and theatrical. A solemn judge pronouncing a sentence of death, a condemned man going to a gallows that stood in a public square, an army marching off to battle in its glittering glory, a master gathering his slaves and making them watch while the lash was laid on, a tavern braggart loudly asserting his superior manhood—all were acting out rituals to be seen and understood. Such people were giving messages, and they expected that others in their world would act accordingly. This was as true of crowd action as of any other aspect of the violence of early American life.

Crowds or mobs or popular uprisings were central to the public life of colonial and revolutionary America. By itself, no single riot can ever make a revolution. In the eighteenth-century world, rioting was often defensive. It was the act of people who wanted to restore or protect something good, not of people who were driven by a vision of change. But popular upheavals were central to the way that British power in America came to its end, and they were central as well to the beginnings of republicanism. We can understand these revolutionary crowds only against their colonial background. But we must also understand that in the Revolution crowds left that background behind. Beginning as a normal, almost functional part of the old order, they played a major part in bringing that order down. The consequence was that they helped put an end to the very conditions of their own quasi-legitimacy.

I

Virtually no place in America was immune from large-scale violence during the second half of the eighteenth century. In the two Carolinas backcountry "Regulators" faced down low-country grandees. There, as well as in Georgia, in Maryland, and on New York's western frontier, the war of independence became a vicious internal conflict. Pennsylvania's interior erupted in 1763, when the "Paxton Boys" murdered peaceful Indians who lived nearby and then marched on Philadelphia. It erupted again in

1792 with the Whiskey Rebellion. Central New Jersey was torn apart in the mid-eighteenth century by land riots. In New York's Hudson Valley, tenant discontent simmered through the 1750s and boiled up into a massive rising in 1766. Settlers from New England clashed with speculators, settlers, and political authorities from New York in the Green Mountains during the late 1760s and the early 1770s and broke free in 1777 to establish Vermont. Not just Massachusetts but much of the rest of rural New England turned to violence in 1786, during the rebellion of farmers and villagers known as Shays's Rebellion.

Nor were the cities any quieter. The streets of Boston and New York witnessed violent and sometimes lethal strife during the imperial crisis. Philadelphians avoided such conflict prior to independence, but they opened fire on one another during the Fort Wilson riot of 1779. In lesser towns, too, people took to the streets, threw brickbats, tore down houses, and defaced property. We will not look at all of the upheavals of the period in this chapter. Some will be passed by, and some discussed later. But to list these few gives an idea of how important violence was during the revolutionary era.

Why was this so? Was it simply that "the mob" turned violent every time its tether slipped? Or was it the expression of some vicious strain that always has disfigured the American soul? There can be no doubt that eighteenth-century crowds sometimes were bloodthirsty. Particularly in matters of racial strife, they helped to set ugly patterns that have reappeared again and again throughout American history. But crowd action had a specific place in the early modern world. It did not usually lead to bloodshed, and when it did, the authorities, not the crowd, were most often the cause. Sometimes crowds turned out at the urging and under the leadership of highly placed men. Sometimes they expressed the frustration and the anger of the "lesser sort" against their "betters." But almost always crowd action rested on a clear understanding of what was right and what was wrong, what ought to be endured and what ought to be resisted. It also rested on well-developed ideas about how resistance ought to be carried out.

Crowd action came very close to being an institution in early American life. In some ways the crowd became an institution of colonial society. Modern police departments did not exist, so crowds that were called sheriff's posses enforced the law; nor did modern fire departments exist, so crowds called volunteer fire companies gathered to save property and lives. Drawn into ranks and given officers, a crowd became a unit of the militia. Yet crowds that were less formal, less organized, and less recognized by officialdom were just as much a part of life. Sometimes they protected a community from a danger that faced everyone who lived in it. In places as far apart as Marblehead, Massachusetts, and Norfolk, Virginia, crowds kept smallpox victims from entering town, so contagion would not spread. When the royal navy sent a press gang into a port to kidnap men into service, it threatened everyone: prospective sailors, because life in the navy was appalling; merchants, because they dared not put their ships to sea; townsfolk and traders, because even small boats bearing food and firewood would not venture out on the harbor. Such a press threatened Boston in 1747, and the crowds that resisted it held control of the town for three days. In times of shortage, crowds kept merchants from exporting scarce foodstuffs. In times of moral outrage, they closed down houses of prostitution. In times of bigotry, they drove out sectarians. If inflated rhetoric, climbing to the heights of principle, was a prime social weapon of the elite, crowd action was a prime social weapon of the ordinary people.

Yet we cannot leave matters there, for eighteenth-century Americans knew crowds of many kinds. Again and again even the most prominent people declared that crowd action could be perfectly legitimate, almost natural. Thomas Jefferson once said that "a little rebellion" was like a "storm in the atmosphere" and spoke of watering the tree of liberty with the blood of tyrants. John Adams used a similar metaphor, comparing "church-quakes and state-quakes in the moral and political world" with "earth-quakes, storms and tempests in the physical." Some linked American rebelliousness with British freedom. "Our happy constitution," said Josiah Quincy of Massachusetts, gave Americans "impatience of injuries, and a strong resentment of insults." Governor Thomas Hutchinson of Massachusetts, whose sufferings at the hands of revolutionary crowds were intense, once observed that "mobs, a sort of them at least, are constitutional."

Men like these usually had crowds of a very specific sort in mind. Characteristically, such crowds drew their membership from the whole spectrum of colonial society. They might claim to be "the people," and they might all be wearing the long trousers and the plain hair of working people, rather than the knee breeches and powdered wigs of the gentry. But among the rioters there would be gentlemen as well as artisans, laborers, and apprentices, and everyone knew it. A "legitimate" crowd was usually urban and short-lived. Its members turned out, did what needed doing, and went back to their homes and their work.

Most important, a "legitimate" crowd acted within the "corporatist" political economy discussed in Chapter 1. In time of shortage, the rich had an obligation to help the rest; in time of trouble, the powerful had an obligation to help the weak. But if privileged men failed in their duty, lesser people might use violence to protect themselves. Poor people's right to a supply of bread at a fair price was more important than a merchant's right to seek his profit where he might. Usually the town fathers saw to it that people got bread by publishing an "assize of bread" that established prices and weights for the brown loaves that ordinary people consumed. But if they failed, the people might act for themselves, demanding what they needed and paying a fair price for it. The same principle held in other dimensions of life. A community's right to keep out smallpox was more important than the right of victims to wander in their misery. Its right to share out work among its members was more important than the right of outsiders to drift in, seeking jobs. Such crowd action was essentially defensive. It was also fairly easily controlled. It placed limits on the power of men who ruled, but it also provided a set of signals from people to their rulers. If the rulers heeded those signals and made appropriate concessions, they could be fairly sure they would retain their power.

We will never know very much about who actually took part in most uprisings. Well-placed observers varied in their descriptions. They often used the phrase "the people"; it was usually a sign of approval. The term "mob" was used as well; it was short for *mobile vulgus*, and it actually tells very little. If a crowd drew disapproval, it might be dismissed as a "rabble of Negroes and boys," whatever the color or the age of the people involved. But in broad terms we can distinguish crowds of two sorts. At times virtually a whole community might rise. Boston's resistance to the royal navy's impressment of sailors in 1747 provides one example, whatever reasons different Bostonians had for joining in. At other times people of a particular kind would act to protect themselves, whatever the rest of the community thought about it. The nighttime destruction of a market house that some Bostonians were building in 1736 was a sign of conflict within the community, not agreement about an external threat. There were occasions when men with motives of their own manipulated crowds in order to get what they wanted. The violent Philadelphia election of 1742 seems a case in point. There were others when crowds themselves decided what to do. The mood of one crowd might have been fearfully serious; that of another might have been to celebrate with familiar rituals. During the Revolution there was no "single" form of crowd action. Rather, the uprisings of the era drew on all these traditions.

II

Upheaval in the countryside was another matter. Throughout the eighteenth century, governments and upper classes responded to rural rebellion with hard repression. They called out the militia and regular troops: against the Regulators in both Carolinas, against Hudson Valley tenants in 1766, against Shays's Rebellion in Massachusetts in 1786, and against whiskey rebels in Pennsylvania in 1792. Their legislatures passed laws that condemned rioters to death without trial. One such was the "Bloody Act" that New York adopted against the Green Mountain Boys in 1774. It was modeled directly on Parliament's response to the Jacobite rebellion in Scotland in 1715. Courts likewise imposed gruesome death sentences: on Hudson Valley farmer William Prendergast in 1766; on Shays's Rebellion leaders twenty years later. The elite took up arms; even Quakers did so as the Paxton Boys approached Philadelphia in 1763. From their viewpoint, urban risings were one thing and rural rebellions were another. How can the difference be explained?

One answer lies in how rioters did what they did. Townsmen almost always went unarmed, except for stones and sticks. They acted and then dispersed. They organized quickly and dispersed quickly, posing no real challenge to institutions of power. Country people, however, were much more likely to be armed, if only because most farmers kept a gun or two for hunting. They were much more likely to attack the symbols of authority. They broke up courts; they kidnapped judges and sheriffs; they opened jails. Crowds acted that way in North Carolina during the Regulation, in New Jersey during the land riots, in the Hudson Valley in 1766, in the Green Mountains through the early 1770s, and in western Massachusetts during the Shays affair. These movements were strong and highly organized. Some of them lasted for years.

Unlike a traditional urban uprising, a rural rebellion offered a challenge to the whole social and political pattern. What that meant varied from place to place. The South Carolina Regulator movement developed as settlers with few or no slaves moved down the interior valleys and began to set up a small-farm society. Most hoped to become slave-owning planters. A frontier can

be a lawless, ugly place, and theirs rapidly became one. The settlers sought representation in Charles Town and could not get it;
they sought courts and sheriffs, and their petitions were denied.
They finally realized that they had to look to themselves; hence
the name they chose. All they wanted, they proclaimed, was to
protect their lives. Yet they challenged the power of the governor, Lord Charles Montagu, who called them lawless. They
challenged the planters in the Commons House of Assembly,
who were more worried about their slaves and about the Stamp
Act than they were about the backcountry. Though Montagu
once sent the militia to put it down, the movement did not lead
to pitched battle, but it did lay bare the differences between
lowland and backland. Those differences would count in 1776.

North Carolina insurgents called themselves Regulators also,
but their situation was much more complex. Their movement
lasted from 1766 to 1771, when eastern militia defeated a force of
western farmers at the Battle of the Alamance. At its height, between six thousand and seven thousand of the eight thousand
farmers who lived in the piedmont counties of Orange, Rowan,
and Anson were involved. As in South Carolina, part of the problem was simply tension between frontier and seacoast. But
more than simple regionalism was at stake. The issue was com-
pounded by questions of land title, political power, economic
development, and public symbolism. Their historian Marjoleine
Kars places the Regulators within a smoldering southern small-
farmer populism that has rekindled unexpectedly in many
places.

North Carolina land became a problem for two reasons.
First, like much of colonial America, the province suffered from
ill-defined boundaries. Second, like much of the colonial frontier, the Carolina interior included enormous holdings that men
of power had assembled. The English peer Lord Granville, de-
scendant of one of the original Carolina proprietors, claimed a
tract of 26,000 square miles. The immigrant speculator Henry
McCulloh headed a combination that received grants in excess

of 1.3 million acres. Neither Granville nor McCulloh intended to run his land as a consolidated estate, but both did plan to make as much money as they possibly could. Whether that money came from quitrents, which were small annual payments due forever to the original owner, or from sales and actual rents was immaterial. These men had a great deal at stake, and they had no hesitation about using force against people who challenged them.

North Carolina frontier people suffered not from an absence of government but rather from the kind of government they had. There were local courts, and the western counties had their delegates to the provincial assembly. But officials tended to be self-seeking adventurers who looked on public office as just one more way to improve their fortunes. One such was Edmund Fanning, a college-educated northerner who worked his way into the confidence of two successive royal governors and who acquired post after post. Among these men, embezzlement, bribe taking, and extortion were so rife that Regulators sang ballads making fun of their climb to wealth. Fanning and his sort, for their part, did their best to act like aristocrats. The provincial assembly spoke their minds when, confronted with public criticism, it refused to "be arraigned at the Bar [of lesser people's] Shallow Understanding."

The North Carolina Regulators' quarrel was with the entire situation of their half-formed society. But the immediate issue that angered them most was the assembly's appropriation of a total of £15,000 to build an elaborate dwelling for Governor William Tryon. "Tryon's Palace" was the scornful name it rapidly acquired. The issue was economic, since taxes had to be raised to pay for it. But it was also symbolic. North Carolina was not yet a society of rich planters, poor whites, and great slave forces, but men like Tryon and Fanning wanted to make it so. At least some of the Regulators, including their leader and spokesman Herman Hubbard, wanted nothing of the sort. Imposing houses for the planters and a palace for the governor were symbols of increasing wealth, but they were also among the means that the rulers of such a society could use to dominate others. The Regulators developed a broad range of tactics, ranging from simple pressure on officials at one extreme to armed confrontation at the other. The fact that the movement ended with a battle between massed troops suggests that it grew out of the most fundamental issues.

The same is true of backcountry movements farther north. What the Paxton Boys of Pennsylvania did in 1763 to peaceful Indians who lived nearby was gruesome, and it was by no means the only such atrocity in the history of white America's conquest of its continent. But the frontiersmen's uprising and their march on Philadelphia were also signs of how wide the gap was that separated them from their rulers. Elsewhere, in the cases of New Jersey, the Hudson Valley, and the Green Mountains, tensions grew over the questions of who should hold the land and how it should be developed.

Part of the problem was jurisdiction. In New Jersey, the area that surrounded Newark and Elizabethtown was claimed under a royal grant by a well-placed group of "proprietors." But it also was claimed under a direct Indian title by the descendants of New England migrants. At first glance that might seem a better basis for possession, but the history of Indian land sales is full of instances of direct title that amounted to outright fraud upon the vendors. In the Hudson Valley, the boundary between New York and its neighbors was uncertain. New York claimed to extend as far east as the Connecticut River in places, and Massachusetts claimed jurisdiction almost to the Hudson. New England townsmen pushed their borders west onto New York manors, and New York manor lords pushed theirs east into Connecticut and Massachusetts villages. Farther north New York, Massachusetts, and New Hampshire all had long-standing claims to the mountainous country that lay between Lake Champlain and the upper Connecticut Valley. The Privy Council resolved the issue in New York's favor in 1764. But by then the New Hampshire government had made many grants to people who wanted to move up from the lower New England provinces.

Jurisdiction was not the only problem involved, however. The presence of New Englanders in all three conflicts is notable, but for reasons more complex than the simple fact that Yankees were one group and Jerseymen or Yorkers another. The real problem was that insurgents and their opponents had different social visions.

The Puritan settlers who came to New England in the seventeenth century were driven by the same powerful forces that tore old England apart in its "Revolution of the Saints." Both Puritans who fled to America and Puritans who stayed behind lived in a complex relationship to the commercial society taking shape around them. In the end, their descendants would become that society's masters on both sides of the Atlantic, but many seventeenth-century Puritans were repelled by their world's crude self-seeking. They were equally repelled by what was left of England's feudal heritage. Cromwell's Parliament abolished the House of Lords, and New Englanders wanted no lords among them. Instead, they founded a society of communal villages where, they hoped, they could live in peace, their lives controlled by a complex relationship of family, church, and town meeting. Some even tried for a time to use the open-field agricultural system of the Middle Ages, with its requirement that a whole community do its work together. These people were not democrats in our sense. They did not believe in human equality, and they did believe firmly in private property. But they were still attempting a utopian experiment on a remarkably large scale. In good measure, their experiment succeeded. New England's greatest achievement was the social peace its settlers by and large enjoyed for almost a century.

But the Puritans paid a high price, part of which was their morbid belief that their jealous, wrathful God watched everything they did, ready to deal out punishment for the least transgression. Another part grew out of their very success. Their population expanded rapidly in the first few generations, thanks to longevity and fertility rates unknown in Europe. By the middle of the eighteenth century, they were running out of space, and that simple fact was forcing their synthesis apart. As land grew short and lost its fertility, the conditions of life changed. The birth rate fell, and the death rate climbed. Town meetings turned rancorous. Congregations split. Fathers lost control over their children. As many grew poor, some found in business the chance to become rich. But the old vision remained, and when new towns were founded to the west and north, they were modeled on the older ones to the south and east. Nucleated town centers, village greens, and town meeting politics all signified that these people wanted to continue their old ways. Their greatest single fear continued to be that they would lose their farms and descend to the status of tenant under the dominion of a great landlord.

The New Jersey proprietors and the rulers of New York were heirs to a different tradition. There was more than a hint of feudal ways in the founding of much of North America. Proprietorships in the Carolinas, Maryland, Pennsylvania, and New Jersey all reflected the union of economic and political power that lay at the heart of feudalism. The philosopher John Locke, at the request of the Carolina proprietors, even drafted plans for a fully structured colonial nobility. Many an early New York land grant carried the hereditary status of manor lord. This never added up to a full-blown feudal society. Locke's Carolina constitution was abandoned; only the Penns retained their colonial governorship and passed it down through the family; New York landlords never held court. Yet the enticing vision remained, and it was clear by the mid-eighteenth century that what was left of feudal practice offered a route to enrichment. As late as 1769 Sir William Johnson sought formal manorial status for his Mohawk Valley estate. By then many a landlord enjoyed a permanent tenant-based society over which he could rule, and others looked forward to establishing one. Some of them were nostalgic for old ways, some paternalistic, and some unashamedly exploitative. Most such men held frontier speculations that they planned eventually to sell off, but they maintained large home estates that they intended to pass on intact to their heirs. They looked on their land as the basis for large-scale gain, gain that someone else's labor would produce. They also enjoyed great political power, as colonels in the militia, council members, and judges. For three New York manors, Rensselaerswyck, Livingston, and Cortlandt, there were even special seats in the provincial assembly, seats that the manor lord or his nominee invariably filled.

The landlord's dream was the New Englander's nightmare. In some, but not all, cases it was also the tenant's distress. By the mid-eighteenth century, there was more and more frequent conflict. Landlords had the power of the New Jersey and New York provincial governments behind them, and they used it. But their opponents knew about fraudulent titles. They loathed the way life was lived on the great estates. They had political resources of their own. Where Massachusetts met New York, border settlers and insurgent tenants enjoyed the active support of the Boston government. In the Green Mountains, people who held New Hampshire titles established towns, courts, and their own militia, despite New York's attempt to impose its form of county government on them. Even in central New Jersey, far from any disputed border, land rioters "built a goal [jail] back in the woods," established their own tax system, elected their own militia officers, and "erected Courts of Judicature."

These movements were closer to insurrection than to riot. Like urban rioters, the people who took part in them chose their targets carefully: Abraham Yates during his term as sheriff of Albany County; jails where arrested rioters were held; settlers claiming the land under title granted by landlords; justices of the peace enforcing landlord law; sometimes the landlords themselves. Only the Green Mountain movement was successful.

During the decade before independence, it became impossible for New York courts to function there and for would-be landlords to build their estates. After a brief reconciliation with New York revolutionaries in 1775, the movement finally established the state of Vermont. By contrast, the New Jersey movement fizzled out in midcentury, and the New York tenant rising was suppressed by military force in 1766.

But from the banks of the Pee Dee River to the shores of Lake Champlain, these rural risings exposed the lines of stress that ran through late colonial rural life. Nineteen of every twenty people lived in the countryside in the 1770s. Their problems, like those of townsfolk, gave shape to their era and to the Revolution they helped to make.

III

From 1765 to 1774, however, the main story of the Revolution was acted out in the towns. It was urban interests that were most threatened by the Sugar Act, the Stamp Act, the Townshend taxes, and the Tea Act. Townspeople, not farmers, had to deal with inquisitive customs men and with the constant harassment of redcoats among them. Except for the Virginia planters, it was town writers who worked out the rationale of American resistance. Townspeople turned that rationale into action. What did they do? How and why did they do it?

Without crowd action, there would have been no resistance movement. Crowds made it impossible to enforce the Stamp Act; they gave power to the nonimportation agreements that merchants adopted against the Townshend taxes; they dumped East India Company tea into more than one harbor. Crowds confronted customs men and soldiers, sometimes at the risk of their members' lives. They captured and destroyed British customs vessels. They forced officials to resign high positions; they gathered in huge, sometimes illegal meetings; they paraded with effigies; they tore down elegant buildings, disrupted concerts, and erected liberty poles. Individuals opposed these crowds at their peril. Some found their property destroyed or defaced. Others found themselves tarred and feathered or ridden on rails. In the end, some suffered not just broken windows but broken lives.

This enduring militancy sprang from people's anger about what the British were doing, but it was more than spontaneous wrath. The energy that drove it had its sources in domestic as well as imperial problems. It gained discipline and direction because of a group of men whose commitment and organization made them, in effect, a revolutionary party. These were the Sons of Liberty.

Let us look at some of the major points of action and conflict. The first two events happened in Boston in August 1765. On the fourteenth day of that month, Bostonians awoke to find that some of their number were presenting a vivid dramatization of what the Stamp Act would mean. Effigies of stamp distributor Andrew Oliver and of a huge boot with a "green-vile sole" and a devil peeping out of it were dangling from a tree near Boston Neck. The boot and its sole were a pun on the names of the hated figures of Lord Bute and George Grenville. Men were waiting by the tree to collect a mock stamp duty from every passerby. They continued all day as carts with goods and foodstuffs rumbled back and forth between town and mainland. No one who passed could fail to learn the lesson: the Stamp Act would make a difference in everyone's life. Estimates of how many did pass by and gather to watch vary from 2,500 to 5,000, and toward evening people who had been standing around paraded with the effigies, marching to a small brick building that Oliver had under construction on the waterfront. Believing it to be the stamp office, the crowd demolished it and then proceeded to Oliver's house. They smashed some windows and tore down some fencing and then entered the house, seeking Oliver himself. At that point Lieutenant Governor Thomas Hutchinson, who was the stamp man's brother-in-law, arrived with the sheriff. The rioters met them with a "volley of stones" and then went their ways.

Twelve days later another crowd gathered, again in the evening. Marching on the houses of two British officials, it did some minor damage, just as the earlier crowd had done to Oliver's. The goal was the same, to force the officials to resign their offices, as Oliver in fact would do. One of them rapidly resigned. Then the crowd went to Thomas Hutchinson's elegant mansion, and for him there were no half measures. By the time the night was over, the house was a shell, its cupola torn off, interior partitions pulled down, and Hutchinson's property scattered in the street. On the evening of November 1, a New York City crowd treated another elegant dwelling in exactly the same way. The Stamp Act was about to take effect, and the crowd had gathered to demand that the city's stamps be locked away and that the stamp distributor resign. It assembled outside Fort George, at the foot of Manhattan Island. The people knew that the fort's guns had been turned to face their town rather than out to sea. Again there were effigies, this time of the devil and Lieutenant Governor Cadwallader Colden. The crowd broke into Colden's carriage house, took out his sleigh and carriages, and burned them and the effigies on a bonfire. Then it marched to a mansion called Vauxhall, occupied by Major Thomas James of the British army. What happened to Vauxhall was just about the same as what happened to Hutchinson's house, and by the time the night was through, it was nothing more than a wreck. This was the first of many times that winter that New Yorkers took to the streets, and in May 1766 they invaded and destroyed another building, a newly opened theater. After driving out the patrons and actors, the crowd leveled the house and then carried the wreckage to the fields, where an enormous bonfire consumed it.

These uprisings took place at the time of the Stamp Act, but if we look at the same two cities four years later, we find a different pattern: Now British soldiers have become the focus of action.

In January 1770 in New York, a week of street fighting broke out between redcoats and civilians. It centered on two places. One was a tavern that faced across "the fields" (now City Hall Park) to tne barracks where many of the soldiers were quartered. Until just before the brawls, a stoutly constructed liberty pole, encased in iron, had stood in front of the drinking house. The other place was Golden Hill, where grain sometimes turned the streets yellow as it spilled from the wagons that were bearing it to the mills and granaries there. Not much more than sore heads resulted from the fighting, and New Yorkers did their best to forget this Battle of Golden Hill.

But two months later similar tensions erupted in Boston, with tragic and lasting results. On March 5 a crowd gathered in King Street to confront troops who were guarding the customs house. Someone began to throw snowballs, and the soldiers panicked. Someone else—his name has never been established—shouted the order to fire, and a minute later five Bostonians lay dying. Many more were wounded. This was the Boston Massacre, and for the next thirteen years Bostonians would gather each March 5 to commemorate it. Only when the Treaty of Paris brought the final guarantee of American independence would they begin celebrating July 4 instead.

For our last two instances, let us look again at these same two cities, this time in the winter of 1773–74. Late in November the merchant vessels *Dartmouth*, *Eleanor*, and *Beaver* entered Boston Harbor bearing East India Company tea. Among the merchants to whom the tea was consigned were two sons of Thomas Hutchinson, who was now governor of the province. Other places had refused company tea: New York's ship turned around at Sandy Hook, and Philadelphians sent theirs back down the Delaware. But the Boston ships tied up, with twenty days to make their customs entries, pay the Townshend duty, and unload. Hutchinson and the consignees refused demands that the ships be allowed to sail with their cargo unbroken, and the governor let it be known that cannon on navy ships and at Castle William would open fire if they tried to put to sea. The demands that the three ships depart had come from an extraordinary continuous meeting that called itself simply "the Body." Faneuil Hall, where the town meeting gathered, was too small for this assembly. So day after day thousands of Bostonians came to Old South Church to consider what to do. After days of fruitless negotiation the body's moderator, Samuel Adams, announced that it could do nothing more "to save the country." This was a signal, and immediately some one hundred Bostonians donned Indian disguise, boarded the three ships, hauled out the tea, and dumped it into the harbor. Among these "Mohawks" was the diminutive shoemaker George Robert Twelves Hewes. The "destruction of the tea" was a most serious event, and the Bostonians knew it. It did not acquire the jolly, dismissive name "Boston Tea Party" until decades later.

More tea was dumped, this time in New York, in March 1774. New Yorkers had forced their first tea ship to turn back, but when a vessel called the *Nancy* tied up, they found there was company tea on board. They set out to follow the Bostonians' example, so a mass meeting debated the issue while a party of "Mohawks" prepared themselves. But while the "Indians" were still donning their war paint, a crowd from the meeting surged onto the ship, found the tea, and disposed of it. Then the crowd paraded with the empty chests to the fields and burned them. It was very much like the parade that another crowd had conducted with the wreckage of the theater eight years before.

By no means is this all that crowds did during the crisis. By no means were Boston and New York the only places where uprisings broke out. But these are among the most striking events, and they show us the range of what happened. We can begin to understand them by looking at what they had in common. Then we can ask how crowd action developed and changed between the Stamp Act and the several times when determined people boarded ships and dumped East India Company tea.

Most obviously, in every one of these instances except the sacking of the theater, the target was tied to British policy. Andrew Oliver and the sons of Thomas Hutchinson were doing the ministry's work. Hutchinson himself opposed the Stamp Act behind the scenes, but in public he supported British authority and denied that people had any right to question or thwart it. Major James was the officer who had been responsible for turning the guns of Fort George so they faced New York City. Lieutenant Governor Colden, a miserably unpopular man, had the task of enforcing the Stamp Act in New York. The soldiers were stationed in the two cities to see that the will of British officials was done. In ways that were different but that were highly visible, all these people symbolized the change that had come over colonial relations after 1763.

Yet there is another dimension, one to which the attack on the theater points. Eighteenth-century Americans did not look kindly on playhouses. The Continental Congress voted a ban on plays as part of its association in 1774, and this was only one of many in the era. Part of the reason may have been a lingering Protestant mistrust of fiction of any sort, but most people disliked the theater for what it symbolized, not for what went on in it.

To colonials who knew they looked dull and provincial, theaters stood for European culture, sophistication, gaiety, and wit. Even for Americans with great privilege, Europe had qualities that both attracted and repelled. A political operator who was ruthlessly self-seeking by the standards of Philadelphia might come back from a trip to London relieved that he did not have to remain in so corrupt a world. An arrogant Virginia planter might find himself at once thrilled and terrified to hear a young minister who was fresh from Cambridge mouth fashionable unorthodoxies. Many an aspiring writer did his best to keep up with European literary fashion, but he always knew that his work was derivative and that London coffeehouse intellectuals would pay it no heed. So, too, with the theater. Even its patrons had reason to doubt that it was right for them to be where they were, despite the *Song in Praise of Liberty* that was on the playbill that New York opening night.

Something more was at stake, though, than provincial morality. The coming of peace in 1763 had brought an end to the overheated war economy that had brought prosperity to many colonials. Imports and exports fell; the poor rolls increased; ships lay idle in the harbors; and tools lay unused in artisans' shops. But in the midst of this depression, some still thrived. The good fortune that Andrew Oliver and Thomas Hutchinson enjoyed was glaringly visible in Boston, where the economy had begun to stagnate as early as 1750. The year 1765 was a bleak one in New York as well, but privileged people still saw fit to grace their summer evenings with outdoor concerts in the Ranelagh Gardens, named after a fashionable London gathering place. Others drove about town in expensive imported carriages, like the ones that the crowd took from Colden's coachhouse. They accepted invitations to dine at houses like Vauxhall. That, too, was the name of a place in London where the lights were bright.

The Chapel Street theater represented, in other words, glittering ostentation and callous unconcern in a time of distress and shortage. The same was true of the Ranelagh Gardens concerts and of the whole refined way of living signified by large houses, silver plate, fine furniture, and good wine. A New York writer who styled himself "A Tradesman" made the point in unmistakable terms in 1767. Why, he asked readers of the city's most radical newspaper, had its coverage of "our distressed situation" lessened? "Are our Circumstances altered? Is Money grown more Plenty? Have our Tradesmen full Employment? Are we more frugal? Is Grain cheaper? Are our Importations less?— Not to mention the Playhouse and Equipages which it is hoped none but People of Fortune frequent or use." Bostonians had similar things to say about Hutchinson and Oliver. As early as

1749, when Hutchinson was involved in a scheme to end the easy circulation of paper currency, his house caught fire. Instead of rallying to put it out, bystanders shouted, "Let it burn!" We know of that incident from Hutchinson himself, but Oliver was never aware of his worst humiliation: It came with the cheering of people watching the onetime stamp man's body being laid in its grave.

This was class resentment, not class warfare. Despite the fears of some highly placed observers, such as Francis Bernard, governor of Massachusetts in 1765, it did not betoken open struggle between rich and poor. There were rich men, like John Hancock, who either joined crowd action or cheered it on. There were poor and middling people who took no part. But what these crowds did makes little or no sense unless we realize they were acting as crowds had long been expected to act in a corporatist society. The likes of Oliver, Colden, and Hutchinson made themselves enemies of the community because they served as British minions, and they made themselves enemies of ordinary people because they were profiting greatly in a time of severe distress.

Similar tensions lay behind the strife between soldiers and civilians. Colonials had many reasons to resent the presence of redcoats. All political theory told them that a standing army was the greatest danger a people's liberty could face. New York had had a small garrison ever since it was taken from the Dutch, but Boston traditionally had none. When the size of the New York garrison was increased at the war's end, when Parliament insisted in 1767 that New Yorkers supply it and suspended their assembly for refusing, and when a large force was sent to Boston in 1768, it all seemed to point in one direction: tyranny. The military itself did nothing to allay such fears. Officers were gracious enough about asking prominent townspeople to dine; such townsmen were glad enough to accept the invitations and to bid for supply contracts. But in New York and in Boston the day-to-day presence of the troops became an endless aggravation. In

Boston especially the needs of the soldiers clashed with the ways of the townsfolk. The garrison had to have a place to stay when it arrived, so it pitched its tents on Boston Common and then commandeered one public building after another. It needed to drill, and when better than a Sunday morning, when trumpets, drums, and shouted orders were sure to disturb the Puritans as they prayed. Soldiers deserted and vanished into the interior, so guard posts were established where people would have to answer a challenge from a foreign sentry in their own streets. Men who had volunteered during the Seven Years War remembered how appalled they had been by the fierce discipline of the British army and by the gulf of social class that separated its officers from the rank and file.

Most immediately, in each town the garrison made the depression's effects even worse. By tradition, off-duty soldiers and naval sailors could seek part-time work where they were stationed. Their own pay and conditions were wretched, and such work made all the difference between bare survival and some comfort. The jobs they took were the ones no one else wanted, and the pay they accepted was less than an American needed to live on. In the prosperous war years, it made little difference to colonials. But now depression had made every job valuable, and there were far more military men competing with the townsfolk for what work there was.

All these tensions fed into what happened on Golden Hill and in King Street. In New York civilians were complaining as early as 1766 about how sailors from ships that were wintering over were taking away work. Local people tried to keep soldiers and sailors out of their taverns and markets. Civilians broke into the ranks as soldiers paraded in the streets. Military men responded in kind. Among themselves, officers dismissed Americans as "boorish peasants," and there were times when local people were beaten up and stabbed with bayonets. Throughout the late 1760s the soldiers made it a point of honor to cut down a liberty pole each time the locals put one up.

In the immediate background to both outbreaks, ideological, symbolic, and economic issues fused. In New York two inflammatory broadsides appeared at the end of 1769. One hammered away at the point that the soldiers were the tools of tyranny and accused the province's rulers of betrayal by finally voting supplies. The other addressed daily reality. "Whosoever seriously considers the impovrished state of this city," it said, "must be greatly surprised at the Conduct of such . . . as employ the Soldiers, when there are a number of [city people] that want Employment to support their distressed Families." It called for a meeting at the liberty pole in the fields. Immediately afterward soldiers destroyed the pole and piled the pieces provocatively in the workingmen's tavern that faced their barracks. This was the incident that brought about the Golden Hill riots.

Precisely the same issue helped bring on the events that led to the Boston Massacre. Boston was already tense at the beginning of March 1770, for the previous month a well-hated customs informer, Ebenezer Richardson, had fired into a crowd demonstrating outside the store of merchant Theophilus Lillie, who was known to be an importer. Possibly they intended to decorate the store with "Hillsborough Paint." Named for the Earl of Hillsborough, who was secretary for colonial affairs, this was no more than raw sewage drawn in buckets from outdoor "necessary houses." Richardson killed a boy of eleven, Christopher Seider. Thousands attended Seider's funeral on February 26. Only a few days later a soldier seeking work went to a south end ropewalk. One of the rope makers taunted him, offering him a job cleaning his own "necessary house." The soldier went for his comrades, and a brawl rapidly developed. At its height as many as forty soldiers were trading punches with workers from several ropewalks.

The people who started to throw snowballs at the customs house sentries a few nights later were men like the rope workers, and they were responding to their whole experience with British soldiers since 1768. Challenges by sentries in their streets, bands marching past while they worshiped their God, soldiers at work when Bostonians could not find it, a son of the town shot dead at the age of eleven—these were memories that stung, and even hard-packed snowballs were a mild enough way to express them. But the soldiers themselves were young men, sent far from home to serve in a place where they were despised for being what they were. They were the dregs of Britain, serving under aristocrats and gentlemen who paid more money for their commissions than a private might ever see in his life. Many things came together in their heads as well, and what the guard detail saw that night was not an outraged citizenry but a vicious, irrational mob. When they heard the order to fire, they did not pause to ask who gave it or why they were there at all. They did what they were told.

IV

Colonials who took part in these events knew that they were confronting Britain and the people who served it. But they were also confronting their own situation. We can see in these uprisings the heritage of protest that people carried in their minds and hearts. Crowd action during the Revolution was often angry and sometimes very ugly, but it was never anarchic. Disguises, effigies, tarring and feathering, bonfires, even tearing down houses were all well understood in the eighteenth-century world. Colonials turned to them because they were familiar acts.

Now, however, several things were different. The first was the developing problem between the colonies and Britain. The second, reflected in the ostentation of Governor Hutchinson's house and in the violence of what happened to it, was the belief of an increasing proportion of the elite that the old ways were of use no longer and that they had no obligation to sacrifice in a time of distress. A third was the presence, in and with the crowds, of men who called themselves Sons of Liberty. From

South Carolina to New Hampshire, the Sons took shape spontaneously in 1765 and 1766. They derived their name from a well-
publicized speech that was given in Parliament by Colonel Isaac
Barré, who was sympathetic to the American cause, and there
were times when the term was used to mean virtually any American who was involved in resistance. But in New York City a core
of committed radicals made the name their own, and they called
on men of similar spirit to establish like groups elsewhere. Such
groups were already assembling; the one in Boston called itself
the Loyal Nine. Their foremost modern student, Pauline Maier,
has found organized Sons of Liberty in at least fifteen places,
and there may have been more. Some of the groups, though
not all of them, were knit into an intercolonial correspondence
union. It centered on the New York Sons and on their secretary,
the instrument maker John Lamb.

No revolution takes place in a simple way. There must be
large grievances, felt by many people. There must be upheaval.
There must be shared ideas as to what is wrong, what needs to
be done, and what a better future might look like. There must
be coalitions among people of different sorts. There must be
organization and discipline and direction, rather than just incho-
ate rage and mindless violence. In revolutionary America the
Sons of Liberty represented both the necessary element of coalition and the equally necessary elements of organization and
discipline.

Three sorts of men were central to the Sons: dissident intellectuals, small intercolonial merchants, and artisans. The intellectuals among them lived by their knowledge, valued ideas, and
enjoyed political argument. Perhaps the best known and most
important was Samuel Adams, in Boston. A Harvard graduate
and a long-serving petty town official, Adams had drunk deeply
both from classical learning and from his Puritan heritage. He
dreamed of making Massachusetts a Christian Sparta, a place
where hardy, self-denying, God-fearing people would think
of the public, not of themselves. Some radicals, such as the

Philadelphia physician Benjamin Rush, shared the Christian element in that vision. Others, like Tom Paine and the wandering revolutionary Dr. Thomas Young, emphatically did not. But whether they thought in secular or in religious terms, these thinkers understood that they had to work together, and that whatever divided them was less important than the cause that they shared.

Artisans and intercolonial merchants had a great deal in common as they faced the imperial crisis. Most of all they shared an interest in making the American economy strong. Intercolonial traders enjoyed the protection of the royal navy, but they were less tied than transatlantic merchants to the network of trade, credit, and legality that formed the empire's economic sinews. They had no friends in Parliament, or correspondents in British ports, or sisters who had married into the British aristocracy. But their common interest in the home economy provided one major reason why these people supported the nonimportation of British goods as a way of protesting British policies. It brought them direct benefit. For the great merchants who organized it, the boycott was a burden to be borne—and to be shed as quickly as possible. But for artisans of any sort and for small traders, it was an opportunity to be seized. It offered the hope that colonial producers and the traders who dealt in their goods could produce a new prosperity for themselves.

Isaac Sears and Alexander McDougall of New York City were small-merchant Sons of Liberty. Both were first-generation New Yorkers, and both came from humble backgrounds. Sears was the son of a Cape Cod oyster catcher. He had married the daughter of a tavern keeper who ran a bar where merchant seamen drank. McDougall's father was a Scottish immigrant who made his living delivering milk. Both men had experience at sea, commanding small vessels with tiny crews and earning not much more than an ordinary sailor would receive. Both had sailed on privateers during the Seven Years War. Each bore the title "Captain," in recollection of those days, rather than the more prestigious "Mr." or "Gent." or "Esq." By the 1760s these men could approach the places where the elite gathered. McDougall had the spare time and the inclination to sit in the gallery and watch the provincial assembly as it deliberated. But such a man could have no expectation that he would ever cross its bar and become a member himself. That was for the Livingstons and the De Lanceys and others like them, who enjoyed everything that McDougall lacked.

Like Sears and McDougall, Paul Revere came from an obscure background. His family were French Protestants; the name had been anglicized from Rivoire. As an aspiring mechanic, Revere had climbed the ladder from apprentice to journeyman to master craftsman. Now, as owner of his own shop, he was a small businessman. But as a master of his trade, he still worked side by side with his own journeymen and apprentices. A successful artisan could lead a comfortable life. Though no mansion, Revere's house in the north end of Boston was spacious enough. Around 1768 Revere commissioned a portrait of himself by the renowned John Singleton Copley. Despite the depression the silversmith was doing well, and the portrait celebrated that. But it celebrated his way of life as well as his increasing wealth. He had Copley paint him in his leather work jerkin, with his tools lying in front of him, while he fingered a teapot of his own making. Fame came to Revere long after his death, when the poet Henry Wadsworth Longfellow gave immortality to the ride he made to Concord in 1775 with the warning that the British were on their way. But Revere's real importance did not lie in that one spectacular exploit. Rather, it lay in the increasing pride and self-assertion that he and men of his kind took in their own lives. Whether they turned out silverware or shoes, men like Paul Revere and the shoemaker Ebenezer Mackintosh knew that their personal welfare and their community's welfare were bound together. Their futures would be very different, Revere as an industrialist and Mackintosh in obscurity. But during the crisis with Britain they had good reason to look in the same direction and to act together.

Such men could organize a popular resistance movement because they occupied a place between the elite and genuine plebeians. As men of some sophistication and occasional leisure, they could understand the abstruse political arguments that elite pamphleteers put forward. Samuel Adams, in fact, always dressed in gentlemanly style, a practice shared by Maximilien Robespierre, leader of the radical Jacobins during the French Revolution. When *he* posed for Copley, it was in a frock coat with his hair powdered and a scroll representing the provincial charter in front of him. But whatever they wore, the Sons knew the ways of ordinary people and the pressures those people lived under. Their great task was to turn traditional crowd action toward the British question and to generate new political consciousness among ordinary Americans. They were not master manipulators, bent on forcing an issue about which most people did not care. Nor were they tribunes of the oppressed, using the problem of relations with Britain as a way to bring internal change. Rather, they began the job of fusing the imperial issue and domestic problems into the one grand question of what kind of place America would be. How they did so varied, for the situation in Boston was not the situation in New York, and neither was it the same as the situation in Charles Town or Philadelphia or Albany.

In Boston the Loyal Nine used several means to generate Stamp Act resistance in 1765. One was to contact Mackintosh, who was the acknowledged leader of one of the crowds that traditionally gathered on November 5, Pope's Day. With the encouragement of the Loyal Nine, Mackintosh rallied both his own followers and their traditional Pope's Day foes to support the open-air political theater of August 14. The devil's effigy that hung in the Liberty Tree was familiar from many a November 5 celebration, but now Satan had Andrew Oliver and George

Grenville for company. When the crowd took to the streets that evening, Mackintosh was in front, carrying a sword and wearing a uniform, general for a day. Questions of ritual and memory, class and culture, and imperial politics had come together to start Boston on the road to revolution.

New Englanders invoked many such memories between 1765 and 1776. Calls for action by the Committee for Tarring and Feathering were signed by "Joyce, Jr." The name referred to Cornet George Joyce, the low-ranking Roundhead officer who captured King Charles I during the English Civil War and who supposedly stood on the royal scaffold. People called up the ghost of Oliver Cromwell; the Loyal Nine themselves were among the first to do so. Cromwell's memory was a horror to orthodox Whigs, who were committed to the political solution established by the Glorious Revolution of 1688. But New England's founders had known and supported Cromwell, and they had given shelter to regicides fleeing England after the Stuart monarchy returned. Their descendants kept those memories alive. Couple upon couple named their newborn boys Oliver during the crisis decade. Even George Washington once found himself being addressed by a Massachusetts farmer as "Great Cromwell." As Alfred Young has pointed out, a Yankee then might have spoken of "Oliver" in the same respectful tone that an African American would today use to speak of "Martin" or "Malcolm." Both the name and the tone in which people invoked it carried the same heavy symbolic burden.

Boston's radicals made the most of this consciousness and these issues. They knew perfectly well what stagnation and poverty meant in their town. But they insisted, in public at least, that local issues should not come to the fore. Their newspaper, the *Boston Gazette*, carried on an endless campaign against the British administration, its policies, and its servants in Massachusetts. Their campaign led to a state of permanent hostility between two successive governors, Francis Bernard and Thomas Hutchinson, and the Boston Town Meeting. When Bernard was recalled in 1769, he sailed away from the humiliating sight of a town that had illuminated its buildings and was ringing its church bells to celebrate his departure. But by then Ebenezer Mackintosh, who perhaps had presented the possibility of genuinely lower-class leadership, had lost his prominence. By 1770 Mackintosh was in debtor's prison, and no Son of Liberty would go to his aid.

In New York the Sons operated differently. The Boston Sons had made plain their disapproval of the sacking of the Hutchinson house, and they took careful steps to prevent anything like it from happening again. But the New York Sons showed no shock at all when crowds destroyed Colden's carriages and Major James's mansion. Admittedly, Colden and James were associated much more visibly with the Stamp Act than Hutchinson was. But neither did the Sons show any opposition to the disruption and leveling of the Chapel Street theater. In fact, Sons of Liberty led it, and members of the crowd cried "Liberty! Liberty!" as they carried the wreckage to the fields. New York's most radical newspaper, the *New York Journal*, dramatized the British issue, but it also carried essay after essay attacking the evils of high rents, rising prices, and short employment. It told of popular uprisings in London to resist the engrossment of grain. It castigated fashionable youth who would not give up their finery. It opposed the imprisonment of debtors. For both the leadership and the people of New York, domestic issues were part of the crisis.

Other groups operated in other ways. In Charles Town the Sons of Liberty developed out of a volunteer fire company. In Connecticut their roots lay partly in sectarian bitterness left over from the Great Awakening, partly in disputes about paper money, and partly in conflicts among speculators. In some places the "wealthiest gentlemen and freeholders" provided leadership; in others, such as Annapolis, Maryland, and the whole province of New Jersey, it came from men now lost in obscurity. In Philadelphia no group emerged at all at the time of the Stamp Act, largely because the artisans themselves were divided. Never, in other words, was there a single pattern. Each group of Sons operated in its own way within its own community. But the Sons of Liberty maintained contact with one another and pledged mutual cooperation. At the end of the Stamp Act crisis, they disbanded their formal organization, thinking their task was over. But the radical leadership that had sprung up among them remained important throughout the era.

Leaders are nothing, however, without followers. Neither the colonial elite nor the Sons of Liberty could have done anything serious against British policy without enormous popular support. It was people in crowds who turned what was happening from a debate to a movement. Crowd action was a fact of life in the whole eighteenth-century world, and the American movement built on all the traditions and customs that made it up. But the sustained popular political militancy on a great political issue that developed in America's towns was something very new.

Four

INDEPENDENCE AND REVOLUTION

During the eight years that followed the Stamp Act, Britain tried again and again to make the colonies serve its interests. Instead, laws and policies proved unworkable. Colonial writers demolished official rationalizations. Colonial people made it impossible for British officials to do their jobs. Twice the British sought a way around colonial objections. The Townshend program distinguished external taxes from internal ones in the hope that Americans would pay one even if they would not pay the other. The Tea Act used the lure of lower prices in an outright appeal to consumer self-interest. But each time the result was new forms of resistance.

In the two years that followed the destruction of the tea, Parliament turned to stronger measures. The colonists had to be taught that they were truly subordinate, that Britain could alter their charters, close their ports, change their rules of law, and billet troops directly on them as it chose. If need be, it would use its immense military strength to make them submit. The Intolerable Acts that were passed to punish Boston for the Tea Party, and the appointment of General Thomas Gage as governor of Massachusetts established these points. These acts needed and received no elaborate rationale; they were a resort to naked force. But the result was not to end contention—it was to rip apart the empire. As the empire was sundered, colonials found reason and opportunity for thoroughgoing political revolution. Their cultural and public agenda, which had turned on conceiving of themselves as fundamentally unequal, as "God almightie in His most holy and venerable Wisdom" had decreed (as the seventeenth-century revolutionary John Winthrop told his fellow Puritans in 1630), was changing to one that regarded "all men" as created equal according to "the laws of Nature and of Nature's God," on which the eighteenth-century revolutionary Thomas Jefferson relied. The problems arising from being British in America had reached the point of having no possible solution. The problems arising from being American were beginning to emerge.

I

The internal revolution and the final collapse of the empire began when the people of Massachusetts decided to resist the punishment rather than pay for the tea. The groundwork for cooperation already had been laid, much though not all of it by Massachusetts itself. That province's assembly had established a committee of correspondence in 1764 to deal with the emerging imperial problem. The Stamp Act Congress of 1765 and a spider's web of agreements among separate groups of Sons of Liberty followed. In 1768 the Massachusetts General Court circulated to other legislatures a letter, written by Samuel Adams, condemning the Townshend Acts. In 1772 the Boston Town Meeting established a committee of correspondence to arouse awareness in the New England interior; Adams had proposed that, too.

Now people rallied. From New York to the Carolinas, provincial assemblies and local communities established their own committees to maintain correspondence. Up and down the coast, people loaded vessels with supplies to relieve the "poor of

Boston." By the summer of 1774, colonials had decided that they needed a Continental Congress that would give direction to their movement. It met in Philadelphia in September, the first "official" gathering of delegates from the different provinces since the Stamp Act Congress nine years before. Some of its delegates were chosen by provincial assemblies, some by local meetings and committees, some by illegal conventions. The congressmen from Massachusetts and Virginia came together to press for strong measures. The ones from New York and Pennsylvania established reputations for moderation. As events were to show, this was a reflection of their own fear of upheaval, not actual opinion in their provinces.

Congress defeated an attempt by Pennsylvania's Joseph Galloway to offer a conciliatory petition to the Crown. Taking the matter further, it voted to "expunge" Galloway's motion from its official record, as if it never had been proposed. Instead of offering conciliation (but after considerable debate about different provinces' special concerns and interests) Congress adopted the Continental Association. Whoever signed it would accept the position that Boston's problems were everybody's problems. The American economy would close. Trade with Britain would end completely. Trade with the rest of the world would drop sharply. Liberty-loving, abstemious Americans would buy no more slaves or Madeira wines. They would race no horses, fight no gamecocks, waste no money on plays or on fine clothes. They would slaughter no sheep, because wool was going to be much more necessary than mutton. Technically this was only a voluntary agreement, as its name suggests. But in order to enforce it Congress called a committee "of association" in every "county, city, and town." A brave person who did not support the cause might hold out. But the pressure to conform would be enormous. The first steps toward destroying British power and toward creating a revolutionary government had been taken.

In their earlier struggles, the Americans had been aided by support in Britain and by turbulence in Parliament. Crowds had rioted in London as well as in New York and Boston, and both Americans and Britons had recognized the connection between the uprisings. John Wilkes, the radical parliamentarian in whose support London crowds had turned out in the mid-1760s, became an American hero. In turn, he encouraged the American cause. The colonials enjoyed support from moneyed men in the City of London as well, and that also helped convince Parliament to retreat. Political instability was an additional factor. Through the 1760s ministries rose and fell as George III searched fruitlessly for leaders able to control the House of Lords and the Commons. At least part of the reason for the repeal of the Stamp Act was that George Grenville, the act's father, was out of office.

But now, in 1774, matters were different. Though Wilkes had become lord mayor of London, the crowds were quiet. In Frederick, Lord North, the king had finally found the prime minister he needed. Plodding and reliable, North would serve faithfully until 1782. He held a "courtesy" title as a peer's son, not a real one in his own right. That meant that he sat in the House of Commons rather than in the House of Lords. When Britain's tiny electorate went to the polls in 1774, the election was fought without regard to the American question. North won an unquestionable majority. Until the end of the American war, there would be angry speeches attacking his policies, but he would win every vote. Until the French entered the conflict, the Americans would stand alone.

When the First Continental Congress adjourned in October 1774, it called for a successor, to meet the following spring. All it expected the new Congress to do was consider how well the association had worked, but by the time it gathered, General Gage had redefined the issue. Under orders from London to make a move and aware (thanks to his spy Benjamin Church) that arms were secreted at Concord, he dispatched a column of infantry to seize them on April 18, 1775. Even had Paul Revere not made his ride, the Concord farmers would have been ready. Since the previous summer they had organized a dense network of committees and message riders. Preparations in Boston were so obvious that the coming of the troops could not have been kept secret. Colonists had their own well-placed informant, most likely Gage's American-born wife, Margaret Kemble. Perhaps all the farmers intended was a symbolic confrontation, before allowing the British to take the few supplies that had not been hidden. But like the troops, these Minutemen were armed. Whoever fired the first shot, the skirmishing and the deadly sniper fire that the redcoats endured returning to Boston marked the end of words and the beginning of war.

Congress convened in Philadelphia on May 10 and started to become a war government. A pickup army of New Englanders soon surrounded occupied Boston. The high price they made the British pay before they were dislodged from Breed's (Bunker) Hill, overlooking Charlestown, confirmed their ability to fight. New Englanders under Ethan Allen and Benedict Arnold captured the forts at Ticonderoga and Crown Point and sent the cannons to Boston. Supplies had to be raised and men and officers recruited from outside New England. Naming George Washington to command the newly created Continental Army recognized Virginia's political importance as much as Washington's talents. Similar considerations lay behind lesser generalships.

Fifteen months of war passed before the Declaration of Independence. During that time Britain announced that the colonies were in a state of rebellion; each side rejected the other's plan for conciliation; Sir William Howe replaced Gage as British commander; and Parliament declared the colonies outside the Crown's protection. Congress declared its reasons for taking up arms, repudiated all links to Parliament, opened American ports to all commerce except British, and on May 10, 1776, ordered the suppression of British government. Some colonies explicitly rejected the idea of independence, but others appointed committees to draft new constitutions. Congress

opened secret negotiations with the French, and Britain worked
out agreements to hire an army of up to twenty thousand Germans. Ships of war blockaded American ports and shelled
both Norfolk, Virginia, and Falmouth, Massachusetts (now Port-
land, Maine). The captured cannons from the Lake Champlain
forts finally arrived at Boston, and Washington placed them on
Dorchester Heights. That made the town untenable, and the
British withdrew on March 17, 1776, regrouping at Halifax.

Until the end of 1775, the word *independence* remained almost unspoken. Even when cutting the tie became a real possibility, it took the whole first half of 1776 for Congress to make up
its mind. The situation was almost like the one that many a di-
vorcing couple must face: Bitterly antagonistic, facing different
directions, the two partners still seek to hold on.

British interest lay in maintaining the mastery of the Western
world, including the colonies, that it had won over half a century
of conflict. But why did it take the colonies so long to make the
break? Part of it was that white Americans did not believe what
was happening. They had long thought of themselves as Britons
overseas, as heirs to the full, proud tradition of British freedom.
Their heritage, their history, and their identity were important to
them. That was so even for colonists whose actual ancestry ran
back to the original Dutch settlers of Nieuw Amsterdam, or to
French Protestants who had fled Louis XIV, or to Germans, or to
Sephardic Jews. Many colonials, especially those who picked up
their pens and tried to work out what was going on, still believed
that the only problem was an aberration in an otherwise com-
mendable state of affairs. They turned readily to the idea that
the source of their troubles lay in a conspiracy of evil men, not
in the existence of the British Empire itself.

They were not paranoid. Rather, as the historian Gordon
Wood has argued, they were trying to work out an explanation in
human terms for the course of the human events that were
swirling around them. An earlier generation might have tried to
understand its tribulations in terms of witchcraft, or God's pun-

ishment for sin, or Satan's malevolence. Many Americans did think exactly that way, but by 1776 an increasing number of people did not. To them, the notion of conspiracy offered a way to make sense of their troubles. Who the conspirators were remained something of an open question. Some blamed evil ministers surrounding and duping their "best of kings." Among such, they thought, were Lord Bute, the Scot who was George III's earliest adviser; George Grenville; Lord Hillsborough, who oversaw colonial affairs after 1768; and Lord North.

Others looked closer to home. New York's lieutenant governor Cadwallader Colden, who supposedly had supported the Jacobite rising in Scotland in 1715, was one favorite target for suspicion. Thomas Hutchinson of Massachusetts was another, especially after Benjamin Franklin discovered his call to London for a curb in the colonies on "what are called British liberties" and published it in Boston. Even the Declaration of Independence carries overtones of this fear of conspiracy in its recital of how "a long Train of Abuses and Usurpations, pursuing invariably the same Object," had shown "a Design to reduce [the colonies] under absolute Despotism." But a conspiracy can usually be rectified: Find the evil men, throw them out of office, undo their work, and all will be well again. By itself, the suspicion of conspiracy could have produced neither independence nor revolution.

What was needed was a radical breakthrough in Americans' understanding of what the British Empire was and meant. By 1775 people had been moving toward that breakthrough for ten years. The distance between the hesitant half-acceptance of subordination that marked Daniel Dulany's writing in 1765 and the sharp self-assertion that runs through Thomas Jefferson's in 1774 is one measure of how far they had traveled. Another, as Pauline Maier has argued, lies in people's understanding of where the much-feared conspiracy lay. Initially suspicious minds located it among ministers and placemen. But gradually its compass spread until it included most of Parliament and finally the king. That is why it is the monarch who receives the blame in the Declaration for "a History of repeated Injuries and Usurpations, all having in direct Object the Establishment of an absolute Tyranny over these States." Even the British people did not escape, for the conviction grew that they were so corrupt that they could not save themselves from their rulers.

Yet it was not in Jefferson's eloquent prose that the most radical American insights found their voice. Rather, it was in Tom Paine's great pamphlet *Common Sense*, published in January 1776, nine months after war broke out. The reception that Americans gave it is the fullest proof that it said what needed saying. Paine's predecessors among American pamphleteers might have been lucky to sell a few thousand copies of their work. But *Common Sense* was reprinted and reprinted, in place after place. Perhaps as many as 150,000 copies came off the presses, and Paine himself exulted in this "greatest sale that any performance ever had since the use of letters." Paine may have been vainglorious, but he was right. In a separate study Pauline Maier has found dozens of provincial, county, local, and private-group calls for independence in April, May, and June 1776. Most came from New England, but the idea was aired everywhere.

Part of the reason for Paine's success was the way he wrote. Even the crystalline purity of Jefferson at his best could not match Paine's combination of passion, insight, and vivid yet straightforward prose. Paine's medium was part of his message. He deliberately wrote for people who would tolerate no condescension but who made no pretense to high learning. What he said, however, was as important as how he said it.

Paine attacked not one policy or another but the whole structure of Britishness, subordination, and monarchy within which colonial Americans had lived. The problem was not to explain what had gone wrong in a good system; it was to explain why the system itself was the problem. Addressing a people taught to revere the British Constitution, with its age-old balance of king and Parliament, Paine attacked the monarchy: "A French Bastard landing with an armed Banditti and establishing himself king of England against the consent of the nation, is in plain terms a very paltry rascally original." To a world that revered antiquity, he wrote of the absurdity of the past: "Monarchy and succession have laid (not this or that Kingdom only) but the World in blood and ashes." In a world built on subordination, he showed where inequality led: "America is only a secondary object in the system of British politics. England consults the good of this country, no farther than it answers for her own purpose." To people troubled as they had never been troubled before, he offered a task of worldwide significance: "Freedom hath been hunted round the Globe. Asia and Africa have long expelled her. Europe regards her like a stranger, and England hath given her warning to depart. O! receive the fugitive, and prepare in time an asylum for mankind."

Perhaps most important, Thomas Paine offered more than just a vivid summary of what Americans were against. He gave them something to be for: a republic. " 'Tis the Republican and not the Monarchical part of the constitution of England which Englishmen glory in," he wrote. "It is easy to see that when Republican virtue fails, slavery ensues. Why is the constitution of England sickly? but because monarchy hath poisoned the Republic." The task before the Americans was not to restore a good state of affairs they once had enjoyed—it was to abandon their old ways so they could build a republic of their own.

Paine's call was exhilarating. *Common Sense* crystallized what events had been teaching Americans about themselves and their world since 1765. It changed the terms of American debate. No longer would the questions be how reconciliation might be won and how the British Constitution might be applied to American reality. Henceforth the issues were the coming of independence and the kind of republic it would bring. Those questions presented a frightening prospect for some. Paine's real power lay less in what he said than in the people for whom he spoke. He wrote *Common Sense* after two years of immersion in turbulent revolutionary politics in Philadelphia and after a lifetime of dissent in his native England. His immediate target was Philadelphia's artisan class; by extension, his intended readership was the whole population of farmers and mechanics who were finding their political voice in the Revolution. Many an American "leader" shuddered at the points Paine was making and at the way he was making them. They shuddered most of all at the thought of power falling into the hands of the people whose voice Paine had become. To understand both these men's fears and other men's hopes, we must look at what the independence crisis meant for the ordinary people who lived through it.

II

For eighteenth-century Massachusetts farmers, late August and early September were a time to slow down. The hay and the winter wheat were safely harvested; the spring wheat, barley, oats, and peas were not yet ripe. It was a brief moment of leisure in their endless cycle of work, but in August 1774 farmers in Worcester County made it a moment of intense politics instead. They knew that soon the county court would open for its new term, the first since the Massachusetts Government Act had abolished the old provincial charter. As if to provoke the people, the judges of the court had sent a message supporting the act to Governor Gage, and in town after town people gathered to decide what to do about it. Fine resolutions would not be enough, for no one thought that Parliament would pay any attention to them. Nor would the old weapon of cutting off trade; Parliament itself had already done that when it closed Boston's port. The only choice was between defiance and submission.

The farmers chose defiance. Early in the month a gathering of their committees of correspondence resolved in favor of "wise, prudent and spirited measures" to keep the Intolerable Acts from going into effect. By the end of August they had decided what those measures would be. The "ordinary course of justice" would be stayed. There would be a "convention of the people" to "devise proper ways and means" of conducting public business. In the days before the court was to open in Worcester, towns voted to go there in whole bodies. Records of the town meeting in the village of Westminster tell us that command of the town's two militia companies passed to officers who would not acknowledge Governor Gage's authority; the same was happening elsewhere. When the judges arrived in their wigs and robes to open the court, Westminster farmers were there, together with people from every other town in the county. They were orderly, drawn into ranks on the Worcester town green. But they were also angry and armed, and the court did not open. Instead, by the end of the day the judges had resigned their posts, reading their statements aloud as they walked bareheaded through the townsmen's ranks. It was a humiliating ritual of submission.

This was Worcester County's moment of revolution, different from any experience American people had known before. Part of the difference was the massive presence of farmers. At last, after nine years, the American movement was no longer an affair of the seaport towns alone. A second part was the direct defiance of both British and colonial authority. Worcester's people were challenging not the rightfulness of any particular law but rather Parliament's legislating for them at all. The judges, the provincial councilors, and the militia colonels whom they were displacing were not Englishmen sent from outside to lord it over the colonials. They were successful sons of Massachusetts itself, basking in the rewards that a lifetime of achievement had brought. Not many New Englanders ended by choosing the king's side, but a disproportionate number of the ones who had enjoyed high favor did.

Perhaps the most important difference lay in the popular committees that organized this defiance. Since as early as 1772, towns throughout the Massachusetts interior had been picking small groups of men to correspond with the world outside and to keep track of political events. These committees of correspondence had no legal standing. They enjoyed no more mandate than the vote of a town meeting. But now they were taking power, acting as if they, not the courts, were where authority lay. As committeemen faced down judges, as militia officers who did not acknowledge Governor Gage confronted militia officers who did, as the General Court itself barred its doors to the governor's secretary, who bore a proclamation dissolving it, Massachusetts found that two sets of institutions and rulers were competing for the people's loyalty. One set rested on old teachings, long-standing customs, well-established habits, and the belief that some people deserved to rule others. The other set was still forming, as people cast off what they had "always" believed, called up seventeenth-century radical memories (including Charles I's closing of Parliament in 1628), and began to act as if all men were created equal.

Political scientists call such a situation "dual power." It is intolerable to any working government, but it is at the heart of the process of political revolution. By the end of that summer, Gage had no power except where his troops dared to march. In name, the whole upheaval was for the sake of keeping the Massachusetts Government Act from going into effect. In name, the committees, the new militia officers, and the defiant General Court did all that they did for the sake of preserving their old provincial charter. But in reality, the old order was collapsing and something very different was taking its place.

Country people joining in, popular committees taking power, old rulers being displaced, and confrontation politics: These were the elements that started to change a limited movement of resistance into a popular movement of revolution. They came together all over America between 1774 and 1776, but how and when this process happened varied from place to place. Though knowing the course of events in Massachusetts may provide us with questions to ask about what happened in Virginia, we will have to turn to Virginia for its particular answers. Everywhere, however, people found they had to face the same problems that the farmers of Worcester County faced that August and September.

Let us look at three instances. The first is a frontier county in New York; the second is Philadelphia, which was the greatest city in British America; the third is the province of Virginia. Tryon County, New York, had been created only in 1771. It was named after William Tryon, who had been transferred that year from governor of North Carolina to governor of New York. The county sprawled west of Albany, as far as the 1768 line of property, and the people who lived in it were farmers, fur traders, and Mohawk Indians. For decades the Mohawk Valley had been the unquestioned domain of Sir William Johnson, but late in 1774 a small group of men began meeting secretly to challenge his family's rule. Among them were small freehold farmers, perhaps resentful of the manorial way of life he had built on his estate of Kingsborough. There were also petty traders, unhappy at the strict control Johnson exercised over commerce with the Iroquois. Farmers and traders alike probably would have been glad to get rid of the Johnsons, their Catholic Scottish tenants, and the Iroquois, and to appropriate the rich lands on which they lived, but the immediate idea was to organize help for Boston.

Not everybody agreed. The Johnson tenants were refugees from the fierce vengeance that Britain imposed on the Scottish Highlands after the rebellion of 1745. But their kilts, their Catholicism, and their Gaelic speech marked them as different from their English, Protestant Scotch-Irish, Dutch, and German neighbors. They had a strong tradition of loyalty to benefactors and chieftains, and those are the roles that Sir William Johnson had played in their lives. Even his abandonment of his own natal Catholicism was a recognized strategy for the sake of a family's survival.

But the Iroquois were more important to both British and rebels than Johnson's tenants. By 1775 the Mohawk, who were the easternmost of the Six Nations, were almost surrounded by white settlement, and they did not like it. Immediately to their west the Oneida and the Tuscarora felt the strong influence of the New England–born and New England–sponsored missionary Samuel Kirkland, who labored among them on behalf of Congress as well as his fierce Presbyterian God. Farther west the Onondaga, the Cayuga, and the Seneca all understood that their interests would be better served on the British side. During the colonial wars the Six Nations had made a strategy of satisfying both European sides, but both their political confederacy and their great league of peace, the Haudenosaunee, had remained whole. Despite their different leanings, all six nations tried hard during 1775 and 1776 to remain neutral, but the pressure from both the British and the Americans was intense. The confederacy and the league finally broke apart, and the ceremonial council fire at Onondaga (now Syracuse) was extinguished in January 1777. The Oneida and Tuscarora joined the Americans. The other four nations chose the British.

The white Mohawk Valley revolutionaries emerged into the open in May 1775, in response to the news of fighting in Massachusetts. A county committee of thirty-two men was elected, but it and what it stood for met the determined opposition of Sir William's loyalist heirs: Sir John Johnson, who had just succeeded his father as baronet, and Colonel Guy Johnson, who had inherited Sir William's post of Indian superintendent. Like the confrontation on Worcester Green, the face-down in the Mohawk Valley was public and dramatic. But unlike what happened in Massachusetts, it pitted evenly matched forces against each other and brought tragic results.

In June 1775 Sir John chanced upon a popular meeting "to choose a Captain agreeable to the resolution of their committee." In the words of one of Johnson's friends, "One Mr. Visher who was a candidate" for the rebel captaincy "became so very impertinent that Sir John could not bear it—but gave him a hearty Horse-whipping . . . and then very cooly got into his carriage and drove [off]." The next month news began to spread that Sir John's county sheriff had arrested a prominent rebel. A crowd of about one hundred men gathered at Johnson Hall to demand his release. The house had been fortified with light artillery. After some shots were exchanged, the ranks of both defenders and besiegers swelled to about five hundred. The rebels sent to Albany for cannons of their own, but the committee there sent negotiators, who arranged a truce. It lasted only until the autumn, when the Johnsons and their closest allies fled to the Niagara frontier. Their flight marked the beginning of seven years of civil war.

In Philadelphia events took a different course. The Quaker City had been noticeably quieter than other port towns through the 1760s, but in 1774 "radical resistance leaders" won "their hesitant, divided community . . . to a determined opposition to London's new imperial policies." The city never had a Sons of Liberty organization, but now a committee movement took shape. The radicals who founded and developed the committee system had to overcome the determined hostility of Philadelphia's traditional leaders, especially its Quaker mercantile elite.

Pennsylvania's old rulers had two bastions. One was the Corporation of the City of Philadelphia, a small group of men accountable only to themselves. They did not have to face either town meetings, as leaders did in Boston, or open elections, as in New York. Instead, Philadelphia's city fathers decided among themselves whom to invite to join them. The provincial assembly of Pennsylvania was the old rulers' other bastion. Unlike Virginia's Burgesses and the Massachusetts General Court, Pennsylvania's assemblymen had steered a course that kept them well apart from the resistance movement. In 1765 they passed some resolutions against the Stamp Act, but they never courted dissolution by defying royal orders, and they never transformed themselves into an illegal revolutionary gathering. Instead, the assemblymen simply tried to keep business going as usual. Governor John Penn followed much the same policy.

After the Intolerable Acts, most Philadelphians accepted the need to support Boston. After all, they had refused company tea themselves. On May 20, 1774, a meeting of the city's leaders voted a boycott of British commerce and named a committee of nineteen to enforce it. Among the nineteen were a number of men who wanted to go slowly but only two who became outright loyalists. Already the hold of the city's genuine conservatives was slipping. As the emerging loyalists lost their ability to influence events, "official" institutions like the assembly came under the control of men like John Dickinson, who believed in resistance but shuddered at the idea of revolution. Dickinson and other moderates did well in several assembly elections between 1774 and 1776, but they rapidly lost influence in the city's growing committee movement. There men of different social background and of a different cast of mind were coming to power.

Philadelphia's committee system went through two phases. First came a "revolution of the elite," and then a "revolution of the middle classes." The first brought to the fore several dozen men who had stood outside the charmed circle of the old order. In general, they were prosperous enough, but they did amount to "a new elite for a new society, chosen (and self-chosen) to perform unprecedented public services." The second phase mobilized several hundred lesser people: German immigrants, Scotch-Irish Presbyterians, and "obscure mechanics in shirt-sleeves and leather aprons." Here, says historian Richard Ryerson, was "a birth of modern American politics."

The confrontation in Pennsylvania was not just between the colony and the mother country; it pitted committee against assembly and people who stood for one order against people who were coming to stand for another. It finally came to a head in June 1776, when, with prodding from Congress, the Philadelphia committee organized the overthrow of the old assembly. Within little more than two years, Philadelphia and the whole of Pennsylvania with it had been transformed. From a city of hesitation, led by men determined not to lose their comfort and their power, it had become the most thoroughly radicalized place in all America.

The burst of scholarship that underpinned the first edition of this book revealed story after story of internal conflict and transformation akin to the ones in rural Massachusetts, the Mohawk Valley of New York, and Philadelphia. But despite intense study, Virginia seemed different. Except for a very few, its white people seemed to be united, not divided, for a number of very good reasons. The vast majority of them grew tobacco. Rich or poor, they governed their lives according to the fifteen-month cycle of intense cultivation and careful preparation of the crop that tobacco required. Even those who did not own slaves wanted to, and all shared the slaveholders' realization that the slaves might revolt. Very few were townsmen, with the different set of interests and orientation toward the world that urban life induces. Most white Virginia men could expect to own enough property to be independent at some point in their life cycle. At the tavern, at the race course, at the polls, on court day, on the dance floor, on militia training day, and even when they worshiped in their Anglican parish churches, they acted out public rituals that bound them to one another. Within a county the same great planter might be member of the House of Burgesses, justice of the peace, militia colonel, and vestryman, unifying all forms of authority in his one person. Among white Virginians the only source of diversity seemed to be sojourning Scots merchants in Norfolk or Alexandria and a growing but still small movement of dissident evangelical Christians. Here was a perfect candidate for a republican society, with one rural way of life, one large economic interest (tobacco), one large social interest (slavery), and powerful rituals of belonging and identity. Small wonder that Virginia produced its remarkable elite, that those planter-statesmen led other white Virginians into revolution with little dissent, and that they created simple, open political institutions with the full expectation that they would continue to rule with their fellow Virginians' consent.

That picture is too simplistic. Colonial Virginia's leaders were not divided among themselves as were the elites in Massachusetts, New York, and Pennsylvania. But by the mid-1760s they were frightened. Just when the Stamp Act was repealed in 1766, the death of John Robinson, speaker of the House of Burgesses and treasurer of the province, implicated many of them in a major financial scandal that he had organized. They feared it meant the decay of their own civic virtue. They recognized as well that militant evangelical Protestants posed a serious cultural challenge to their entire way of life. Some planters dealt with Baptists and Methodists the same way that Sir John Johnson tried to deal with Mohawk Valley revolutionaries, riding into open-air meetings flailing their whips at the congregants.

Historian Woody Holton suggests that more was at stake among the planters than fear and self-doubt. In his reading, the Virginia elite found themselves under pressure from four different directions. They were not just landowners but avid land speculators beyond the Blue Ridge, and they faced hostility to their acquisitions from both Indians and Parliament. Though wealthy men, they saw little hard coin from year to year, and their accounts with Norfolk and British merchants usually ran far in arrears. Despite the shared culture of tobacco, all the marks of their own social class separated them from their yeoman and tenant neighbors, and the "lesser sort" resented it. Most frightening of all, the planter class claimed to own the bulk of the two-fifths of all Virginians who were enslaved. Slaves had more common sense than to risk their lives in futile romantic gestures of rebellion. But in 1775 some slaves saw their moment to act, encouraging Governor Lord Dunmore to offer them freedom and then rallying to him as well as they could. Under all these pressures Virginia's patriot leaders are better seen as forced into the militant stance they took than as leaping into it.

In Virginia even more than in Massachusetts, the top echelon of leaders did choose loyalism; 57 percent of the councilors and high administrative officials ended up on the king's side. But save for these, most of Virginia's elite chose the Revolution. As in Massachusetts, the provincial assembly became a core of resistance, confronting the governor above it rather than the popular committees below. Lord Dunmore dissolved the House of Burgesses at the end of May 1774, for voting a day of "Fasting, Humiliation and Prayer" against the Intolerable Acts. But its members simply reconvened as a provincial congress. Then they set in motion a campaign to win the backing of lesser white Virginians, inviting them to join in rituals of virtue and commitment. Virginians of the "middling and lower classes" stood patiently at county court houses while condescending orators explained how "on the virtue . . . of the people does it depend whether we shall be happy or miserable." Others turned out in good order for ceremonies like the return from the Continental Congress in 1775 of Peyton Randolph, its president. As one account, noted by Rhys Isaac, put it, they surrounded "the FATHER of his COUNTRY, whom they attended to his house, amidst repeated acclamations, and then respectfully retired."

Change did come. The crisis demanded sacrifice: food, so Boston's poor would not starve; private pleasures like horse racing, dancing, and gambling, so austere virtue could be demonstrated; and private dissenting opinions, so the world would see a united Virginia front. As Virginians armed to resist Britain, they changed the terms on which they dealt with one another. The change from ceremonies of hierarchy to ceremonies of commitment gave lesser men the chance to narrow the distance between themselves and greater ones. Politics became more contentious, but much of the narrowing took place at the symbolic level. The best example was when great men bowed to public pressure, doffed their habitual elegant costumes, and agreed that a plain hunting shirt and a tomahawk would be the emblems of commitment to the cause.

These examples show us immense variety in what happened, but they do not show us everything. Worcester County's response was like that of most of the rest of Massachusetts, but the Mohawk Valley's was not like that of the rest of New York. Elsewhere in that province, some counties plunged wholeheartedly into involvement, some were divided, and others remained overwhelmingly loyal. New York City's revolution was very much like Philadelphia's. That is not surprising: The two cities were similar in many ways. But Maryland's revolution was unlike that of either Pennsylvania, to its north, or Virginia, to its south, despite the fact that the province had elements in common with each. Though in the end Virginia planters kept control of lesser whites, Carolina planters did not. Backcountry people there were still bitter in the aftermath of the Regulator movements, and when the British invaded the lower South in 1779, the whole Carolina interior broke into vicious civil war.

Once raised, fundamental questions are not easy to answer, and from 1774 to 1776 both prominent people and obscure people agonized about whether to support the British or the patriots. Prominent New Yorkers John Jay and Peter Van Schaack, who had been friends since their time at King's College (now Columbia University), debated the matter in 1775–76 and parted ways. Despite Jay's reputation as a "conservative," he threw himself into the movement once he made up his mind. Meanwhile farmers gathered in the forbidding Helderberg escarpment, west of Albany. Most were tenants on the manor of Rensselaerswyck. They were alienated from their landlords and from the patriot leadership in Albany, and they retreated to the hills to decide in privacy what to do. A patriot informant was among them, which is how we know that one of them, John Commons, finally put the question. "Those who thought Congress was in the right," Commons said, "should go and those who thought the king was right should stay." But to put the question was one thing, to answer it was another, and Commons himself "did not know who was right."

Congress finally accepted the need for independence in the summer of 1776. On July 2 it voted in favor of a "resolution of independence" that Richard Henry Lee had offered almost a month before. The resolution proclaimed "that these United Colonies are, and of right ought to be, free and independent states, that they are absolved from all allegiance to the British Crown, and that all political connection between them and the State of Great Britain is, and ought to be, totally dissolved." Two days later Congress approved the Declaration, which a five-man committee led by Thomas Jefferson had been drafting since early June.

Independence could not have come earlier. Breaking the emotional, political, economic, and intellectual ties that held colonials to Britain took time. For many, the ties were never broken. Loyalists never formed a large percentage of the American population, but they constituted a significant minority. In a few places, such as the area surrounding New York City, they were an overwhelming majority. In others, including the Hudson Valley and Maryland's Eastern Shore, they were strong enough to wage extended guerrilla resistance. In the Carolina and Georgia backcountry and on New York's western frontier, they were so numerous that the Revolution became a war of American against American. When "one people" broke the "political bands" that had "connected them with another," a fair-sized minority of that people dissented and broke the social bands that had connected them to neighbors, friends, and even relatives.

The Declaration of Independence is divided into three parts. The first proclaims high principles: that all men are created equal, that they all have unalienable rights; that among these are life, liberty, and the pursuit of happiness, whatever happiness may be. Thomas Jefferson's draft of this part is virtually what Congress adopted, and it shows him at his most inspired. This is the part that still resonates, but the Declaration's most recent historian suggests that it counted for relatively little in 1776. The second part declares why the Americans are altering their political order. Mounting charge after charge, it indicts "the present king of Great Britain" with planning "an absolute tyranny over these states." Charging the king alone reflected Jefferson's own belief that only the Crown had bound the colonies to Britain; to him Parliament never did have any American authority. It also reflected the fact that Congress had abjured all parliamentary authority in December 1775. The bill of indictment was mostly Jefferson's work, and his training as a lawyer is apparent. Jefferson knew that no absolutely clinching evidence of the king's personal culpability could be found. The indictment had to persuade its readers by its own rhetorical device of piling one piece of circumstantial evidence upon another. Building momentum as it moved from charge to charge, the indictment began with the king's refusal to assent to laws "the most wholesome and necessary for the public good" and culminated with outright acts of war.

Both Jefferson's preamble and his bill of indictment have the ring of psychological truth. They did express their author's deeply rooted and firmly held beliefs. But toward the end of the indictment the prose falters. The next-to-last count charges the king with bringing "on the inhabitants of our frontiers the merciless Indian savages, whose known rule of warfare is an undistinguished destruction of all sexes, ages, & conditions." Jefferson knew better. Frontier war was brutal, but Indians were not the king's puppets, and since the first whites appeared Indians had been receiving just as much "undistinguished destruction" as they wrought. Jefferson wanted to close the indictment by blaming the king both for the fact that slavery existed in America at all and for trying to rouse the slaves themselves in rebellion. This was the first of many public writings where Jefferson would touch upon the problem of slavery only to find that his own prose betrayed his personal misgivings. There were elements of literal truth in the count. The king had rejected Virginia statutes against the African slave trade, and his agent Lord Dunmore had encouraged slave rebellion. But in contrast to Jefferson's usually cool writing, this count labors under capitalized words ("a market where MEN should be bought"), inflammatory adjectives ("piratical warfare, the opprobrium of *infidel* powers"), and the sheer illogic of blaming the supposedly tyrannical king for encouraging real slaves to seek their freedom. Its psychological truth is simply that slavery did bother Jefferson, and many of his fellows, as it had not bothered their fathers. Congress dropped the count. Jefferson would say that the reason was pressure from South Carolina and Georgia, which still wanted to import Africans. But there were many Virginians who wanted Africans, too; otherwise the slave traders would not have bothered with the Chesapeake market. Had this count remained in the Declaration, particularly as framed in Jefferson's fevered language, its subsequent reputation as a charter document of human freedom would have been badly soiled. Even as it stood, the London literary figure Samuel Johnson still could ask in acid tones "how is it that we hear the loudest *yelps* for liberty among the drivers of Negroes?"

The third part of the Declaration sunders the tie: The colonies are "free and independent states," entitled to do everything "which independent states may of right do." For purposes of international law, this is what counted most. Unlike Paine's *Common Sense* the Declaration did not attack the principle of monarchy. Jefferson probably would have been glad to do so, but he and Congress understood that the king of France represented their only real hope of assistance against the "present king of Great Britain." The fraudulent Bordeaux trading firm of Hortalez et Cie. already was providing clandestine French aid. Perhaps appropriately, the company was run by Pierre Caron de Beaumarchais, whose *Marriage of Figaro* was one of the great works of democratic art of the era. Now, if the Americans did not suffer defeat, French assistance might become open.

Congress did appoint a committee to begin establishing foreign relations. But as soon as independence was declared most of its members turned their attention to their own states, where the task of shaping a new order loomed.

III

Only two things were certain in 1776. One was that the new America would be republican. The Revolution was not for the sake of installing a different monarch, like its "glorious" namesake in England in 1688 or like the Jacobite uprisings in Scotland in 1715 and 1745. It did not replace one king or one ruling house with another; it abolished monarchy and ruling houses altogether. The other certainty was that the new states would have written constitutions. In metaphorical terms, colonials killed their king in 1776. In very real terms, they destroyed the whole ancient pattern of institutions, beliefs, habits, and usages that had made up the British Constitution in America. To replace it, everyone agreed, there would have to be special solemn documents laying the basis for future public life.

With that much understood, agreement stopped and intense debate began. What was at stake was not just ideas; it was also power, interest, property, and the course of the future. The struggles that developed around the making of the state constitutions reveal the internal lines of stress in the revolutionary coalitions. They show how groups and individuals who had agreed there had to be a break with Britain were divided and in conflict about what should follow.

Fourteen states—including Vermont—adopted constitutions between 1776 and 1780. But the documents that were produced in Pennsylvania, Maryland, New York, and Massachusetts show the range of argument and the problems to be overcome. Pennsylvania's constitution established a simple democracy in which "the people" came very close to being their own rulers. Maryland's created complex, restrictive institutions designed to keep citizens and rulers as far apart as possible. New York's constitution of 1777 represented the second thoughts and the cool deliberations of men with much to lose. So did the Massachusetts constitution of 1780. But in that document we can see the working out of procedures that would become standard practice for creating popular sovereignty, not just in America, but in many other postrevolutionary nations.

We cannot say that "the people" of any one state were either "radical" or "conservative." In every state there were some people who wanted simple democracy and some people who feared it. Each state constitution reflected the balance of power at the time of its writing as well as the honest search of men trying in good faith to find the best way. People across the political spectrum were exhilarated by their chance to be the founders of a new order.

Radical democracy triumphed in Pennsylvania because its men of moderation were routed. Letting fear turn into panic, they forfeited leadership precisely at the moment of independence. Some, like the colonial political leader Joseph Galloway and most of the Philadelphia Quaker elite, moved into outright loyalism. Benjamin Franklin, once Galloway's firm ally, chose independence, but he was busy with Continental matters. The spokesmen for the center were men like pamphleteer John Dickinson, whose fear grew as the crisis deepened, the wealthy merchant Robert Morris, and the Scots-born rising lawyer James Wilson. Though they knew that independence would come, they would have been happy to delay it. With Pennsylvania's genuine loyalists already gone, centrists made the provincial assembly their power base in 1775 and early 1776, which proved a disastrous mistake. In the spring of 1776 radicals in Philadelphia, aiming at internal change, united with radicals in Congress, aiming at independence, to undermine them. In May, when Congress called for the abolition of all institutions that still accepted royal authority, it was aiming at Pennsylvania's moderates. The people of the province responded, bringing the assembly down. Neither genuinely Tory nor really revolutionary, the moderates suddenly had no place to stand.

So Thomas Paine's people found themselves in control. Paine himself did not take part in writing the state's 1776 constitution, but the plan he sketched in *Common Sense*—"Let the assemblies be annual, with a president only"—was in perfect harmony with it. Among the authors of the constitution were a number of Paine's friends, including James Cannon, a teacher and scientist from Scotland; Timothy Matlack, a disowned Quaker and the son of a brewer; Christopher Marshall, a retired druggist; and Dr. Thomas Young, a radical physician who had practiced medicine and politics in Albany, Boston, and Newport before coming to Philadelphia. They wrote their document under the authority of a convention that had been chosen at polls open to every adult militia member. The militiamen had a program of their own, which they announced through their committee of privates. They wanted as much equality as possible between men and officers; they wanted the officers to be elected, not appointed; and they wanted no exemptions from service, whether for Quakers with conscientious objections or for wealthy men who could buy substitutes. Most of all, as James Cannon put it in a broadside that was published in the privates' name, they wanted no man in power "who would be disposed to form any rank above that of freeman." The radicals had their own lines of stress. One ran between the free thought represented by Young and Matlack and the stern piety typified by Marshall, who maintained his Quaker faith despite his revolutionary politics. Not everyone who had been militant in bringing down the old government liked either the new constitution or the policies the new government adopted. But the major point is that in the summer of 1776 Pennsylvania's old elite abdicated, allowing new men representing new constituencies to take its place.

The state's democratic constitution emerged out of that situation. It established no governorship and no upper house at all. Instead, an executive council under an annually elected president would administer affairs, without taking any part in the making of law. The House of Representatives would be elected annually as well, and every adult male taxpayer who had lived in the state for one year would be eligible to vote. The only qualifications for election to the House were to be "noted for wisdom and virtue," to have two years residence in the constituency, and not to "hold any other office except in the militia." To keep officeholders from developing into a separate caste, no man could be elected to the House for more than four years in any seven. Perhaps the most startling provision was the constitution's attempt to bring Pennsylvania's people directly into the process of making laws. Once a bill was considered by the representatives, it was to be "printed for the consideration of the people" before it was "read in general assembly the last time for debate and amendment." Except "on occasions of special necessity," that final reading would take place at the assembly's next session. In the interval, the people would have the chance to let their representatives know what they thought of their work—if necessary, by refusing to reelect them.

In Maryland great planters led the province into independence. They were fully equal in wealth, sophistication, and, as events showed, political skill to the Carters and Lees of Virginia, but they lacked the Virginians' secure self-confidence. The Calvert family, which held the proprietorship of the colony and among whom the title Lord Baltimore descended, retained enormous economic power through the whole colonial era, even though they lost political control. Some Maryland planters, such as the Carrolls, were Catholics, hence disqualified by their faith from prerevolutionary public life. Perhaps most important, white Maryland had more reason to be divided than white Virginia. Baltimore was a real town, and its people had town dwellers' interests. The Eastern Shore, between Chesapeake Bay and the Atlantic, was a farming economy much more than a planter one. The farther north and west one went in Maryland, the more likely one was to find free labor, both black and white, producing wheat, rather than slave labor producing tobacco.

Unlike Virginia, Maryland experienced serious "disaffection" outright. The militia proved unreliable; Tory guerrilla bands roved freely; state courts could not open; blacks and poor whites talked of making common cause. While popular loyalism gath-

ered force, other Marylanders were generating an intense republican radicalism. In July 1776 the militia of Anne Arundel
County put forward its members' ideas about government. The
militiamen wanted a two-house legislature, each house to be
elected annually under a broad suffrage. There would be a governor, rather than a president as in Pennsylvania, but he would
have no power to veto laws. Local officials would be elected, not
appointed. The tax system would be based on "a fair and equal
assessment in proportion to every person's estate." The militia
were not alone in their radicalism: In August almost nine hundred freemen of the same county instructed their delegates to
write a constitution along similar lines, adding that the suffrage
ought to be open to every taxpayer. In the state's revolutionary
convention there were figures such as John Hall and Regin
Hammond who spoke for such men.

But Maryland adopted a constitution that suited its planters
and reflected their own sense of being beleaguered. The planters' correspondence, largely centered on Charles Carroll of Carrollton, reverberates with danger and near-panic, and so does
their constitution. It put real distance between Maryland's people and their government. While annual elections would be held
for county sheriffs and the members of the lower house of the
state legislature, state senators would be picked for seven-year
terms by a college of electors. The governor would be chosen for
a one-year term by the senate and the lower house acting together. To sit in the assembly or to be an elector for the senate,
a man had to be worth £500; to be a sheriff, a senator, a con-
gressman, or a member of the executive council, the sum was
£1,000. To become governor, one had to have a fortune of at least
£5,000. These were daunting requirements that only small mi-
norities of white adult males could meet.

Like its Pennsylvania counterpart, New York's old elite broke
apart along lines that had been etched by a long history of internal dispute. They had to face enormous popular discontent. The
elite patriots were helped by two elements beyond their control.

The first was that from 1768 to 1775 the provincial assembly was in the control of men who were moving toward outright loyalism, centered on the De Lancey family of New York City. Elite patriots—the Livingstons, Van Rensselaers, and Schuylers of the Hudson Valley and urban figures like John Jay and Gouverneur Morris—were in no hurry to win independence, but unlike the Pennsylvanians they could not use the assembly to stave it off. When the assembly collapsed at the end of 1775, the patriots had already shifted operations to provincial congresses, where they mastered the art of delay. They were also aided by the British invasion of New York City in August 1776. The coming of the redcoats scattered the artisans and the Sons of Liberty of New York. The invasion also forced all New York revolutionaries to see their first problem as simple: defending themselves against hostile troops.

The new patriot leadership centered on Jay, Morris, the ambitious merchant William Duer, and the young lawyer and landowner Robert R. Livingston. They appreciated the task in front of them and made the most of their chances. As early as 1774, as he watched a committee election, Morris compared "the mob" to "poor reptiles" basking in the morning sun: He was sure that "ere noon" those reptiles "will bite." But in Livingston's words, his own sort used "well-timed delays, indefatigible industry and minute . . . attention to every favourable circumstance." Heeding the warning of their loyalist mentor, the jurist William Smith, they understood that their place was "rather to the Cabinet than the field." Later Duer reminisced to Jay about their labors on the "Council of *Conspiracy*." Livingston summed up both their methods and their goals with a metaphor of "swimming with a stream it is impossible to stem" and of yielding "to the Torrent" in order to "direct its course."

Their sense of danger was justified. In May 1776 the organized mechanics of New York City demanded that the people ratify any state constitution that might be written. They also wanted the constitution to allow the election of popular committees whenever people might want them. The first draft in New York's revolutionary constitution called for a president, not a governor, and for direct election of most officials. One observer, a future popular politician, called the draft a "child of heaven." But another, making up his mind to be a loyalist, feared the power it gave to "the peasantry."

The constitution that John Jay wrote and that New York adopted was realistic rather than reactionary. It created a two-house legislature. The assemblymen would be elected annually in county delegations, and the members of the state senate would be chosen at staggered four-year intervals to represent four "districts," apportioned roughly by wealth. The governor would be chosen for a three-year term. Except for the assembly's exclusive right to initiate money bills, the two houses would have equal powers. A "council of revision," made up of the governor and highest judges, would have a veto on laws unless two-thirds of each house voted to override. Patronage would be in the hands of a "council of appointment," made up of the governor and four senators. There were no property qualifications for office, but a freehold worth £40 or a renthold valued at twenty shillings was necessary to vote for the assembly. A freehold worth £100 was required to vote for state senators or for the governorship. Proposals did circulate for a qualification of £10,000 and a New York City residence to sit in the upper house; these came to nothing. Men from across the political spectrum joined Jay on the drafting committee and sat in the convention that finally approved and proclaimed the document. Using a physical image different from Livingston's "Torrent," Jay observed that "another turn of the winch would have cracked the cord." The upper-class patriots had gone far enough. Moreover, they had no doubts about who would fill the state's high offices: themselves.

Massachusetts took longest to create a constitution. Its old order dissolved in 1774, but there was no new constitution until 1780. While Massachusetts people waited, they argued incessantly about both the shape their government ought to take and, especially, about the manner in which it ought to acquire its form. When the General Court defied the governor's order dissolving it in 1774, it simply pretended that it was upholding the royal charter of 1692. But far to the west mountain dwellers who became known as the Berkshire Constitutionalists began to insist that the commonwealth needed a firmer basis. These people started Massachusetts toward the constitution it finally adopted, just as the mechanics of New York City were the first to broach the idea of popular ratification. As long as the legal standing of the government was in doubt, the courts stayed closed. People made do with arbitration under county conventions and town committees. The towns of Ashfield and Middleborough and an anonymous pamphlet called *The People the Best Governors* (which apparently originated in Pennsylvania) all proposed that Massachusetts adopt simple, direct institutions. Elections would link the people to almost all their officials, and there would be no property requirements for voting. There would be no real power higher than the one-house assembly; a council might exist, but only to advise, not to take part in making the laws. In Ashfield's plan, as in Pennsylvania's constitution, the voters would have the right to pass judgment on the assembly's actions. Under that plan and in *The People the Best Governors*, judges would be elected, not appointed. Middleborough's plan made no proposal for courts at all.

But Massachusetts ended up with a very different settlement. In 1778 the interim government wrote a constitution and offered it to the towns. From Boston to the Berkshires, they rejected it, partly because of its content, which was like Maryland's, and partly because the temporary rulers had no authority to write it in the first place. In 1780 a convention elected with special powers wrote another constitution. Under it a man had to have a freehold worth £60 to vote. Assemblymen would represent towns, but the state senate would be apportioned according to the value of property in any district, not according to its population. Senators would have to possess at least £300 in real property or £600 in personal property, and to become governor a man would have to be worth at least £1,000. The governor would enjoy considerable power, both in appointments to public office and in a qualified veto over laws. Samuel Eliot Morison showed long ago that the towns actually rejected this constitution, and that the convention, desperate to establish a permanent government, juggled the figures so it could declare ratification. But in principle Massachusetts had resolved a problem that had plagued constitution writers in every state. The special conventions and the plebiscites on which postrevolutionary political orders have been founded ever since have their beginning here.

All these problems and debates echoed and reverberated throughout America. In Vermont the Green Mountain Boys found their chance to break free of New York and its hated land system. As Ethan Allen's brother Heman put it to a town meeting, "If we submitted to the mode of Government now forming in the state of New York . . . we could not get off in a future day." Being "without law or government," it was up to the Green Mountain people to create their own forms as they saw fit. Vermont did not receive "official" recognition from Congress and acquiescence from New York until after 1790. But from 1777 onward its existence was a reality that even New York could not ignore. Vermont's self-founding was the only time in the eighteenth century when backcountry rebels got the chance to do everything they wanted. They chose to adopt Pennsylvania's radical democracy.

They did so at least partly at the suggestion of Dr. Thomas Young. Young had grown up in New York's Hudson Valley. In the early 1760s he made friends with Ethan Allen, who was running an ironworks just across the Connecticut line. They talked about the evils that great landed estates brought and discovered that neither believed in Christian revelation or in the power of the church. They wrote a deist tract. Decades later their book became known as *Ethan Allen's Bible*, and it made Allen's name hateful to orthodox ministers all over America. Young moved to Albany, where he was practicing medicine at the time of the Stamp Act, and then on to Boston, Newport, and finally Philadelphia. His name comes first on a roster of Albany Sons of Liberty from 1766. In Philadelphia he associated with Tom Paine, and he helped to draft the Pennsylvania constitution of 1776. When the Vermonters declared their own independence, he suggested it to them as a model, calling it "as near perfection as anything yet concerted by mankind." Even then Young was still berating the "men of some rank" who wanted to re-create in America "the system of Lord and Vassal, or *principal* and *dependent*." The Vermonters followed his advice. They added a clause abolishing slavery in their new state. The number of slaves actually reached by Vermont's abolition cannot have been greater than a few dozen. But for the first time in the whole history of the western hemisphere, there was a place where being black automatically meant that a person was free rather than a slave.

Even titles of office took on significance in state constitution making. The word *president* turns up again and again: in New York's first draft; in Tom Paine's call to "let the assemblies be annual, with a president only"; and in the actual state constitutions of Delaware, New Hampshire, and South Carolina, as well as that of Pennsylvania. The choice was deliberate. Unlike *governor*, the word carried no overtones of distant monarchical power. It suggested that the job of the officer who bore it was to preside rather than to rule. The people of Ashfield, Massachusetts, had the same point in mind when they announced that they wanted no governor save the "Goviner of the Univarse." Spelled in standard form, that phrase also turns up in the Pennsylvania constitution. The people who used it did not see their God as either a father or a king but rather as a republican magistrate. Their revolution had taught them to think of themselves not as sinners in tearful exile but rather as citizens of the grandest republic the mind could imagine.

We can see, then, how tangled was the process of destroying the remnants of the British Empire and erecting the first structures of the American Republic. At the point of independence Americans had only one question to answer: which side they were on. But they came to that point by joining in coalitions that linked regions, interests, classes, and individuals, all with their own points of view, their own fears, and their own visions. That the coalitions started to come apart as soon as independence was declared should not be surprising. That the shaping of the state constitutions was affected by questions of balance and tactics within each state should not be surprising, either. Their shared commitment to independence and republicanism gave Americans something to agree on. But their differences were many and, naturally, gave them something to argue about. The arguments would continue well after the new state governments had begun to function.

Five

FOURTEEN STATES

Careful, self-controlled, always pondering consequences, reining in the fierce passions that drove him, John Adams was not a man to let himself go. But in May 1776, when Congress called for new state governments, his joy knew no bounds. "It is independence itself," he exulted in private, and in his pamphlet *Thoughts on Government* he crowed over his generation's privilege. "How few of the human race have ever enjoyed an opportunity of making an election of government," he wrote, "more than of air, soil, or climate for themselves or their children." Adams and his kind would be the fathers of a new order. History would speak of them as it did of the heroes who founded the city-states of the ancient world.

Yet exultation was not the only mood in Adams's heart. He knew that cutting the tie with Britain meant cutting many ties among Americans. When crowds closed courts, towns elected committees, militiamen debated with their officers, and Tories took flight, Adams was appalled. With characteristic clarity, he defined the problem and worked out a plan to resolve it. "To contrive some Method for the Colonies to glide insensibly from under the old Government, into a peaceable and contented submission to new ones" was "the most difficult and dangerous Part of the Business Americans have to do in this mighty Contest."

If we stand back far enough, it looks as though John Adams's plan worked. States wrote their constitutions and put them into effect. Congress became the center of a national system of sorts and finally gave that system form in the Articles of Confederation. Together they won the war. When postwar problems grew too large, a suitable and enduring remedy was found in the federal Constitution. Not for Americans, it would seem, the agonizing disorder that has plagued so many other peoples seeking to emerge from revolution.

But it was not so simple. The long struggle over the formal shape of the new state and national governments only began to resolve the question of what kind of place independent America would be. During the war years, from 1775 to 1781, and the Confederation period, from then until 1788, American society confronted immense problems. Raising and disciplining an army was hard enough, for the surge of military enthusiasm that followed Lexington and Concord tapered off quickly. Financing the war was worse: Congress had no taxing power at all, and the states had little, so the only recourse was to borrow abroad and to print paper currency at home, with the promise that someday the loans would be paid and the currency would be redeemed. The new governments had to deal with loyalists and neutrals, enough of them in some places to make it impossible to exercise any real authority.

Almost everywhere people debated about how, for whom, and by whom the new order would be run. This great decade-long debate took place in many arenas. It went on in legislative chambers, in the rooms where popular committees met, and at polling places. It went on in newspapers, in broadsides, and in private correspondence. It also went on in city streets, where people sometimes rioted, and in the fields of western Massachusetts, where people finally rose in arms ten years after independence. Shays's Rebellion, as this backcountry uprising was called, was no aberration. It marked the most extreme aspect of a general conflict.

I

From the skirmish at Concord in 1775 to the final battle at York-town in 1781, the revolutionaries' immediate problem was to keep Britain's military might from destroying the American movement. The first theater of conflict was New England, where farmer-soldiers besieged British-occupied Boston until the redcoats withdrew in March 1776. After regrouping at Hali-fax, the British invaded lower New York State in August 1776, with the greatest seaborne army the modern world had seen. They captured New York City easily and held it until the end of 1783. Washington's skill at retreating kept defeat from becoming disaster and kept the American army in existence to fight again. Preserving the army, fighting only when he felt sure of victory (though he did not always win), and retreating whenever he had to would be the core of his strategy until the war's end.

In 1777 the British came close to cutting the country and the rebellion in two when General John Burgoyne led a massive col-umn south from Montreal along the Champlain and Hudson valleys. He was defeated at Saratoga, north of Albany, by Ameri-cans under Horatio Gates, who once upon a time had been his fellow junior officer in the same British regiment. A lesser British force coming from the west was stopped in a frightfully bloody engagement of neighbors and cousins at Oriskany. The failure of this attempt to cut New England off gave the French their chance to recognize the independent United States and enter the war. The British occupation of Philadelphia that win-ter meant humiliation and terrible suffering for the American troops encamped not far away, at Valley Forge. Fierce warfare continued where white settlement met Iroquois Indian country. But the Revolution had not been split in two, let alone defeated. The war shifted south in 1779. From then until General Wash-ington and Admiral François Joseph de Grasse trapped the army of Lord Cornwallis at Yorktown in 1781, the southern interior was the main scene of conflict. It took two more years to make a formal peace, which was signed in Paris on November 29, 1783.

The notion that a virtuous American nation of citizen-soldiers accomplished it all by putting aside their plows and picking up their guns does not stand up. After an initial burst of martial enthusiasm in 1775 and 1776, most people went back to their farms and shops. Both the officers and men of the Continental Army came to think of themselves as a caste apart from ordinary citizens. In some places, these people fought the war by the rules as eighteenth-century gentlemen understood them. British officers were gentlemen by definition, and many American officers decided that their rank made them gentlemen, too. But by no means did all of them behave as their code required, and for many "lesser" men the rules never held. The Massachusetts farmers who sniped at redcoats marching back from Lexington and Concord set the pattern. They were more interested in survival than in glory, and they knew that firing from behind a rock or a tree made their chances of survival a lot better. They had to learn, however, that faced with totally disciplined British and German soldiers, they sometimes needed total discipline themselves. In places as far apart as the Georgia and Carolina backcountry and the western frontier of New York, the war became a vicious guerrilla struggle. In those places, the devastation and the bloodshed were frightful, and the British, the revolutionaries, and the loyalists all bore a share of the responsibility.

Keeping the army intact was as important as winning battles. In the face of enormous adversity, this was George Washington's great achievement, but he did not do it alone. Part of his problem was internal discipline and organization. After Lexington, farmers all over New England did drop what they were doing and join the siege of British-occupied Boston, but such a haphazard, informal army could not last long. When Washington took command in July 1775, he was appalled to find that latrine trenches often were dug very close to field kitchens. It took years of effort, experiment, frustration, and mistakes before Washington genuinely commanded the "respectable" army he had wanted from the start. It also took the services of a host of other officers. The generals, whether Americans like Nathanael Greene, Henry Knox, Philip Schuyler, and Benedict Arnold, or foreigners like Gates, his fellow Englishmen Richard Montgomery and Charles Lee, the German drillmaster Friedrich von Steuben, or the French marquis de Lafayette, are the best known. But there were many lesser men—colonels, majors, captains, and lieutenants—who also came to think that they were the Revolution's heroes.

Winning the war required the willingness of thousands of very ordinary men in the ranks to put up with disease, danger, physical conditions that often were horrifying, and discipline that grew steadily more severe, all in a war that must have seemed as if it would never end. As with the regular British army, this meant recruiting people for whom civilian society seemed to offer little, including slaves who wanted to win their freedom. There were black men in the pick-up force that surrounded Boston after the Battle of Lexington and Concord, but Washington tried to bar them from service in the Continental Army. The ban could not last, both because free black men did want to serve and because masters of slaves wanted to use them as substitutes. David Humphreys of Connecticut, who became one of Washington's closest personal friends, was in command of an all-black company in 1781. "Women of the army" were usually with the troops, accepting military discipline, receiving (or being promised) half a private's pay, cooking, mending and washing clothes, nursing the sick and wounded, and sometimes coming under fire themselves.

The other problem that Washington had to face was supply. Shoes, clothing, food, firearms, ammunition, tents, cooking equipment—all these and more had to be found on a massive scale. The French provided generous help, especially after Louis XVI recognized the United States and signed a treaty of

amity and commerce in February 1778. But the vast bulk of supplies had to come from Americans themselves. How to provide
them was the first great problem that confronted the revolutionary conventions, congresses, and committees. The complications to which the task led formed a great continuing problem
that plagued the state governments.

From the start, the question was more than just one of physically finding supplies. Bad enough in the first stages of the war,
the problem worsened and became more complicated in 1777,
1778, and 1779. One reason it worsened was people's loss of
their initial enthusiasm. Another was that the demands of three
armies, French and British as well as American, created a vastly
increased market for what American farmers and artisans could
produce. A third was the fact that the two foreign armies could
pay with hard coin, gold and silver, whereas the Americans had
none. Instead, both Congress and the states paid their bills with
paper money, in which people had less and less faith. At first the
inflation was slow, but in January 1779 a Continental dollar was
worth only an eighth of its face value. By November its worth
was one-fortieth, and Congress had no choice other than to virtually repudiate it. Until recently the phrase "not worth a Continental" could still be heard occasionally in American speech.

The armies' demands and the British blockade brought real
shortages: of meat, grain, and salt; of cloth, shoes, and gunpowder; and of imported goods like tea, spices, and rum. But in good
part the problem was politics and distribution, not absolute lack.
Washington's army froze, starved, and bled at Valley Forge over
the winter of 1777–78 and again at Morristown, New Jersey, in
1779–80. But twenty miles from Valley Forge the British troops
who had occupied Philadelphia were enjoying festive indulgence
with their American collaborators. Civilians faced the same
problem. All over the northern states they could not get what
they needed, not so much because it was not available but because their dollars could not buy it. To deal with the problem,
they turned to their long-standing tradition that the good society

was cohesive and "corporate." Merchants who played the market or held back goods and speculators who depreciated the currency became "monopolizers" and "hoarders." Crowds, often made up largely of women, gathered and acted out the rituals of popular price setting that people of their time knew so well. Hearing that a trader had a supply of tea or salt, the crowd would visit him and offer a price its members thought just.

Only if the trader refused would his store be sacked, and even then the "just price" would be left behind. It happened in Ulster and Dutchess counties, New York, in the Connecticut Valley, and in seacoast Massachusetts towns like Beverly, Salem, and Marblehead. In Boston a figure who called himself "Joyce, Jr." led crowds of up to five hundred people that carted monopolizers about town and enforced price controls. The same name, with its echoes of the seventeenth-century Puritan revolution, had been signed a few years earlier to calls for action by the Committee for Tarring and Feathering.

The ethos that a community's need had primacy over an individual's chance for profit was nothing new. But now this old tradition joined with the power of popular committees and with the radical politics of equality and involvement that they embodied. A crowd could act, but a committee could set and execute a policy; a crowd would dissolve, but a committee could adjourn. One unfortunate New York State storekeeper learned the difference in 1777, when he was visited for the second time by angry women bent on seizing his stock. When he protested, they told him that "they had orders from the Committee to search his house."

People founded the original committees to resist Britain, not to change America. But resistance and corporatism went together. The initial response to the fact of war in 1775 was to unite, to submerge self into community. Towns and counties elected new committees, created new militia units, and started raising supplies. Military associations passed from hand to hand, and the worst punishment a nonsigner could face was the contempt of the community. Men laid lesser quarrels aside. Perhaps the most striking example was the appearance of the Green Mountain leaders Ethan Allen and Seth Warner before the New York provincial congress in 1775. Both men had been condemned to death, in colonial New York's "Bloody Act" of 1774, for leading their people's insurrection. Now Allen and Warner pledged cooperation and accepted New York commissions.

In this heady atmosphere, it was easy to do what needed doing and to announce that the burdens would be shared as equally as possible. But to the extent that that slogan became reality, it was because of pressure from below. The militiamen in Virginia and in Philadelphia who demanded plain hunting shirts as a standard uniform understood that point. So did committeemen, who were insisting as early as 1775 and 1776 that for the good of the community they had to control the price and the supply of necessities. The Pennsylvania constitution summed up the political experience of the committee movement, insisting that it was good that "more men . . . be trained to public business." It likewise summed up the movement's political economy, noting an expectation of times when the government would have to "lay embargoes, or prohibit the exportation of any commodity."

Most people probably expected that the committees would fade away when new regular state governments appeared. New York's constitution said as much, calling the committees "temporary expedients . . . to exist no longer than the grievances of the people should remain without redress" and condemning the "many and great inconveniences" that they brought. But that state's new government swiftly found that it could not do without the committees, and they persisted there until well into 1778. When the inflation reached its worst in 1779, people spontaneously revived their committees all over the northern states. The revival began in Philadelphia and spread to the Hudson Valley, the New England interior, and Boston.

Throughout the North the late 1770s saw people linking together patriotism, direct involvement, and corporatist economics. "As soon as the authority of your committees ended, knavery showed its head, villains of every class came forth and practiced with impunity," said a New York writer in 1779. A Massachusetts almanac reminded its farmer readership of "how you asserted your rights as freemen" against the British. It contrasted that heroic record with "the vile practice of extortion" that now seemed rife, and it called monopoly and hoarding "incompatible with private interest and public liberty." In Philadelphia a broadside signed "Come On Warmly" showed contempt for a few "overbearing merchants, a swarm of monopolizers and speculators, an infernal gang of Tories." All were enemies of the commonwealth. A general meeting of Philadelphians resolved that public control of the marketplace was the very "spirit of liberty." Bostonians issued a circular letter that linked "the many happy consequences which have been derived from the appointment of committees" with the Revolution itself.

This was a resurgence that the Revolution's leaders dared not ignore. Governor George Clinton of New York, a man of undistinguished background who owed his high office to the votes of farmers and soldiers, went out of his way in 1779 to call the state legislature's attention to the "sense that your constituents loudly express of applying some suitable remedy" to the currency crisis. In Pennsylvania a club formed to support the constitution of 1776 made acceptance of corporatist economics one of its conditions of membership. But there were other people, some in positions of great power, who saw the committees and the attempt to control the marketplace as foolish or worse. We cannot understand what went on in the sovereign states unless we understand what these men stood for and the ways they responded to the popular movement.

II

By the time of the American Revolution, corporatism was under severe criticism. John Locke's *Treatise of Civil Government*, which asserted the primacy of private property rights, was not available in an American edition prior to 1773, more than eighty years after it was published in England. Adam Smith's *The Wealth of Nations* appeared in England in 1776, but the earliest American imprint was 1789. But their ideas were available through magazines, newspapers, and imported British copies. Smith presented a powerful argument that a society of free individuals, all seeking what was good for themselves, would offer the best way to achieve the good of everyone. Smith's vision was exhilarating and, in its time, profoundly liberating. Tear down controls, set individuals free, let them strive for what they wanted, and all of society would gain. This was not abstract speculation. It was the fruit of the enormous, transforming burst of energy that the modern capitalist age was setting loose in the Atlantic world. Nor was it necessarily coldhearted. Smith believed that men of sociability and good will could achieve what they wanted without hurting their fellows.

Merchants, politicians, and other thinkers came around increasingly to this position, but ordinary people did not necessarily see things the same way. The consequence was struggle between people who had decided that corporatism was archaic nonsense and other people who saw it as a necessary means of self-defense. In England that struggle took place over many decades; in America, as later in France, it was compressed and intensified by revolution.

During the first enthusiasm of 1775, loyalists were virtually the only people who rejected the dictates of committees and congresses. Some insisted that the community had no right to tell the individual what to do. The New Englander Timothy Ruggles invited signatures to an association in defense of "our undoubted . . . liberty, in eating, drinking, buying, selling, communing and acting what, with whom and as we please." One New York Tory wrote that "no man can be in a more abject state of bondage, than he whose Reputation, Property and Life are exposed to the discretionary violence . . . of the community." A

Philadelphian described the committees as "gigantic strides to set the resolves of the populace above the law." In April 1776 ninety-odd Philadelphia merchants "petitioned the Committee of Observation and Inspection, denying its power to regulate prices and announcing their intention to refuse further cooperation." A month later the committee of Albany, New York, hauled a trader before it on a charge of raising his prices. His sly defense was that the prices of his goods had remained the same and that the two shillings he now asked in addition were "for his trouble in weighing."

Loyalists, neutrals, and tepid patriots were not alone in thinking this way. By the late 1770s a position was emerging that combined four separate principles. First, committee power and interference in the marketplace had to end. Second, the best way to combat inflation was by unremitting taxes to dry up the excess money. Third, complex, balanced political institutions offered the best means to achieve sound social policy. Fourth, the needs of the Continental Army and of the national economy that the army was generating were more important than the needs of any local community.

From the northern Chesapeake to New England, men who held this position faced the same problem. How they dealt with it, however, differed from state to state. In Maryland and New York the men who had built the new institutions realized that their next task was to make those institutions take hold. They learned swiftly that it could not be done by simple force or by pushing too fast. In Pennsylvania the shape of the institutional structure became the central issue. Pennsylvania's men of property loathed their state's democratic constitution, and they worked to put an end to it even as they worked to end committee power and to secure a free market. In Massachusetts similar men had everything they wanted after 1780, both in institutions and in policies. But the reaction to their policies proved so strong that it became a reaction against their institutions as well.

The Maryland elite confronted the problem most swiftly and with least cost to themselves. They succeeded in building their "fortress of institutions," but the spectacle of blacks and poor whites who were moving toward each other, courts that could not open, and loyalist banditry on the Eastern Shore showed how weak the planters' position was. Even people who accepted the Revolution were in an uproar. Some militia captains led their own men in salt riots, on one occasion seizing what they needed from a member of a revolutionary convention. In other units men deserted rather than serve under officers they disliked. One such officer, a Captain Watkins, had physically beaten his men. Queen Anne County militiamen, "induced to believe they ought not to submit to any appointment but those made by themselves," refused the officers appointed to command them. Anne Arundel County militiamen complained of their "Captain and Ensign speaking in public Company against the poor people in general." The captain, Richard Chew, had said that "no poor man was entitled to a vote, and those that would insist upon voting . . . should be put to death." Chew's brother believed that "a poor man was not born to freedom but to be a drudge on earth." There may have been a time when poor Marylanders put up with such arrogance. But that time had passed.

The most astute member of the planter leadership, Charles Carroll of Carrollton, began to see "the wisdom of sacrifice." He understood that if men of his kind did not make substantial concessions, they might lose everything they had, and that the most important thing an intelligent conservative could hold on to was his ability to influence events. Carroll argued his case in endless correspondence with men of his kind, most notably his father, Charles Carroll of Annapolis. The younger man realized the need for major concessions on matters of taxation and finance. He called for taxes that would place greater burdens on the rich than they had ever borne. He wanted cheap paper currency that would let debtors pay back far less than they had actually borrowed and still call the debt clear. To his father it was madness, surpassing "in iniquity all the acts of the British Parliament against America."

The son realized that "great revolutions" did not "happen without much partial injustice and suffering" and that some things had to be endured. "I entirely agree with you as to the injustice of the law," he wrote, "but I can not follow your advice to withdraw: where should I withdraw?" The younger man proved right. Once the government demonstrated that it was not in the business of oppressing its citizens, disaffection tapered off, the militia became reliable, and popular loyalism started to fade.

In New York both the situation and the solution were similar but more complicated. The constitution of 1777 was proclaimed over a broken state. New York City, Staten Island, Long Island, and the southern part of Westchester County were held by the British. The western frontier was at war with itself. Two counties and part of a third had gone their own way to form Vermont. In the Hudson Valley armed loyalists roamed at will. Some twenty-three hundred men there had been disarmed for loyalism and "disaffection." And despite the constitution's description of the committees as temporary expedients, they refused to disband.

New York had its men who recognized the dimensions of the problem and who knew that resolving it would not be easy. At the center of the group stood the young, highly educated landowners and lawyers who had written the state constitution, such as Robert R. Livingston, Egbert Benson, and John Jay. These men had found a political identity during their brilliant holding action of 1776 and early 1777. Now they commanded the high courts, with Jay as chief justice and Livingston as chancellor. Benson, elected to the assembly, was certain that he could control it as well. But already they had overreached themselves. Their first setback came when the landowner Philip Schuyler, who was their candidate for governor, lost the election to the much more plebeian George Clinton. Though surprised, they were still confident. "They may chuse who they will, I will command them all," Schuyler had boasted in private. Over 1777, 1778, and 1779 he and his kind learned otherwise.

At first these men thought that asserting authority was all that was needed. Tories had to be controlled, so there would be a political police, called the Commission for Detecting and Defeating Conspiracies. Taxes had to be raised, so there would be laws to do it with as little threat as possible to the property of the rich. The power of the committees had to end, so Jay, Livingston, and Benson insisted that the laws of the state make no mention of it. But the Tory problem remained, taxes were not paid, and the committees would not go away.

When the committee movement boiled up again in 1779, the state government made a series of dramatic policy changes. It stopped trying to control the loyalists and began to punish them instead. The most important step was confiscating the estates of some seventy of them, whom the act named. These included some of the greatest names of the colonial era, such as the De Lanceys of New York City, the Philipses of the lower Hudson Valley, Colonel Guy and Sir John Johnson, and Philip Skene of the northern frontier. The act made it easy for the state to seize the property of others as well. This began a body of anti-Tory legislation large enough to fill a sizable volume by 1784. The government enacted price controls and imposed an embargo on scarce goods. No longer would personal property and land held empty for speculative gain go untaxed. Instead, each county would have a quota. Assessors would decide what a person owed on the basis of "circumstances and other abilities to pay taxes, collectively considered." This system was anything but elegant and caused endless debate, especially when each year's quotas were being set. But for the first time in New York's history, the landowning elite would face tax bills that reflected what they really owned.

The picture is much like the one in Maryland. Adopting radical policies enabled conservative institutions to take hold. Loyalism started to diminish; the popular committees faded away; taxes began to be paid. There was, however, one big difference: New York had no Charles Carroll of Carrollton, grasping the wisdom of sacrifice and persuading others of his kind to accept it. Instead, the pressure for the turnabout came from Clinton, the outsider who had become governor, and from the obscure committee veterans who were entering the state legislature.

These men did not come to power with any awareness of themselves as a particular group or with hostility to other patriots. In 1776 and 1777, when they were trying to rule a state torn to shreds, nobody could afford internal bickering. But by 1779 they were acquiring their own consciousness. People like Jay, Livingston, Schuyler, and Benson resisted the turnabout as long as they dared. When they finally realized they could not win, they accommodated. The high judges who sat on the Council of Revision began to allow radical laws to pass. Benson, who had greater technical skills than any other man in the legislature, began to draft bills that he loathed on behalf of others. But these same men quickly began to pull out of a situation they no longer could control. By 1780 they would be gone: Jay to be the American minister to Spain, Livingston to be secretary for foreign affairs, Benson to a seat in Congress. Other men, of much different background, would lead New York through the end of war and the coming of peace. When the elite politicians returned, it would be from the high ground of national affairs, a ground that by then they had made securely their own.

In Pennsylvania the lines of confrontation were clearly drawn. Philadelphia's merchants and lawyers, its Robert Morrises and James Wilsons, had lost their political position in the spring of 1776, but by the autumn they were regrouping. They were determined that the state's constitution should not endure, and they kept up their pressure until 1790, when they finally got their way. Fairly quickly, these men began to call themselves Republicans, to signal the difference between themselves and their

Constitutionalist opponents. By 1779 each group was organized as a formal political party.

Almost from the start the Republicans were aided by men who until independence had stood in radical ranks. Perhaps their foremost recruit was Benjamin Rush, physician, politician, and writer of talent. Rush decided quickly that radical democracy was no way to run a republic, and he decided almost as fast that free-market economics worked better than corporatism. Others joined him, including to some extent Tom Paine himself. Paine did not give up on democracy; nor, in contrast to Rush, did he pull away from Philadelphia's common people. But Paine had grown up in the same Britain that produced Adam Smith. Paine's call for American freedom, *Common Sense*, and Smith's call for economic freedom, *The Wealth of Nations*, both were published in 1776. Paine found himself thinking Smith's way.

It took time, for Paine did become part of the effort to use committee power to control the economy in 1779. Joining forces with the Constitutional Society, Philadelphia's citizen-soldiers petitioned in May for price controls and called a mass meeting. The meeting elected one committee to put controls into effect and another to investigate the dealings of Robert Morris. Paine, like Timothy Matlack, David Rittenhouse, and Charles Willson Peale, was named to both committees. Daniel Roberdeau, the militia brigadier general who chaired the meeting, summed up a position on which militiamen and Constitutionalists agreed: "Combinations have been formed for raising the prices of goods and provisions, and therefore the Community . . . have a natural right to counteract such Combinations, and to set limits to evils which affect themselves." But Philadelphians had reached a point of serious division.

One did not have to be among the elite to accept the free-market case. The city's leatherworkers—tanners, curriers, and cordwainers—decided that price controls did them nothing but harm and published a broadside saying so. "Trade should be as free as air, uninterrupted as the tide," they wrote. Not everyone who worked in the leather trades joined them. One Whig shoemaker claimed that the broadside had originated among people who had collaborated with the British during their occupation of the city, and there were two shoemakers and a tanner on the price-control committee. In October about twenty prominent free-market men, including Robert Morris, gathered in the house of James Wilson, a man "obnoxious to a large portion of the community" because of his opposition to price controls and the state constitution. A militia unit besieged the house, just as a crowd of several hundred had surrounded the home of Whitehead Humphreys, a man of similar stance, in July. Someone inside Wilson's house fired on the militiamen. A serious riot was averted only when Joseph Reed, the president of Pennsylvania, and his fellow Constitutionalist Timothy Matlack arrived at the head of an elite militia unit called the City Light Horse. As Benjamin Rush noted, Matlack and Reed had drawn their swords against the very people they had long led.

With that confrontation at "Fort Wilson," the effort to control prices by popular action went into decline. It may have been the nakedness of the clash. It may have been the abandonment of the militiamen by Reed, Matlack, and other prominent radicals such as the artist Charles Willson Peale. It may have been that a schism was opening between the artisan intelligentsia and ordinary people. Whatever the cause, the same decline was starting to take place in New York and New England. But the end of the movement to control the market did not mean the end of division. Throughout the 1780s Pennsylvania's Republicans and Constitutionalists would compete to control the state.

Disorders went on longest and perhaps cut deepest in Massachusetts. Working out the system of a special convention to write a constitution and a popular vote to ratify it was a major achievement, but the state refused to settle down. By the time Massachusetts resolved the shape of its new order, both the first euphoria of independence and the perils of open warfare were fading. The British withdrawal from Boston in March 1776 and their defeat at Saratoga in October 1777 ended serious military danger to New England, although the British stayed in Rhode Island for two more years and coastal raiding continued. Instead, the great issue was the deteriorating economy. Controlling prices was as much on people's minds as whether to have a strong senate and whether the governor should have a veto on laws. Records of meetings in such towns as Upton, Westborough, Sturbridge, and Petersham show people debating both issues.

The complicated, balanced government Massachusetts adopted marked a victory for the coastal port communities over the farming towns of the interior. The ports won a series of such victories, first in the old General Court, which governed the commonwealth until 1780, and then in the new state legislature. Both institutions confronted the economic crisis with hard money and demanding taxation. After 1780 there was no legal tender in the state save gold and silver, which were impossible to find. Failure to pay either debts or taxes could lead to lawsuits, imprisonment, and worst of all, the loss of a man's land. It was the very nightmare that the men of the interior had feared since the time of the Stamp Act. Then they had blamed distant Britons and an elite whom the British had seduced. Now the cause seemed to lie within their own republican government.

Matters grew worse after the coming of peace. Under the terms of the Treaty of Paris, British creditors were free to call in their American debts, and British merchants were free to dump their goods on the American market. The result was a quick boom and then a deep depression, as credit contracted further and further. Even in states like New York, where soft money and anti-British laws gave people some protection, the effects were serious. In Massachusetts they were devastating. Pressed by London, Boston merchants called in their debts from traders in county towns like Worcester and Springfield. The traders then demanded what was owed them by storekeepers in small villages. The storekeepers told farmers and artisans to pay or face legal action. The same farmers found themselves faced with impossible tax bills from their government.

For men who understood commerce, it was all regrettable but unavoidable. But for farmers who traded mostly for necessities and who had no hard coin, it was disaster. With more time, with a different background, and perhaps with a little more money in their pockets, they might have mounted a campaign for their representatives to protect them by changing the laws. In terms of sheer numbers, the towns could control the lower house easily, but that smacked of partisanship, which was an evil word in these people's vocabulary. Moreover, each town had to pay its own representative, and if individual farmers could not pay their debts and taxes, how could the towns they lived in find the money to send a man to Boston? If they did send someone, he would be raw and green, no match for the eminent, self-confident Harvard graduates who had been elected in places like Salem, Newburyport, and Boston itself. And even if they could win the lower house, there was still the senate and beyond it Governor James Bowdoin, who was very much a hard-money man.

So they chose another way to protect themselves. Town meetings and county conventions had served them well enough during the crisis with Britain. Let them serve again. The resolutions that the farmers voted and the actions that they took rested on the good, classic republican principle that if a community acted together, it could solve its problems. The interior people knew about the differences between poor and rich, and between men of agriculture and men of commerce. But they did not think of themselves as a group that had to do battle with other interests, or as a class that was locked in struggle with other classes. They did want the capital moved westward so it would be closer to them; some wanted an end to or changes in the state senate, with its special representation for property. But most of all they wanted to close the courts for a time so they could work things out among themselves, not lose their land and sink into tenancy.

It seemed not too much for a farmer to ask, especially if the land had been in his family for generations and he had fought in the war. Late in 1786 they finally took action, gathering in arms much as they had in 1774, and once again closing the courts. This was Shays's Rebellion, named for one of its leaders, Daniel Shays, a western Massachusetts hill farmer and former captain in the Continental Army.

As the British historian J. R. Pole notes, their rebellion did not amount to much. But the state repressed it with all the force it could muster. General Benjamin Lincoln led a force of eastern volunteers against the rebels. He was not interested in killing or destruction for its own sake, but he did intend to show the farmers where power lay. Chief Justice William Cushing handed down death sentences on four of the leaders. "Instead of a due reverence to authority, and submission to government, enjoined in the holy Scriptures as indispensable duties upon all Christians," he intoned, "have you not endeavoured . . . to overturn all government and order, to shake off all restraints, human and divine, to give up yourselves wholly to the power of the most restless, malevolent, destructive, tormenting passions." Over the winter of 1786–87 individuals and whole towns begged forgiveness. "True it is that I have been a committee-man," wrote one, but "I can truly say that in draughting any papers of a publick nature, I have ever endeavoured . . . —not to have anything therein— . . . which might reflect upon authority, or strike at the dignity of government, and if any thing of that nature in fact appears, I am sincerely sorry . . . —and hope it will be overlooked and pardoned." The pride and self-assertion with which such men had stood up first to Britain and then to their own rulers seemed completely lost.

But the governor pardoned the convicts, just as kings regularly pardoned such unfortunates in Europe. The goal was the same: to win gratitude that would turn into loyalty. Soon it was time for new elections. Former rebels and people who sympathized with their cause took full advantage of their right to vote.

Three times as many people turned out for the election for governor as had the year before. Despite the pardons, James Bowdoin found himself replaced by John Hancock. Sixteen new people appeared in the forty-member senate. Two hundred twenty-eight towns sent members to the lower house, far more than in any previous session, and 60 percent of these were new men. This was not an internal revolution. Hancock, like Bowdoin, was an easterner and a man of commerce, and the government made no dramatic switch from hard money to paper currency. In fact, by the time the new legislature met, people's attention was focused not on Boston but on the federal convention that was about to meet in Philadelphia. But it was still a fact that Massachusetts had changed. A government that the rich had created largely for their own protection and benefit had become something that lesser people could capture and try to use for themselves.

Four separate stories; four separate courses of events; four separate outcomes; one set of problems: This is what emerges from the records of Maryland, New York, Pennsylvania, and Massachusetts during the first years of independence. We could find the same problems in New Hampshire, Vermont, Rhode Island, Connecticut, New Jersey, and Delaware. Questions of ideology, of institutional balance, of power, and of economics intermingled in different ways but with a single underlying trend. The wrenching experiences that had made up the revolutionary crisis were forcing people to think hard about who they were and to find new ways of dealing with the complexities of their world. Farther south the problems were different, but the transformations were just as real.

III

Events spared the Deep South the worst of the inflation, but it was spared little else. Georgia and South Carolina became the main theater of war after 1779, and in 1781 fighting moved north into Virginia. The South faced severe disaffection and militant loyalism. Class, race, culture, and region contributed to people's decision to stay neutral or to fight for the king rather than Congress. In Maryland those elements came together most powerfully on the Eastern Shore, separated by Chesapeake Bay from the planter mainland. Farther south planter control was weakest in the deep interior, where the most serious trouble erupted.

The new British commander in chief Sir Henry Clinton took the war to Georgia in 1779, capturing Augusta and Savannah. Charles Town fell on May 12, 1780, with the surrender of fifty-five hundred American troops. The coastal communities gave Clinton virtually no opposition. They had little choice—the main American military force was far away, and there was no question of the planters arming their slaves to drive Clinton's troops back. Congress suggested in 1779 that Carolina and Georgia black men be made soldiers and given their freedom for serving, but the state governments would not even think of it. Instead, the revolutionary governments fled and their people either joined the flight or knuckled under. In Charles Town whites of all classes signed a congratulatory address to Sir Henry in the hope he would let them get on with their lives. Artisans and shopkeepers soon found that stronger gestures, including joining the loyalist militia, were necessary, for the conquerors would allow only men who were overtly loyal to practice their trade. For all their assertive rhetoric during the imperial crisis, the lowlanders rapidly settled down to a life of submission.

The interior was another matter. Already soured in the aftermath of the Regulator movements, its people had not been enthusiastic about the Revolution even in 1775 and 1776. In South Carolina a team of lowland political missionaries found themselves preaching their gospel of liberty to a largely uninterested audience. The team's leader, William Henry Drayton, promised men who enlisted a share of Cherokee land and a chance to enslave captured Indians. But he had to negotiate a

treaty in order to prevent a pitched battle between his supporters, numbering about one thousand men, and a larger force of
the disaffected. North Carolina revolutionaries and loyalists
faced one another for the first of many times at the Battle of
Moore's Creek Bridge in February 1776. The backcountry was
not united for the king; it was divided against both itself and the
seaboard.

When the British invaders dealt with low-country grandees,
they treated them as gentlemen. But the rough men of the interior were another matter. The British released the backcountry's
tensions and set off the immense wave of violence that swept
through it between 1779 and 1781. Sir James Beard pointed the
way early, when he ordered that rum privileges be taken from
every soldier under his command "who [took] a prisoner." Beard
once slaughtered more than a dozen rebels himself, despite their
surrender. He set a pattern that was followed through 1780 by
such officers as Lieutenant Colonel Banastre Tarleton and Major James Wemyss. Leading loyalists on a 170-mile dash, Tarleton caught retreating Virginians at the Waxhaws on May 29,
1780. He paid no attention when the Americans tried to surrender and even had his soldiers pull apart piles of bodies so that
living men at the bottom could be bayoneted. Tarleton's creed
was clear: "If warfare allows me I shall give . . . no quarter."
Wemyss, meanwhile, was devastating an area seventy miles long
and as much as fifteen miles wide between Georgetown, on the
coast, and Cheraw, well inland and near the North Carolina
line.

Such brutality reignited passions that backcountry people
knew well. Patriot partisan groups took shape under men like
Thomas Sumter, Andrew Pickens, and Francis Marion, the
"Swamp Fox." Tory guerrillas formed similar groups of their own
under officers like William "Bloody Bill" Cunningham. Which
side slaughtered more of the other cannot be said. Revolutionaries victorious at King's Mountain shouted "Tarleton's Quarter"
and killed the loyalists whom they had captured. Cunningham's

loyalists, for their part, once chopped to pieces twenty Whigs who fell to their mercy. These are only two of many instances. Lord Cornwallis, to whom Clinton gave the southern command, did have all of South Carolina under control for a brief time, but he could not hold it. Nor could he pacify North Carolina after he invaded it in September 1780. His move into Virginia in the spring of 1781 admitted his frustration farther south. But on June 4 British troops very nearly captured Governor Thomas Jefferson near Charlottesville. Then they marched to Yorktown, where they fortified themselves and awaited seaborne reinforcements and supplies.

Virginia's strongest tension was between blacks and whites. But as the war moved northward toward the Chesapeake, even Virginia saw outbreaks of white popular loyalism. It was strongest in the far southwest of the state, where Bedford, Henry, Montgomery, Pittsylvania, and Washington counties experienced genuine popular uprisings. Why the outbreaks happened is uncertain. It may have been that as Lord Cornwallis and his army drew near, people just wanted to be on the side that seemed to be winning; that had happened in northern New York, as General Burgoyne drove southward from Montreal in 1777, and in New Jersey, when Sir William Howe marched his troops through. It may have been simple proximity to the tortured Carolina piedmont. It may have been that the social tensions behind Virginia's evangelical dissent were finally becoming openly political. Methodism certainly had a strong appeal in Maryland's loyalist-ridden Eastern Shore, and it was in the southwestern frontier counties that Virginia's own evangelical movement had first begun to take shape. Whatever its roots, however, popular loyalism came to far less in Virginia than in either Maryland or the Carolinas. Planter control remained strong, and Cornwallis's surrender to Washington at Yorktown firmly established which side actually had won.

With peace came new problems. As early as 1783 British merchants were beginning to regain control of southern commerce. They had what planters needed: slaves and familiar goods to sell, markets for plantation crops, and credit to make up for the planters' lack of hard cash. Virginia never had had a merchant community of its own, and in South Carolina the planters used the power of the state to give British traders a privileged position. There was intense anti-British feeling in Charleston (formerly Charles Town) after the war, which took political form in the activities of groups like the Marine Anti-Britannic Society. It is tempting to think that had such groups won the contest, artisans and local merchants might have become the basis for a pattern of development that did not depend fully on slavery. Charleston might have joined New York and Philadelphia on the course of differentiation and rapid growth that turned those northern ports into great nineteenth-century cities. It is equally tempting to think that its people might have joined with nonslaveholding small farmers in the interior to create a South Carolina different from the one that emerged.

But almost as soon as peace returned, the planter-dominated South Carolina government began giving benefits to British traders and manufacturers at the expense of local ones. It extended citizenship rights freely; it allowed aliens on trial before a Carolina court to have other noncitizens on the jury; it established a city government for Charleston that took as its first priority the crushing of anti-British action. All the planters really wanted was sure markets for what their plantations produced and cheap goods. They knew that British traders could supply these and that American traders could not. But what they did committed South Carolina to a course that would leave it a colony in everything but name. In 1850, as in 1750, it would be a society based on unfree labor, producing primary goods for people in places far away to process and to market. In 1850, as in 1750, Charleston would be a small port, serving its hinterland but enjoying little economic life of its own. The planters gained, immensely in some cases. But the society they ruled lost, for it would reap almost none of the benefits that rapid transformation would bring to the North. Whether or not the planters intended it, they were condemning their world to permanent underdevelopment.

It probably could not have been any other way than it was. Historian Rachel Klein demonstrates convincingly that even before the Revolution would-be planters, not family farmers, were becoming the dominant group in the South Carolina backcountry. It is no accident that among their leaders was John C. Calhoun's father, Patrick. The father's candidacy for the colonial Commons House of Assembly in 1769 sprang from the same tensions that created the province's Regulator movement. Rather than wanting to overthrow coastal planter dominion, let alone the plantation system, he wanted an interior that would be safe for aspirant planters like himself. His crop was tobacco, and by the middle 1780s tobacco culture was triumphing in the piedmont. Even before Eli Whitney's invention of the cotton gin, the division of South Carolina into a lowland region of plantations and an interior region of small farms was coming to an end.

South Carolina society had been wracked by the Regulation and then by the Revolution; now it would be united around the institution of slavery. Now it could become the very center of pro-slavery feeling. It dominated the importation of slaves from Africa during the twenty-year interval in which the federal Constitution forbade its closing. The historian of these last Africans enslaved for the North American market, James McMillin, estimates their number as just short of 170,000, of whom 100,000 came through South Carolina ports. In the time of Andrew Jackson, South Carolina would force the issue of a state's right to nullify a federal law. In the time of Abraham Lincoln, South Carolina would be the first state to secede from the union and would ignite the war to destroy the United States.

Even policies that in the North might have betokened a small-farmer triumph marked planter gains here. The South was as troubled as the North in 1785 and 1786 by glutted markets and tight credit. There were places where southerners took the first

steps along the road to rebellion that backcountry Massachusetts farmers were starting to walk; in May 1785 popular action
kept a judge in Camden, South Carolina, from trying suits for
debt. South Carolina's government responded with a series of
laws that reflected everything the Massachusetts farmers could
have wanted. But their net effect was to benefit planters, not
small farmers. A law that allowed debtors to tender property
rather than money, as long as assessors agreed on the property's
worth, is a good case. Rich men who owned useless land in the
pine barrens had no trouble discharging their debts by offering
it. The assessors were local men, and usually they would agree
with the owner's exaggerated statement of its value. But people
"without different kinds of property had to offer creditors something of value, at least to them," and they were likely to lose it.
The act looked like populist legislation, but it was the planters
who gained from it.

But in the South as in the North, the Revolution brought
marked changes in how rulers and the people whom they ruled
dealt with one another. In the colonial period, people had either
deferred or rebelled, and most often they deferred. By contrast,
suggests Jerome Nadelhaft, in the 1790s people "did not politely
or humbly request anything. They described their condition and
expected that the people who were no better than they but who
happened to sit in the legislature would act." "That," Nadelhaft
argues, "was the Revolution."

Something similar happened to Virginians. Their colonial social order had been organic and hierarchical. Its rituals, ceremonies, and patterns had served both to link people to one
another and to show that some were above and some were below. But in the state's revolutionary settlement such structure
and hierarchy disappeared. Rhys Isaac's portrait of Virginia's
transformation suggests that postrevolutionary Virginians lived
lives that were much more private and self-contained than had
their forebears. Gone were the lavish hospitality for the whole
neighborhood and the open display that had marked great-house

life. Gone was the enforced Anglican worship that the planters had used on occasion to assert their own worth. Only court day and the militia muster remained as occasions for the community to gather.

As Isaac shows, the planters put an end to their effort to force their own cultural patterns on people who were unlike themselves. Thomas Jefferson's act establishing religious freedom, made law in 1786, marked the change. So did Virginia's fierce conflict in 1788 over whether to accept the federal Constitution. Virginia's greatest planters would remain immersed in a "proud, assertive culture," but other Virginians would not be obliged to share it. The Baptist faith would triumph across the South, and it would remain egalitarian. But Southern Baptists made their peace with slavery. Lesser whites would think of planters as people who perhaps were more fortunate and powerful than they but not intrinsically any better. On that basis, their version of American republicanism would be built. On that basis as well, slavery and the society it produced would spread westward. Virginians, Carolinians, and other white southerners would find it possible to think of themselves both as equal citizens in a republic and as members of a master race.

IV

As republican Americans confronted the problems of revolution, war, and peace, the ideology they tried to live by told them one set of things about their world, but the reality they were building told them another. All good republicans knew that the first duty of a citizen was to forgo selfish interests and to seek the common good. But experience was teaching them over and over that the common good was elusive, and that if people did not assert themselves, they would be crushed. What they were learning and how they were learning it found its reflection in political action. In the 1760s and early 1770s people rioted. As we have

seen, one major justification for crowd uprisings was the belief
that if rulers forgot the public good, the people would remind
them of it. In the late 1770s people formed committees. These,
too, rested on the ideological basis that a single public good existed and could be determined. But now there was a difference.
Instead of rioting in the hope that rulers would set matters right,
the rioters acted like rulers themselves.

Within both crowd action and the committee movement, the
notion of a single, clear public good was on the decline. The imperial crisis demonstrated that the old pieties about Parliament
protecting the interests of Englishmen everywhere were false.
Being a colonial Briton in America and being a real Briton "at
home" just were not the same. A similar lesson slowly emerged
from the attempts at radical democracy that followed independence. Some Americans had their doubts about simple democracy from the beginning. The complexity and the balance that
these people tried to put into the state constitutions were
needed, they thought, to protect different kinds of people from
one another. Paradoxically, radical democrats began to learn a
very similar lesson: Using committee power to stem the economic crisis did not work. Partly it was that the crisis was too
great. Partly it was that the interests of traders, consumers, and
different kinds of producers not only were not the same; they
did not even seem reconcilable. And partly it was the combined
recognition that the crisis of 1778 and 1779 originated in the
emerging national economy, that it needed a large-scale remedy,
and that local attempts to close local economies could only hurt
the Continental Army and thus endanger the Revolution.

These hard-learned lessons explain why a very different form
of political action began to take shape in the 1780s: open, com-
petitive partisanship. It would be an overstatement to say that a
fully formed party system was in place anywhere by, say, 1785.
There were no national or state committees, no carefully
worked-out platforms, and very little orchestrated campaigning.
In only one state, Pennsylvania, were there party labels that men

proudly wore. There was not even any real understanding that party politics offered a way for people to get what they wanted. Parties were "the dangerous diseases of civil freedom, the first stage of anarchy, clothed in mild language." Voters should "distrust men of violent party spirit," for they "would wish to split the state into factions." "The sooner we can effectually destroy the Spirit of Party in Republican Governments, the more we shall promote the Happiness of Society," wrote one observer. Let there be a time "when all Party and Animosity will be absorbed in the general and Generous Sentiment of promoting the Common Good," said another. Practically every voter and every officeholder agreed: Political parties were Bad Things.

But by the mid-1780s such talk was one matter and political reality was another. From Georgia to New England, people with interests in common were learning that they would do well to act together. They were realizing that they could expect opposition from others who were unlike themselves. The process moved more quickly in some places, especially New York and Pennsylvania, and less quickly in others, especially Massachusetts. But it was under way everywhere.

It happened fastest in Pennsylvania. There the Constitutionalist Society and the Republican Society amounted to political parties as early as 1780. During the war years the Constitutionalists were a continuation of the coalition that had overturned Pennsylvania's old leadership in 1776. The group included Philadelphia artisans, backcountry farmers, and self-conscious radical politicians. It even recruited a few members of the old elite who at first had opposed the constitution of 1776. The party had an ethnic and cultural dimension as well, for it drew a great deal of support from evangelical German pietists and Scotch-Irish Presbyterians. The Republicans began as little more than the patriot wing of the old elite. But they gained support, first among former radical politicians like Benjamin Rush and then, more slowly, among Philadelphia's working people.

Without doubt, there was a class dimension to the contest.

Both sides said so often enough. But how they understood the world was also important. The Constitutionalists tried to hold fast to the classical republican belief that in a good society the only real interest was the public interest. That meant, for them, the interest of the small producers and small consumers from whom they drew their support. For the Republicans, however, commerce was as much the way of the world as productivity. In their eyes, it was just as legitimate to seek wealth by manipulating money as it was to seek personal independence by producing food and objects that people could use. In 1784 Benjamin Rush actually used the phrase "productive property of this state" to mean money for investment rather than tools or land or draft animals.

One of the largest immediate issues was the Bank of North America. Chartered in 1781 under the aegis of Robert Morris, it was the first bank in the United States. It was also the perfect symbol of the aggressive, commercial society that Morris and his sympathizers wanted America to be. It was the perfect means of furthering the interests of people who were close to its directors and whose reputations and policies the directors approved. Among the enemies that the bank acquired were some men who disapproved of banks on principle, seeing "enormous wealth in the hands of a society who claim perpetual duration" as a danger to the republic. There were others who were simply envious, or perhaps angry because their own applications for loans were refused. In 1785 the bank's enemies won control of the Pennsylvania legislature, and they repealed the bank's charter. The bank promptly launched a campaign to reestablish itself, hiring Tom Paine to make its case. Its friends, the Republicans, won the election of 1786, and soon the bank was back in business.

The affair of the bank illustrates the way that Pennsylvania's party system was changing by the middle of the decade. It was not just that the Republicans and the bank recruited Paine. It was also that their case seemed more and more appealing. They understood far better than the Constitutionalists that there were many sorts of Pennsylvanians and that the state's future would have to be built on that fact. Self-assertion, not self-denial, would be the basis of people's lives. The Philadelphia leather-workers began the shift when they refused in 1779 to support price controls, and now others were following. The result was that the Constitutionalists became more and more a party of inland farmers, without significant urban support. Farmers were still the vast majority of Pennsylvanians, but the tide was running against the Constitutionalists. By 1790 they would be finished as a political force.

Let us look in detail at only one other state, New York. There it took time for parties to develop. The social elements were much the same as in Pennsylvania: artisans and small farmers for whom the Revolution was a political awakening, and the mercantile, landholding, and professional elite. But conditions were different. With New York City occupied by the British until the end of 1783, neither merchants nor artisans had a base from which to operate. As a result, a coalition of freehold and tenant farmers became the democratic core. When New York City artisans entered state politics in 1784, their alliance with upstate radicals would be only tenuous. A second contrast was that the state's institutions never became an issue, for almost everyone accepted the constitution of 1777. Nor were New Yorkers as quick as the Pennsylvanians to develop party labels. Historians sometimes write of "Clintonians" and "Anti-Clintonians," referring to the central position that Governor George Clinton came to hold on the democratic side. Clinton was reelected to his office repeatedly through the war and Confederation years, and that would not have happened if he had not been a politician of consummate skill. But people of the time never used his name as a political label. The earliest use of any label at all came in 1787, when a farmer-politician named Henry Oothoudt described his own side as "the Republican party." What he meant by it was nothing like what the Pennsylvania Republicans meant, and he was using the phrase in private correspondence.

Labels are one thing; consciousness and organization are another. Partisanship first began to develop in the New York state legislature in response to the issues that came to a head in 1779. Confiscating loyalist land, controlling prices, taxing by "circumstances and abilities"—these were all policies that hurt someone. The elite's response to the fact that it could not stop them was to pull away, but that only opened the way for more. In 1782, 1783, and the spring of 1784, dealing with the loyalists was the prime issue. Under farmer and artisan control, the legislature put a stay on all Tory suits against patriot debtors. It allowed disputes to be settled by referees drawn from the revolutionary side, rather than by court trials. It discharged all wartime interest and allowed payment in cheap paper currency rather than in specie. Patriots who had fled the New York City region could bring damage suits against people who had used their property, even if the British occupying forces had authorized its use. Loyalists were burdened with double taxes. Anyone who suspected anyone else of trading with the enemy could seize the property in question and bring the person to trial, hoping to win half of what had been seized for himself. "Zealous Friends" of the Revolution who had "done Acts . . . not conformable to the strict Letter of the Law" were protected from damage suits by their victims. An act "to preserve the Freedom and Independence of this State" disqualified from voting or holding office anyone who had aided the British. At the war's end, the liberated southern counties found themselves burdened with a special tax as "a compensation to the other Districts" that had carried the long struggle through.

By the autumn of 1784 the issues were shifting from retribution to reconstruction. Most especially, the popular party sought to reform the old elite's institutions. Trinity Church, the immensely wealthy Anglican congregation in New York City, came under attack. So did the city's chamber of commerce and King's College, later renamed Columbia. The men who wanted to reform these institutions were also likely to favor granting a charter of incorporation that the artisans of New York City sought for themselves. These years also brought changes in how the state disposed of public land. Before independence, land operations had taken place behind closed doors, and getting in on them had been a gentleman's privilege. Now sales were open, on the basis of clear surveys, and only minimal fees were due to the officials involved. Gentleman's privilege had become citizen's opportunity.

But most of the state's gentlemen had little liking for what was going on. By the mid-1780s they were beginning to return to state-level politics, with a view to putting an end to it. At their center stood Alexander Hamilton. His own ascent from obscurity into New York's aristocracy showed that by no means were the aristocrats a closed group. When Hamilton left the army in 1781, he began to look hard at the state's affairs. In the many essays that he wrote for publication, and in the long letters that he wrote to others who shared many of his views, he worked out an analysis and a program. He wanted the easy readmission of loyalists to citizenship, especially if they had money and trading connections. He wanted the market, not the state, to determine "the prices of all commodities." He wanted an end to the state's "radically vicious" system of taxing. Most of all, he called on "all those who have anything to lose" to take steps so that "the power of government" would be "intrusted to proper hands." "For their own defence," the "principal people" had "to endeavour to put men in the Legislature whose principles are not of the levelling kind."

Hamilton got a good part of what he wanted. People in sympathy with his policies organized. They set out to win popular support, and they succeeded in forcing some of the radical politicians out of the legislature. In so doing, they were laying the basis for the Federalist movement, not just in New York State but to some extent in the whole country. The success of that movement was to be their great triumph, and we will look at how they achieved it in the next chapter. What is immediately important is the change in the way New Yorkers were going about their public affairs. The issues were real; so were the divisions; so was the transformation of public life. People had learned two lessons in the course of the Revolution. One, the lesson of radical democracy, was that the public arena belonged to everyone. The other, the lesson of emergent capitalism, was that to get what they wanted people would have to organize and compete.

New York and Pennsylvania are the two states where the new politics of the 1780s has been most fully studied. But the massive body of writing that the historian Jackson Turner Main produced on the war years and the Confederation era demonstrates that what happened there was happening in most of the other states as well. New men poured into the state legislatures. They were veterans of popular committees, former crowd leaders, and militia officers who owed their rank to enlisted men's votes. They were farmers and artisans and small traders. They were men who had found themselves in the Revolution. Unsure neophytes at first, elected for the most part because they had proven themselves in the resistance movement, they gradually learned to work with one another, to speak with their own political voice, and to organize continuing popular support. Others who were unlike them also sought office and frequently won it, especially in the larger towns. By roughly 1786 one could tell from the roll-call votes of almost every legislature who was on which side. By about the same time one could tell from what happened at the polls who would control the next session. The development of this politics of openly competing parties was not an accident. It grew out of trends and changes that had run through the whole Revolution. The same transformations would lie behind the way the federal Constitution brought the era of fundamental uncertainty about what institutions should wield power in America to its end.

Six

ONE REPUBLIC

The creation of the American Republic forms the last great drama of the Revolution. Just as we can mark the Revolution's beginning at 1765, when the people of the British provinces made it impossible to enforce Parliament's Stamp Act, so can we mark its end at 1787 and 1788, when the people of the American states accepted their federal Constitution. Events, it seems, had come almost full circle. Instead of Parliament, with its House of Lords and its House of Commons, there would be Congress, with its Senate and its House of Representatives. Instead of a king, there would be a president. For as long as George III survived and George Washington wanted the office, both king and president would bear the same name. Washington's own official style was quasi-regal. Had anything really changed? Had a quarter century of turmoil, disruption, and upheaval simply led the American people back to where they had begun?

One of the greatest and longest-running debates in the writing of American history has turned on those questions. Throughout the nineteenth century most people who thought about the Revolution regarded the Constitution as its fitting result. The Founding Fathers, or Framers, who met in convention at Philadelphia to write it were the very men who had made the Revolution. There was George Washington, in the chair. There were Benjamin Franklin, Alexander Hamilton, James Madison, John Dickinson, Gouverneur Morris, Robert Morris, and William Livingston among the members. Of the top American leaders, only a few, such as Thomas Jefferson and John and Samuel Adams, were absent. All three of them did, in fact, support ratification, though Sam Adams had his doubts for a while. George Bancroft drew the obvious conclusion in his enormous, and enormously influential, *History of the United States*: The Revolution had been a struggle to secure American liberty, and the Constitution was liberty's greatest protection.

But in 1787 and 1788 not everyone was so sure. Rhode Island sent no delegates to the Convention. Along with North Carolina, it refused to ratify. Opinion ran heavily against the Constitution in much of Virginia and New York, and it seemed as if these states, too, would reject the document. In Massachusetts, South Carolina, New Hampshire, and Pennsylvania people were seriously divided. The historical geographer Orin Libby published maps in 1894 that showed how widespread opposition had been. His work transformed our understanding of how the republic came to be. No longer could the Constitution be taken as the Revolution's foregone conclusion. Instead, it was a problem to be solved.

Two decades later the historian Charles A. Beard followed Libby's lead. Beard's book *An Economic Interpretation of the Constitution of the United States* became, in Jack Greene's words, "one of the half dozen most influential books ever written in American history." Taking the Founding Fathers down from their pedestal, Beard asked what they had stood to gain if the Constitution took effect. He found that they owned a great many paper securities whose value had depreciated to almost nothing. The backing of a strong government determined to raise taxes and to pay off debts would raise the value of those securities. The case seemed proven. For Beard, the Constitution marked not much more than a triumph for men who were on their way to wealth at other men's expense.

Beard's argument opened up whole new dimensions of the history of the 1780s. For Bancroft, and for his nineteenth-century colleague John Fiske, the decade had been a disaster, "the critical period of American history." The Articles of Confederation, under which the country was governed until 1788, represented total political foolishness. State studies written in Beard's shadow chipped away at Bancroft's and Fiske's understanding of the Confederation years, and by the 1930s Beard's theory was the one taught in most American college classrooms. In 1940 Merrill Jensen published an account of the Articles of Confederation that was very different from Fiske's, arguing that this document, not the Constitution, represented the democratic spirit of 1776. In *The New Nation* Jensen went on to examine the record of the 1780s and found achievement, not failure. Jensen's student Jackson Turner Main expanded that point in many different directions, beginning with his sympathetic account, *The Antifederalists*, and culminating with his reconstructions of 1780s politics, *The Sovereign States* and *Political Parties Before the Constitution*.

But in the 1950s Beard's work received a terrible pounding from historians. Most notably, Forrest McDonald used Beard's own methods to demonstrate that opponents of the Constitution had stood to gain as much from it in monetary terms as its supporters. Clinton Rossiter's *1787: The Grand Convention* put the Founding Fathers back on their pedestal. Stanley Elkins and Eric McKitrick found them to be the "Young Men of the Revolution," driven not by self-interest but by their own youthful energy and by their frustrations as congressmen, diplomats, and ranking army officers. John P. Roche turned them into modern politicians who understood the need for reform and who carefully calculated the best strategy for achieving it.

Yet Beard's voice remained alive. In the mid-1960s Staughton Lynd baldly described New York's Federalist leaders as a "governing class on the defensive" and traced the interplay in the Constitution's making among owners of merchant capital, great landed estates, and large slave forces. Gordon Wood's massive, prize-winning *Creation of the American Republic* pays honor to Beard from another direction. Examining the intense political debates of the late 1770s and the 1780s, Wood finds that the Framers did indeed repudiate the democratic politics of 1776. In so doing, they created a lasting "American Science of Politics" rather than a financial windfall for themselves. But the debt to Beard is still apparent: The republic as we know it was born in disagreement and struggle, not in consensus and continuity. Gary Kornblith and John M. Murrin have described the Framers as the core of a national ruling class that made itself during the revolution, triumphed with the Constitution, and then fell apart under the pressures of democracy. Wood's more recent book, *The Radicalism of the American Revolution*, suggests a similar process, as monarchy yielded to republicanism and republicanism to democratic public life. Yet the older view of complete agreement during a moment of special historical privilege does remain, most especially in the legal-historical belief that it is possible to establish the Founders' "original intent" when they brought the Constitution and the first ten amendments into effect.

On one matter Beard was certainly wrong: Far more was going on than simple pocketbook calculation. As Lynd notes, what was under way was the settlement of a revolution, and it settled as it did because some men and some groups wanted it that way. What, then, led to this settlement? Who were the people who drove events? How did they diagnose their society's ills, and what cure did they prescribe? Most important, what kind of America did they want, and how did they convince others, people unlike themselves, to accept their diagnosis, their prescription, and at least a part of their vision?

I

With hindsight, we might easily say that the colonies moving toward independence and the states traveling toward the Constitution were both following clearly marked roads. The milestones and the intersections seem perfectly visible, and each destination seems certain. In fact, the metaphor is deceptive. Both roads led people into territory that was not even explored, let alone well mapped. We cannot understand independence without understanding the anxiety, the turmoil, and the fear arising from the Stamp Act, the Townshend taxes, the Boston Tea Party, and the outbreak of war. Similarly, we cannot understand the Constitution without understanding the major points of conflict and crisis that lay between 1776 and 1788.

When the Continental Congress appointed a committee to draft a declaration of independence, it named two others of equal importance. One had the task of beginning foreign relations, especially seeking recognition and aid. Its great success came in 1778, when it found both in France. The other's responsibility was to establish a firm, enduring basis for the union of the independent states. The result was the Articles of Confederation. The committee presented its draft of the Articles to Congress in 1777, and the document was finally accepted by the separate states in 1781.

The Articles gave legal form to the ramshackle structure that events had already thrown together. "The United States in Congress Assembled" was the official title of the central body. Though a state might send as many delegates as it pleased, it enjoyed only one vote. Congress had some of the qualities of a national government, but in other ways it was more like an alliance of sovereign republics. The Articles gave it alone the power to make war and peace, and it was in Congress's name that a peace was finally negotiated with Britain in 1783. To that extent, the states were one nation, dealing with other nations as equals. But Congress had no power to tax, and no power to enforce its will.

It might levy requisitions on the states, but they could pay or not pay as they chose. It might insist that its own decisions and the treaties its envoys made overrode state law, but state courts would decide whether that really was so. It took the votes of nine states to make major decisions of policy. It took the consent of the legislatures of all thirteen to change the Articles in any way. To prevent congressmen from becoming a separate caste, no person could be a member for more than three years in a row. A state legislature could recall a delegate whenever it might choose. Were these men representatives? Were they ambassadors? No one could really be sure.

One major reason why the states took so long to accept the Articles was the problem of western lands. Some states, Virginia most of all, had inherited British grants that stretched from sea to sea. Others, like Pennsylvania, were limited by clearly established western boundaries. At the very end of the colonial period, Virginia and Pennsylvania had been in sharp dispute over the upper Ohio Valley. Still other states, such as Connecticut, had *both* fixed boundaries *and* remote claims in the West. States without a hold on the West were jealous of states that had one. States claimed ownership and even jurisdiction over land that lay within what appeared to be the boundaries of others. Speculators everywhere scrambled for advantage in this battle of ambiguities.

In 1781 the main issue was finally resolved when the states with sea-to-sea colonial charters surrendered their claims to Congress. The effect was twofold: A major reason for contention between the separate states came to an end, and Congress, agent for the people of all the states, acquired rights over the vast domain that lay in the interior. Whatever its relationship to the founding states along the seaboard, Congress now was sovereign over the West, provided that the British, who had troops there, and the Indians, who had possession of most of the land and their own ways of life upon it, agreed. The British did agree in the Treaty of Paris that ended the war.

The treaty placed other responsibilities on Congress. The British had insisted that loyalists be subjected to no further punishment and that penalties already imposed on them be revoked. The American diplomats—John Jay, Benjamin Franklin, and John Adams—knew that neither they nor Congress could promise so much, for the states alone made loyalist policy. The final treaty was a compromise: It bound Congress to "earnestly recommend" that the states confiscate no more Tory property and that they return confiscated property if the loyalist owners had not actually taken up arms. It was an empty formula. Confiscations tapered off, but it was because the passions of the war years wound down, not because of the treaty. Returning property already seized was out of the question, for both large-scale speculators and ordinary people had a direct stake in preventing it. Congress may have been sovereign over its western lands, but its treaty commitments meant nothing if they conflicted with the policies of the original states.

Congress also ran into trouble on matters of revenue. Throughout the war years it had had to get by with its depreciating paper, with whatever unpredictable revenue the states might grant, and with aid from the French and loans from the Dutch. It never could raise enough. The supply and pay of the army were always a disgrace, whether we look at the early campaigns, at the misery of Valley Forge and Morristown, or at the final encampment at Newburgh, New York, in 1783, before the army disbanded. When the army did break up, its men took with them pay for only one month in coin and for two months more in certificates. Small wonder that two Connecticut regiments mutinied in May 1780, that four thousand Pennsylvania troops marched on Congress in January 1781, that hotheaded officers in the Newburgh encampment toyed with the notion of a *coup d'état* in March 1783, and that another band of soldiers surrounded Congress in June 1783.

George Washington must be given a great deal of credit for the fact that the threats of military takeover faded. He repressed the enlisted men's mutinies sharply, and when he learned that his officers were gathering to discuss their discontents, he preempted the meeting and held it to a republican agenda. The states, in turn, began to take responsibility for paying what Congress owed their citizens. But an immense debt was still owed overseas, and Congress did not have enough revenue even to pay the interest, let alone the principal. Three times—in 1782, 1784, and 1786—Congress tried to solve the problem by asking the states to let it collect duties, or "imposts," on goods arriving in American ports. Three times the proposal failed. Rhode Island said no in 1782, and New York refused on the two other occasions. In both states opposition to the Constitution would be strong.

New York in particular had everything to lose if the impost was granted. Its great harbor at the Hudson River's mouth was the port of entry for northern New Jersey as well as western New England. The state collected duties on all goods that came in, whatever their final destination. That had happy consequences for the tax bills of its own citizens but ill ones for its relations with its neighbors and with Congress. With no sure revenue to pay foreign debts, Congress faced a world of diplomacy and international finance that treated it with little more than contempt. The severe recession that fell on the North Atlantic market in the war's aftermath only made matters worse. In no way was the downturn Congress's fault, and it began to lift well before the Constitution was written. But to people who felt its effects, the link between economic depression and the political order seemed unmistakable.

By 1785 or 1786 few people with political awareness would have denied that the Articles of Confederation needed serious change. By then even fewer people held any hope that change could come by the method that the Articles required, originating in Congress and winning acceptance in all thirteen legislatures. The repeated failures to secure an independent revenue were evidence enough. Many observers drew the parallel between a single state's ability to block change and the *liberum veto*, which allowed a single member of the Polish nobility to block any policy that displeased him. The infant United States did not have Poland's misfortune of sharing borders with Russia, Prussia, and Austria-Hungary, but the British still ruled north of the St. Lawrence. Despite the Treaty of Paris, they would occupy forts that were legally American until well into the next decade. The Spanish Empire, sprawling to the south and west, was weak, but who was to say that it would not regain its vigor? Neither power was friendly to the United States, and no one with any sense wanted to take a chance on sharing Poland's unhappy fate. Some other route to change would have to be found.

The first steps were taken in 1785, when commissioners from Virginia and Maryland met at Mount Vernon, the home of George Washington. Their immediate subject was the river that flowed almost past their feet, for if navigation on the Potomac was to be developed, Virginians and Marylanders would have to do it together. Though Washington was not a delegate to the gathering, serving merely as its host, and though he dreaded the thought of being seen to profit from a public enterprise, the idea of "improving" Potomac navigation and linking the river to the Ohio interested him greatly. But the commissioners had a larger purpose in mind, and the main result of the conference was a call for delegates from all the states to meet the next year at Annapolis, the capital of Maryland. Their task would be to discuss the commercial problems that the whole country faced.

Despite the halo of patriotism and prestige that hung over Mount Vernon and its owner, only five states responded to the call. But New York and Virginia were among them, and Alexander Hamilton and James Madison were among the delegates who gathered in September 1786. Over the next two years Hamilton and Madison would form one of the most effective political partnerships in the history of the United States. Though they were later to separate, that in no way detracts from what they accomplished now. Each had been preparing himself for years for the task that he knew lay ahead. Each worked out a detailed analysis of what was wrong, and each had clear ideas about what was to be done. Neither was prepared to let wishful thinking or received wisdom interfere with his conclusions. Each was not only an incisive thinker and a masterful writer but also a skilled politician, adept at timing moves and arranging alliances.

Their first step was to convince the Annapolis meeting to step beyond its brief. The meeting had assembled with the task of improving American commerce. It broke up with a call for a convention that would propose amendments to the Articles of Confederation, to meet the next year in Philadelphia. If no more states sent delegates than had responded to the call for the Annapolis meeting, the project would be doomed. So the men behind the call persuaded Congress to second it, and then set out to make sure they would be present themselves. Already suspicions were rising. Alexander Hamilton got himself elected to the New York state assembly so he would be in a position to go. The legislature agreed that he should be a delegate, but it also sent Robert Yates and John Lansing, both of whom were at odds politically with Hamilton. They numbered among the many New Yorkers who had no faith that a strong central government could work or that one was even needed. Their task was to keep Hamilton in check.

The Convention assembled in June 1787 with twelve of the thirteen states represented. Rhode Island's absence was, in fact, a victory for the men who wanted change; it meant that one certain center of opposition would have no voice in Philadelphia at all. The makeup of the Convention marked another triumph. A few men present—Yates, Lansing, Luther Martin of Maryland—had fundamental suspicions about what was going on, and some others decided afterward that they did not like what the Convention had done. But in no way was their number proportionate to the people who would be doubtful when it came time to ratify. For the most part, the Convention's members agreed that thoroughgoing political change was needed if the country's immense problems were to be resolved. It was because they already agreed on so much that they also could agree to meet in secret, so they could argue out their differences among themselves and then show a single face to the world. In terms of democratic political practice, it was a long step backward, for one change the Revolution had brought was the end of just such secrecy among the rulers of the states. But from the point of view of the Convention's ability to get things done, that secrecy was an immense benefit.

When the Convention assembled, Madison was ready to seize the initiative. He had worked out "amendments" to the Articles that, in effect, eliminated the Articles themselves and started from the beginning. The first step in this Virginia Plan was to end the possibility that one state's veto could prevent any change at all, no matter how much the other states might want it. That was accomplished by taking an initial resolution that the new Constitution be submitted not to the state legislatures but rather "to an assembly or assemblies of Representatives, recommended by the state legislatures to be expressly chosen by the people, to consider & decide thereon." The original proposal said nothing about unanimity, and the final draft required the approval of only nine of the thirteen states. A naysayer or two might remain outside, but it would take at least five states to keep the "amendments" from going into effect.

The substantive changes in the Virginia Plan truly were sweeping. Its original version would have established a central government considerably more powerful than the one that the United States Constitution eventually created. There would have been a two-house legislature, with the lower house elected by the people and the upper house chosen by the lower. A chief executive and judges for the courts would have been chosen by both. The states would have been reduced to little more than administrative units. The central government would be able to veto acts of their legislatures and to interfere directly in cases

where the "states are incompetent or in which the harmony of
the United States may be interrupted," with military force if
necessary.

These proposals set the terms of debate for the whole summer. The Convention would propose sweeping changes, not
piecemeal amendments. Hamilton wanted to go well beyond the
Virginia Plan, and in a six-hour speech he called for a government centered on a monarch elected for life. None of the other
delegates took him seriously. But many did listen carefully when
William Paterson of New Jersey offered a plan that was much
closer than Madison's to the existing state of affairs. In it, Congress would remain as it was under the Articles but would be
given the right to raise its own revenue and to control interstate
and foreign commerce. It would have the power as well to elect
"a federal Executive" and to appoint a federal judiciary, and its
acts and treaties would be "the supreme law of the respective
states."

The Virginia and New Jersey plans defined the limits of debate. The central problem was not whether to give the government more power; almost everybody agreed that was necessary.
The New Jersey Plan first used the phrase "supreme law" to describe how treaties and federal law would stand in relation to the
laws of the states. Neither Paterson nor Madison wanted to see
a continuation of a single state's ability to frustrate treaty obligations. The question was what, or who, would be represented in
the federal legislature. If Madison's plan won, the central government would be truly national, owing its power to direct election by the people. But Paterson's proposals would leave it
federal, deriving its authority through the states rather than from
the people themselves. The states would continue to be sovereign corporate entities. Whether Congress's members were representatives of the people or ambassadors from the states would
remain unresolved. As Madison put it in response to Paterson's
move, "the great difficulty lies in the affair of Representation;
and if this could be adjusted, all others would be surmountable."

By 1787 the revolutionary generation had grown used to arguments about political representation. That had proven "the great
difficulty" in shaping the state governments as well. Now three
separate dimensions of the problem intersected: population,
wealth, and the corporate existence of the states. None was easily resolved. If simple numbers became the basis of representation, the smaller states would be eliminated as political forces.
To Delaware, New Jersey, Connecticut, and New Hampshire,
not to mention Rhode Island, that was unacceptable. Moreover,
the reason Virginia was by far the largest state and that South
Carolina, North Carolina, and Maryland stood well up on the
population table was the presence in each of many slaves. State
law regarded those black people as not much more than objects,
liable to punishment but lacking almost every legal right that a
free citizen enjoyed. For purposes of federal law, were they to be
counted nonetheless as full human beings? To many northern
delegates, the notion seemed preposterous, for the law itself
gave the slaves no political identity or will. The reality was that
counting slaves among those to be represented would mean
nothing more than recognizing the special interests of the owners of one particular form of wealth.

One state constitution after another had tried to find a
way to give special representation to wealth. But none of the
schemes had proven successful, and the more insightful members of the Convention knew that there was not much point in
further experiment. Madison, a sizable slaveholder himself, tried
to skate over the issue by suggesting that in one house of the national legislature only free people be represented but that in the
other representation be "according to the whole number counting the slaves as if free." But Gouverneur Morris pointed out
that if the Convention accepted one special interest it would
have to accept others. New England, with its fisheries, and the
middle states, with their commerce, were just as central to
America's economic life as the South, with its slaves. Morris did
find human bondage distasteful, and he understood how anom-

alous it would be if slavery were to enjoy representation. The great flaw in republican American society and the line of stress along which the political fabric would finally rip apart in 1861 lay bare for the whole Convention to see.

In 1787, unlike 1861, compromise was possible. The New Jersey Plan had already pointed the way with a proposal that three-fifths of the enslaved population be counted for purposes of requisitions on the states, should the federal government have to make them. This, in fact, drew on a policy of revenue apportionment that Congress had used as early as 1783, at James Madison's own suggestion. In mid-July Connecticut's three delegates used it to work out a way around the problem, proposing to make this three-fifths rule the basis of representation in the lower house. This would be joined to an upper house in which all the states would enjoy equal weight, regardless of size or wealth.

The proposal met heavy resistance. On the first vote to count three-fifths of the blacks, only four state delegations voted yes and six voted no. Gouverneur Morris may have spoken for many northerners and even for some southerners (the problem was recognized in Virginia by more than Jefferson) when he declared that he was "reduced to the dilemma of doing injustice to the Southern States or to human nature, and [I] must therefore do it to the former." Madison put the central issue, telling the Convention that "it seemed now to be pretty well understood that the real difference of interests lay, not between the large & small but between the N. & South. The institution of slavery & its consequences formed the line of discrimination." But on July 16 the Convention accepted Connecticut's proposal. The tension between large and small states and the tension between North and South had simply disappeared. How did this come about?

There is no absolutely conclusive evidence, but the answer seems to be that during the second and third weeks of July not one but several agreements were reached. Staughton Lynd has suggested that the real compromise was not over any particular issue but rather with the great principle of 1776 that "all men are created equal." There can be no doubt that the Constitution gave a special protection to slavery that it gave to no other single interest. The first step came on July 12, when the Convention reconsidered the three-fifths formula and decided to accept it by six ayes to two nays, with two state delegations divided. The states that changed from nay to aye were next-door neighbors Pennsylvania and Maryland. The ones that changed from nay to a divided vote were the geographical and social opposites Massachusetts and South Carolina. The one had abolished slavery entirely and had been against any representation for slavery at all. The other still was importing slaves. It had hoped to see its many slaves count for representation as the equals of freemen. Other steps came later, as the Convention included a clause to assist masters of runaways and another to forbid interfering with the slave trade for twenty years.

The slaveholders had won enormous gains, but they had to pay a price. It may be, as Lynd has argued, that they paid it not at the Convention but elsewhere. The day after the Convention adopted the three-fifths compromise, "the Continental Congress, meeting in New York City, adopted the Northwest Ordinance," with its clause forbidding slavery north of the Ohio River. As Lynd admits, there is no absolute proof that the two actions were tied together. But considerable circumstantial evidence suggests that they were. What is certain from the records of the Convention is that the tide of regional tension that had been running so high suddenly ebbed. It took only four days to move from the three-fifths compromise to the compromise on the structure of the Senate and the House.

With the matter of representation worked out, other questions proved less contentious. No one doubted that there should be an executive and a judiciary, but how to choose them caused some headaches. Madison's original idea, that the executive be chosen by the two houses of Congress together, was only a point of departure. By July he was arguing that "if it be essential to the preservation of liberty that the Legisl: Execut: & Judiciary power be separate, it is essential . . . that they should be independent of each other," and that "the Executive could not be independent of the Legislure, if dependent on the pleasure of that branch." He made that point when it was still thought that the legislature would elect the executive, speaking against a proposal that the executive be eligible for reelection. But his logic pointed just as readily toward having it derive its power directly from the people, in the manner of the governorships of New York and Massachusetts. The actual method of electing the president, by electors chosen in the states, was devised by a small committee that was appointed late in the Convention's life to deal with "postponed matters." As John Roche has suggested, the Electoral College was "merely a jerry-rigged improvisation." The Convention itself expected that the college would fail to deliver a majority "nineteen times in twenty" and that the House of Representatives would normally be the place where the president would be chosen.

By mid-August the Convention was well on the way to completing its work. At the end of the month an eleven-man committee was named to deal with all unfinished business, and on September 8 a five-man committee was appointed to give the document a final polish. It included Madison and Hamilton, but the main task was done by Gouverneur Morris, and the committee presented its report on September 12. Finally, on September 17, after a last round of speeches, the members signed the document and adjourned. As they were on the point of dissolution, Benjamin Franklin supposedly drew attention to an image of the sun that was painted on the chair Washington had occupied. He had often looked at it, he said, "without being able to tell whether it was rising or setting: But now at length I have the happiness to know that it is a rising and not a setting Sun." With that, the Convention offered the nation its work.

II

What the Convention had done was illegal by any standard that held when it first assembled. Its first illegality was the decision to bypass the whole procedure that the Articles specified for amendment. Its second was the delegates' decision to abandon their assignment of proposing amendments and to draft a whole new document. Linked to that was its assumption that the Convention had the right to speak for the whole nation. "We the People of the United States of America" begins the Constitution's preamble. But in fact the delegates had gone to Philadelphia to represent their separate states, and they had voted in the Convention on the basis of state equality. As opposition to ratifying the Constitution took shape, many a critic, including some people who ended up supporting ratification, noticed these points. "I confess, as I enter the Building, I stumble at the threshold" was how Samuel Adams put it.

Anticipating such objections, the Convention did its best to bow in the direction of the dying confederation. On September 10 Elbridge Gerry of Massachusetts had announced his objections "to proceeding to change the government without the approbation of Congress," and Alexander Hamilton, of all people, concurred. He proposed that "the plan should be sent to Congress in order that the same, if approved by them, may be communicated to the State Legislatures, to the end that they may refer it to State Conventions." It was window dressing, for nothing could hide the fact that the Convention had far exceeded its mandate. In Hamilton's case, it was outright hypocrisy, since no person held the confederation Congress in greater contempt than he. But it was smart politics, the first step toward turning the Convention's work from an extralegal proposal into the "supreme law of the land."

Congress cooperated, resolving unanimously to send the Constitution to the states. At the least, the opposition would not be able to claim that the Convention had wholly ignored Congress. Then the men behind the document—now starting to call themselves Federalists—set out to make the state conventions ratify it. Understanding the importance of momentum, they saw to it that the first states to convene their conventions were ones that were certain to be in favor. States that were highly commercial, that were weak in the existing order, or that had been badly ravaged during the war were likely to favor a strong new government, and Delaware, New Jersey, and Georgia each fitted at least one of those descriptions. The conventions of all three ratified by unanimous votes, the first two before 1787 was out, and the third on the second day of the new year. Pennsylvania also ratified rapidly, by a margin of two convention votes in favor for every one against. The victory reflected the strength that the state's "Republican" party enjoyed. It marked a repudiation of the radical democracy of 1776 as much as a vote for a stronger central government. But it also expressed the Federalists' political astuteness. A big state was needed, and by calling a fast election, they denied their numerous backcountry opponents the chance to organize. Connecticut followed, ratifying by an overwhelming margin. It had everything to gain from a central government that would help it escape New York's economic and political shadow. Maryland and South Carolina took longer, not ratifying until the end of April and late May respectively. But in neither state was the outcome in doubt. The margin in Maryland's convention was 63 to 11, and in South Carolina's, 149 to 73. With ratification readily accomplished in seven states, only two more were needed to make the new government a reality.

Massachusetts had in fact already come into the fold, but ratification did not come easily there. The margin of victory was narrow, with 187 delegates in favor and 168 against. During the months before the ratifying convention, newspapers carried essay after essay on both sides of the question. The debate went on not only in the Boston press but also in inland sheets like the *Worcester Magazine* and the *Connecticut Courant*, which had a large Massachusetts readership. The convention divided along roughly the same line of stress between town and country that had run through Massachusetts life for a decade. But some prominent men from the coastal towns joined inland farmers in having their doubts. Among them were Sam Adams and Governor John Hancock, who probably had enough influence between them to tilt the balance against ratification. That would have been disastrous for the Federalist movement. The men who wanted the Constitution had to avert the possibility of an alliance between westerners and eastern waverers. The convention dragged on interminably, examining the Constitution line by line. While the delegates debated, supporters of ratification put all the pressure they could on Adams and Hancock.

For Adams, the deciding element was the decision of Boston's artisans to support the Constitution. We will look later at what the artisans did and how they did it. In Hancock's case, vanity seems to have tilted the balance. He was offered the chance to propose amendments to the Constitution, and he began to hear hints that he was the logical choice for vice president. Should Virginia not ratify and George Washington thus not be eligible, he might be the right man for the presidency itself. He and Adams both swung, and Massachusetts ratified.

Only one more state was needed, but whether it would be found was by no means certain. Rhode Island clearly would not ratify, and North Carolina elected a convention that was overwhelmingly hostile. Virginia was almost evenly split, and when New Yorkers voted, they chose 46 delegates against the Constitution and only 19 in favor of it. Had either of those major states rejected the Constitution in the spring, the whole project might have been lost. But their conventions debated well into the summer. That gave Federalists their chance to turn the question from whether there would be a republic to whether Virginia or New York would have a part in it.

They found their opportunity in New Hampshire. The state had all the makings of a stronghold of opposition. It was remote; its way of life was essentially noncommercial; it had no Great

Men to throw their influence behind the Constitution; it had suffered little during the war; unlike Connecticut, Delaware, and New Jersey, it did not live in the economic shadow of a powerful neighbor. Not surprisingly its people instructed their convention delegates not to ratify. When the convention met in the dead of winter, it followed those instructions. Had matters rested there, no United States might ever have existed. The convention did not, however, actually reject the Constitution. Instead, it adjourned until June, without taking a final decision. The delay gave the state's people a chance to reconvene their town meetings and decide whether they wanted their instructions to stand. Supporters of the Constitution raised the issue in town meetings up and down the state. Planning intensively for the day when the convention reassembled, they linked New Hampshire into a communications network that stretched south to New York and Virginia. Now the Constitution's friends in all three conventions would know what the others were doing. According to historian Forrest McDonald, the New Hampshire convention finally ratified on an afternoon when men in favor of the Constitution got a number of their opponents drunk enough at lunch to miss the session. Whether or not that is so, New Hampshire's decision to ratify on June 21 established that the Constitution would go into effect.

That still left New York and Virginia. Each was vital, for reasons of wealth, population, strategic location, and the political importance of its leaders. Each had powerful forces and well-known men publicly opposed to ratifying. Among them were Virginians Patrick Henry, Richard Henry Lee, and George Mason, and New York's governor, George Clinton. By the time their conventions met, opponents of the Constitution had finally learned the necessity of organization, and they had a well-coordinated structure of committees in operation. It was centered on Clinton and his downstate political ally John Lamb. These men, too, had couriers ready to ride between Portsmouth, Poughkeepsie, and Richmond, where the three conventions sat. But in the end, they were outflanked.

One reason was the array of talent and prestige that the Constitution's supporters mobilized. Washington, Madison, Hamilton, George Wythe, Robert R. Livingston, and John Jay topped the list. A second reason was sheer hard politics. At one point in the Virginia convention, Madison so thoroughly demolished a claim by Patrick Henry that Jefferson, absent in France, opposed the Constitution that Henry was left looking like either a liar or a fool. In New York there came a point when Hamilton openly threatened to separate New York City and the surrounding "southern district," which supported the Constitution, from the rest of the state, which did not.

Two other elements proved equally important. One was the quality of argument in the Constitution's favor. Whether or not major political decisions ever turn on purely intellectual conviction, the New York campaign generated some of the most sophisticated political writing in American history. It emerged as the eighty-five *Federalist* essays that Madison, Hamilton, and Jay produced between October 1787 and August 1788. Addressed "To the People of the State of New York" and signed by "Publius," *The Federalist* was a masterpiece. Its title marked the capture of high ground by its authors. Logically, the term came closer to describing the Constitution's enemies than its friends; emotionally, "Federalist" was an extremely positive word in the language of the time. Yet by making it their own, the Constitution's supporters forced its enemies onto the defensive. The opponents thrust about, looking for a word of equal power to describe themselves. "Anti-Federal" was the label most of them ended with, but the term could not help sounding simply negative. Others, such as "Democratic Federalist" or "Federal Republican" or "Impartial Examiner" or the now antiquated "Son of Liberty," simply did not work. Playwright and historian Mercy Otis Warren, the only woman who intervened in this war of print, called herself "Columbian Patriot." The Federalists, as we now call them, had seized a symbol that had every possible political virtue.

The other element in their victory came with their handling of the issue of amendments. Opponents of the Constitution had different reasons for wanting to see it changed. For some, that offered a way to reconvene the Convention and raise once again all the issues that the Federalists had thought were finally resolved. Others understood that ratification with conditions could amount to no ratification at all; it was exactly the same trick that New York's legislature had used in 1786 to stem the drive for an independent revenue for Congress. Others were happy with a great deal of what the Constitution offered and simply wanted some tinkering and additions. One of the most common objections was that, unlike most of the state Constitutions, the federal document had no bill of rights.

The issue of amendments became most pressing in Virginia and New York. In both states the Federalists averted the disaster of a ratification with conditions. What they secured instead was an unconditional ratification, combined with a strong statement of each convention's desire to see the Constitution modified. Virginia's instrument of ratification called for a lengthy bill of rights and for a series of changes in the main text of the document. New York's declared that the state ratified "in full confidence" that the amendments it proposed would "receive an early and mature Consideration." It called on the state's "Representatives . . . to Exert all their Influence, and use all reasonable means to obtain" a long series of changes. In both cases, the formula came very close to the position of some Anti-Federalists, while retaining all that the Federalists needed. In both places other opponents remained unconvinced. But in both states enough men with objections were mollified to make ratification possible. Eleven states were in, and Rhode Island and North Carolina found soon enough that they had no real choice about joining as well. The Anti-Federalists had lost, and opposition to

the Constitution dissolved. But it was they who pointed strenu-
ously to the need for a bill of rights as a protection for citizens
against the government. That such a bill was swiftly adopted in
the form of the first ten amendments to the Constitution is owing largely to them, even though James Madison wrote the text.
As Saul Cornell describes them, the Anti-Federalists were "the
other founders."

With the Constitution's acceptance, the period of political
revolution and institutional instability was over. Where a seemingly solid but in fact deeply flawed British Empire had once
stood, there was now a republic, itself of imperial dimensions.
As the subsequent century would show, it was a republic with
an immense capacity for growth and development. But as this
narrative suggests, it was by no means certain even as late as the
spring of 1788 that there would be any such republic at all. If the
story of the Federalists' victory constitutes the Revolution's last
great drama, understanding why it happened presents the Revolution's last great problem.

III

We can begin to understand if we compare the Constitution
with what went before. The contrast with the Articles of Confederation is obvious, but Gordon Wood and J. R. Pole have
shown that the real frame of reference lies in the states. The
Framers wrote a document that bore a strong resemblance to
the New York constitution of 1777 and to the Massachusetts
constitution of 1780. Like them, it provided for an executive that
would be much more than simply a means for carrying out the
legislature's will. Like them, it established a legislature of two
houses, roughly equal in power and neither dependent upon the
other. Like the Massachusetts constitution, it rested its claim to
legitimacy on having been written by a special convention and
then ratified in a manner that approached a decision by "the

People." The Constitution was most emphatically a republican document. It established a political order that came as close as possible to having its basis in the consent of the people whom the government would rule.

But even by the standards of the day, it was not democratic. Consent is not the same as involvement, and the Constitution aimed to limit involvement, not encourage it. The president would owe his power to the people, but the Electoral College and possibly the House of Representatives would stand between them. The senators would owe their office to the state governments, not to direct election. That and their six-year terms would give them considerable immunity from popular pressure. Because there would be only two senators from each state, it was a fair prediction that only a man of considerable prominence could hope to win a seat. Even the House of Representatives was a far remove from the state assemblies. Initially, it would have only sixty-five members, making it not much more than a quarter the size of the assembly of Massachusetts. The House would represent constituencies as large as thirty thousand people, which was nearly the population of the whole state of Delaware. Like would-be senators, aspiring congressmen would need considerable local visibility.

Wherever these men met to do their business, it would be far from where most of the people they represented lived. Though the journals of the two houses would be published, there would be little of the close, almost day-to-day observation of what the legislators were doing that had become possible in some of the states. The two-year term of the representatives would be twice as long as the terms of most state assemblymen. Again and again the framers of the state constitutions had insisted that the representative assemblies should be "exact miniatures" of the people of the state itself. Again and again they had insisted that officeholders should never forget that they were only the people's servants, and that political practices should keep them from becoming a separate caste. But United States representa-

tives, senators, and the president all would know that exceptional was just what they were. The methods of their election,
the size of their constituencies, and the lengths of their terms
would all serve to insulate them from what "the people" might
want.

During the confederation years "exceptional men" had had a
rough time in political terms. What Jackson Turner Main has
called the "democratization of the legislatures" meant that artisans, small traders, farmers, and men with mud on their boots
had come to power. They had passed tax laws, Tory laws, currency laws, land laws, debt laws, and a host of other laws that
worked against the material, social, and economic interests of
the old colonial upper class. To a large extent, what they did also
worked against the interests of modernizers, developers, and
men of new money. The elder Charles Carroll ranted on about
the evil policies of Maryland's wartime legislature, and Robert
Livingston Jr., lord of the Hudson Valley manor that bore his
name, did the same in New York. Though both had chosen the
Revolution, each was a living symbol of what once had been.
But Robert Morris and Alexander Hamilton, harbingers of the
new capitalism, were equally appalled. The Pennsylvania assembly annulled the charter of Morris's Bank of North America because the bank seemed a threat to all that a republic should be.
To Morris and his friends, the bank was necessary to create the
kind of society they wanted.

The final straw was Shays's Rebellion. Though this rising of
Massachusetts farmers was brief and easily suppressed, it exposed a line of stress that ran through all the states. Would independent America be organized around law, contract, and the
needs of large-scale commerce? Or would it be organized around
custom and the needs of local community? Put another way,
could a republic survive if it had within it interests that were in
fundamental conflict? Men of property and commerce in Massachusetts had taken every step to guarantee both that their republican government would be stable and that it would protect

them and their needs. Now it seemed that even the most careful arrangements could achieve neither of those goals, at least in one state by itself.

Here was one social driving force behind Federalism: Men with land, men with fortunes, men with visions of development and wealth, men with far-flung connections, men with memories of the surety with which their fathers had ruled, all were developing the distaste for state-level democracy on which Federalism fed. In Pennsylvania they had been working together for a decade and called themselves Republicans. In Massachusetts they were the men of commerce in the port towns. They had won a great victory in 1780, and they understood the relentless logic of the Atlantic market, but by 1787 neither their victory nor their logic seemed to count. In New York they were the urban merchants and professionals and the upstate landlords who came together in response to the legislature's mid-1780s radicalism. In South Carolina they were men used to power who bemoaned the loss of the "harmony we were famous for." In Maryland they were the planters who had written the archconservative state constitution of 1776.

But not all of Federalism's support can be explained in those terms. For men who had experienced the Revolution at the center of affairs and in the highest offices, Congress and the states alike were simply the components of a nightmare. To men who had had to raise military supplies, it seemed that the policy of the states had been "to starve the army at pleasure." To diplomats who had served the new nation abroad, the way the states frustrated the treaty of 1783 was a disgrace. To men who had been colonels and generals in the Continental Army, their own heroism and dedication seemed to have been taken for granted. The popular outcry against "aristocracy" when former officers tried to organize themselves into the Society of the Cincinnati was evidence enough. To men who had spent the war in Congress, struggling endlessly to win cooperation from states that would not give it, the fault lay with the states.

Let the case of Alexander McDougall of New York illustrate the point. Before independence McDougall had been a popular street leader. John Lamb, his comrade of those days, was at the center of organized Anti-Federalism in 1788. McDougall's broadside of 1769, *To the Betrayed Inhabitants of the City and Colony of New-York*, brought him an extended and highly publicized imprisonment at the hands of the colonial assembly. His defiance when the assembly called him before it led one member to threaten him with the "long, hard penalty" of being crushed to death with rocks. (It also led future governor and Anti-Federalist George Clinton to quip that the Assembly could throw McDougall "over the Bar, or out of the Windows, but that the Public would judge of the Justice of it.") In 1773, when the tea crisis was impending, McDougall baited the cautious lawyer, council member, and future loyalist William Smith by proposing that "we prevent the landing [of the tea] and kill [the] Govr. and all the Council."

But during the war McDougall's fortunes soared, and his opinions cooled. He reached the rank of major general in the Continental Army, and disgruntled fellow officers picked him several times to argue their case before Congress. He spent some time in Congress as a New York delegate. When the war ended, he accepted the presidency of the Bank of New York, a project dear to Alexander Hamilton's heart. McDougall's daughter married John Lawrence, a merchant and politician who was one of Hamilton's close associates. McDougall died in 1786, but it is easy to predict where he would have stood in the debates of 1787 and 1788. At his death he was at the same time a veteran of the popular revolutionary movement, a committed republican, a man with a nationalist perspective, and a man fully in tune with the capitalist order that was rapidly taking shape. The same was true of his old street associate Isaac Sears, who died in 1786 in Canton, China. Sears had organized the first American direct voyage to the Middle Kingdom, and his body was buried there. Only John Lamb among the pre-independence New York City street leaders was alive in 1788. He did oppose the Constitution, but he was so out of step that a Federalist crowd demonstrated outside his house after the Poughkeepsie convention declared New York's ratification.

What was the appeal of the Constitution to men whose lives ran parallel to McDougall's? For some, it may have been the expectation that they would find themselves elected to Congress or the Senate. For others, it may have been the relief of having a government that would not change its laws from year to year and that would not let the class interest of lesser people be translated into public policy. The powers that the Constitution gave to Congress were appealing. Its mandate to regulate foreign and interstate commerce meant an end to state tariffs. Its powers to establish a uniform bankruptcy law, to coin and regulate money, to "fix the standard of Weights and Measures," to regulate patents and copyrights, and to establish a network of post offices and post roads all pleased the entrepreneurial mind. So did its guarantee that "full faith and credit" would be "given in each state" to laws and court decisions of other states and that the citizens of any state would enjoy equal "privileges and immunities" in all the others. With the Constitution in effect, states would be unable to "emit Bills of Credit; make anything but Gold or Silver Coin a Tender in Payment of Debts," or "pass any . . . Law impairing the Obligation of Contracts." Clearly, the Constitution established political conditions that were extremely favorable to the way that the American economy would develop during the next century.

The Constitution was thus a social document as well as a political one. Like the state constitutions, it was the product of a specific coalition and reflected the interests and the problems of the different groups that made up that coalition. To say as much is not to denigrate the Framers' achievement. The fact that the structure they established has endured for two centuries is evidence enough that they understood the needs of their own society and planned well for the future course of American development. The Constitution's acceptance, and the rapid end of opposition to it, are evidence that even in its own time the document satisfied people other than former generals who felt themselves slighted, great landlords annoyed at finally having to pay taxes, and merchants who saw prosperity and radical democracy as natural enemies.

IV

By themselves, all the discontents in the world could not have established the new government. The tasks of defining what was wrong, working out a remedy, and justifying that remedy to the world were carried out by a remarkable group of writers and thinkers. Political intellectuals debated the problem of republican government throughout the 1780s. They had inherited an "Atlantic republican tradition" of political thought that stretched back to seventeenth-century England and Renaissance Italy. But by the time ratification was completed, they had overturned practically every idea within it. They developed instead a framework of understanding that served two functions, both of immense importance. One was to mediate between the direct interests of people who stood to gain from the Constitution and the overriding ideological imperative that the final settlement be republican. James Madison expressed their understanding perfectly when he wrote of the need for "a republican remedy for the diseases most incident to republican government." The other function was to make possible a reconciliation between the interests of the few and the experience of the many. There were writers in the Federalist camp who turned out nothing more than special pleading. But the best of them tried to understand their whole revolutionized society.

From the beginning, Federalist writers possessed the self-confidence and intellectual independence that characterized Paine and Jefferson but that had been so lacking in the early anti-British pamphleteers. No longer awkward provincials worrying what London might say, these people knew that they were carrying out the most advanced political analysis the world had yet seen. Among the most noteworthy of them were Jefferson, James Wilson, Noah Webster, John Adams, and Benjamin Rush. Jefferson incorporated sharp criticisms of the settlement in his own state in his *Notes on the State of Virginia*. Wilson, Webster, and Rush carried on a running criticism of Pennsylvania-style radical democracy. Adams's *Defence of the Constitutions of Government of the United States of America* was a monumental compilation of the whole history of republican experience and thought. Surrounding these were many others who turned out pamphlets, newspaper essays, and books. Among the contributors to the debate must be counted the "other founders," the major voices of Anti-Federalism, such as Richard Henry Lee of Virginia, Melancton Smith and Abraham Yates of New York, and Mercy Otis Warren of Massachusetts. They, too, wrote at length; the so-called *Complete Anti-Federalist* takes five full volumes to survey what they turned out. The major Federalist thinkers made their breakthroughs in an atmosphere of argument, not in one of calm reflection.

Of all the voices, those of Hamilton and Madison resounded loudest. Hamilton was a rank outsider whom good fortune had brought to New York City and to King's (Columbia) College in the early 1770s. While still a student, he was writing anti-British pamphlets. He was barely out of King's when he became first a captain of artillery and then served as Washington's aide-de-camp until nearly the end of the war. His experience of telling generals what to do and his marriage to Philip Schuyler's daughter established his social point of view. Madison's career, if less spectacular, was also marked by early success. Born into Virginia's planter class, he studied at the College of New Jersey (now Princeton) and was only twenty-four when he became chairman of his county's revolutionary committee. Between 1775 and 1783 he served in various Virginia conventions, on Virginia's

Council of State, and for three and a half years in the Continental Congress. When he was in Congress, its problems with the states were at their worst.

Despite their similarities, the two men came to Federalism by different routes. Hamilton's analysis was shaped by his immersion in New York's world of commerce and Madison's by his experience as an upper-class white Virginian. Neither was friendly to slavery, but Hamilton freed the black people his marriage had brought him and joined the New York Manumission Society. Madison remained a slaveholding planter, though he did embrace the cause of sending free black people "back" to an Africa they never had seen, joining the American Colonization Society and eventually becoming its president. The collaboration between the New Yorker and the Virginian represented the way Federalism brought together emergent capitalism and enlightened planter republicanism.

Hamilton's route to Federalism led, as we have seen, from his frustrations on Washington's staff during the war through his experience of the problems of the New York elite during the 1780s. From a very early time he looked to Congress to find a remedy for what was wrong in the states. In his "Continentalist" essays of 1781 and 1782 and his "Letters from Phocion" of 1784, he argued the importance of Congress's having its own revenue and of the peace treaty's terms being honored. His public writings consistently took the high ground of principle and constitutionalism, but from the start he understood that Congress could gain political strength only from a strong commercial economy. Hamilton sympathized with much of the emerging ideology of the free market, especially with its critique of the way corporatism sought to use political power in order to achieve social welfare on a local scale. But he also had sharp things to say about the gospel according to Adam Smith, for he understood that without public support and protection, an independent American economy could never take shape. That theme emerged most powerfully in the *Report on Manufactures* that he wrote in

1791, when he was secretary of the treasury, but it also is present in much of his earlier writing.

In the mid-1780s Hamilton's prime concern was to restore New York City's commercial life. During the war he had been as willing as anyone to take harsh measures against the Tories, but now he wanted a rapid end to their persecution. His correspondence in 1783 shows why. Tory and neutral merchants, fearful of the victorious Revolution, were lining up to leave with the British. They were taking their capital and their skills and their business connections with them, and these losses outweighed any amount of republican zeal. "Many merchants of the second class, characters of no political consequence, each of whom may carry away eight or ten thousand guineas have I am told lately applied for shipping to convey them away. Our state will feel for twenty years, at least, the effects of this popular phrenzy" was how he put it to Robert R. Livingston.

We have seen already how Hamilton turned his close attention to state politics, rallying merchants and landlords and "those who are concerned for the *security of property* . . . to endeavour to put men in the Legislature whose principles are not of the *levelling kind.*" His other passion, besides putting the upper class back in power, was for predictability and order in the making and enforcement of the law. He understood one of the Revolution's central lessons, which was that American liberty was "the *right* to a *share* in the government." But in general, Hamilton was at pains to defend the liberty to be left alone rather than the liberty to take part. An artisan's interest was not to have a real voice in the making of the laws. It was "that there be plenty of money in the community, and a brisk commerce to give it circulation and activity." The "true sense" of liberty was "the enjoyment of the common privileges of subjects under the same government."

The driving force behind both the writings and the actions of this man was his need to realize a program that was made up of many different elements but that was held together by a dominant vision. The elements were a market that was free from the government's interference but still protected by the government's power, the quiet reintegration of former Tories, predictable taxation and secure credit, rule by the best, and a citizenry that stayed out of politics except when it was time to vote. The vision was of a strong central government under which all these specific goals could be achieved. A centralized, energetic republic and a prosperous capitalist economy were the two causes to which he devoted his career. The enormous contribution that he made to the Federalist argument represents his effort to bring those causes together.

If Hamilton was the Constitution's prophet, crying out for the need for change throughout the 1780s in his essays and his endless correspondence, Madison was its evangelist. His great task after the Convention adjourned was to explain why the changes the Constitution made were the ones America needed. Both men did, of course, assume something of both roles. It was Hamilton who instigated *The Federalist*, who invited Madison and John Jay to join in writing the series, and who wrote two-thirds of the total text. Conversely, Madison spent an extended period just before the Convention working out his own analysis, partly in his unpublished *The Vices of the Political System of the United States*, which amounted to his notes for seizing control of the agenda in Philadelphia, and partly in his correspondence with the absent Jefferson.

Madison shared most of Hamilton's concerns, but he had a way of putting the same points with a different inflection. In Hamilton's vision, the overriding element was commercial prosperity and development; in Madison's, it was making sure that the republic did not prove a failure. The Virginian began the serious development of his ideas later than the New Yorker, writing *The Vices of the Political System* immediately before the Convention. He accepted the argument that the problem lay in the states more than in Congress, and he built on two central themes that had emerged in what was becoming Federalist writing. One, developed especially by the Pennsylvania jurist James Wilson, was the dissolution of the traditional distinction between a subject people and a sovereign ruler. In place of that distinction, Wilson was beginning to locate sovereignty in the people themselves. The notion was fully implicit in the making of the state constitutions, but the older view died hard. That older view saw a constitution as a *contract* between people and their chosen rulers, rather than as a special act that stated the terms on which people would rule themselves. The older view was central to much of the Anti-Federalist argument against the Constitution.

The other theme pitted "the people against the legislatures." As Gordon Wood has suggested, when Federalists developed this thought, they came close to hypocrisy, for one of their major goals was to get ordinary people out of the legislatures. Their argument ran that despite every effort to make the state legislatures servants of their people, they had become the masters, and capricious, uncontrollable masters at that. Thomas Jefferson put it most succinctly in his *Notes on the State of Virginia* when, referring to the size of the state's legislature, he observed that "173 despots would surely be as oppressive as one." The ideas that Madison developed drew on both these lines of thought.

As Douglass Adair and several other scholars have noted, Madison also drew on the ideas of the Scottish historian and philosopher David Hume. Writing in the middle of the eighteenth century, Hume addressed one of the oldest problems in republican political theory: How large and complex could a republic become before its own contradictions drove it to destruction? The very word *republic* suggested an answer: It had to be small and simple. Derived from the Latin phrase *res publica*, meaning "public thing," the word implied that a society stood a chance of ruling itself only if its size was limited and if it had no conflicting interests within it. Let it grow larger, let more interests develop, and conflict could not be avoided. Let conflict erupt, and tyranny was foreordained. All history seemed to say so, and so did all republican thinkers from Machiavelli to Montesquieu.

Hume thought otherwise. He speculated in 1752 not only that a republic was possible in a large and complex society but that size and complexity themselves might be the keys to the endlessly vexing problem of how a republic could survive. The great difficulty was that once people began to think *for* themselves, they also thought *of* themselves, and selfishness and republicanism could not avoid conflict. Eighteenth-century people called it faction, putting one's own interests before the interests of the community. But, wrote Hume, though "it is not easy, for the distant parts of a large state, to combine in any plan of free government," there was nonetheless "more facility, when once it is formed, of preserving it steady and uniform, without tumult or faction." In Hume, it was simply a suggestion that some "large state, such as France or Great Britain," might be "modelled into a Commonwealth." For Madison, it resolved the whole problem of what the future of other large states, such as Massachusetts, New York, and Virginia, would be.

Madison developed his argument in *The Federalist* and especially in papers Number 10 and Number 51. For him, the basic reality was that the states were already too large and complex. Each had several interests within it, and it was the clash of those interests that posed the problem. If an interest, or faction, included only a minority of the people, there would be no difficulty: "relief is supplied by the republican principle, which enables the majority to defeat its sinister views." But "when a majority is included in a faction, the form of popular government . . . enables it to sacrifice both the public good and the rights of other citizens." How could those rights be secured without losing "the spirit and the form of popular government"? It would be easy enough to remove "the causes of faction . . . by destroying the liberty which is essential to its existence." It might be possible to do it "by giving to every citizen the same opinions, the same passions and the same interests." But the first remedy was "worse than the disease," and the second was "as impracticable as it would be unwise."

Instead, Madison offered other solutions. The first was to use a large political system "to refine and enlarge the public views by passing them through the medium of a chosen body of citizens, whose wisdom may best discern the true interest of their country." The larger the republic, the greater the probability that such men rather than fools or demagogues would come to the fore. Size alone would sort out the best, a task at which property requirements and complex electoral arrangements had so clearly failed. The second solution was more innovative. A single "public good" could not be obtained even in as small a state as Rhode Island, let alone in Pennsylvania or New York. It was "sown in the nature of man" that parties would develop in such places. The danger was not parties; it was that in a small society one party could much more easily become the majority, and then "the more easily will they concert and execute their plans of oppression." But in a really large republic the danger diminished, for "among the great variety of interests, parties and sects . . . a coalition of the majority of the whole society could seldom take place on any other principles than those of justice and the general good." America's future would be as a society in which interest confronted interest in an unending struggle for self-preservation and gain. Its "public good" would take the form of people's surety that they would not be crushed and that they would enjoy stable conditions in which to continue the struggle. Surety and stability would emerge as different interests, all self-seeking, balanced one another off and canceled one another out.

Madison understood that faction could have many causes, but he agreed with Hamilton that at the root of the problem lay social class. "The most common and durable source of factions," he wrote, "has been the various and unequal distribution of property." Pressed hard enough, he would have had to admit that the "majority factions" he criticized were most likely to be made up of debtors and people without property. His analysis also had much in common with Smith's *Wealth of Nations*, for his argument that the conflict of many factions would bring political stability was very close to Smith's position that competition in a free market offered the best way to abundance and low prices. Whether or not Smith was correct about the benefits that free-market capitalism would bring, he did foresee the course of Western economic development. The United States was to be in the forefront of that development, and Madison's greatest achievement may well have been to recognize the political sociology of a system in which capital would be safe. As Gordon Wood has put it, the Constitution marked a "repudiation of 1776" in its rejection of radical democracy. To that extent, it marked not only the end of the Revolution but also a reaction against it. Yet politically "conservative" though the Constitution was, it was also fully in tune with the needs of what were then the most progressive economic forces in the world. The structure it created would serve those forces well.

The Constitution would serve the needs of many people, however, besides landowners, planters, and emergent capitalists. It reflected not just the needs of one or a few social groups but also the experience that the Revolution had given to Americans of many kinds. Had it been a truly unpopular document, or one that contradicted how most ordinary Americans understood their world, the ritual of ratification would never have given it the widespread acceptance that it so quickly won.

Seven

REPUBLIC, CITIZENS, AND EMPIRE:

THE NEW AMERICAN ORDER

Between 1783 and 1788 the Revolution's national leaders worked out the institutions that still form the republic's living bones. Their discussion was intense and creative. While they were talking and writing about the country's problems, other people of many sorts were trying to work out their own terms for belonging to this new entity that was the United States. We can hear many of their voices: the extraordinary group whom Americans honor as the Framers and the Founding Fathers; ordinary white women and men; Indians who had opposed the Revolution, who had favored it, and who had been neutral; free black people who were forging their own difficult paths in life; and the many more black people who remained enslaved.

At the most fundamental level, the questions they raised were the same ones that had torn America out of the British Empire. People were struggling and arguing over the terms for being themselves, for dealing with others both like and unlike themselves, and for belonging to something larger than themselves. Yet the new argument about belonging to America was different from the old dispute about belonging to Britain. Part of the difference was who was taking part. In a way, the debate had fewer participants than the old debate, because the British were gone and the loyalists were either gone or silent. In another way, it had more participants, because of all the American people who had found their voices. Part of the difference was having no place outside America to look for a final answer. Part stemmed from the basic premises that now underpinned the whole discussion.

I

As the war of independence wound down, America's future was still up in the air. The victory at Yorktown in the autumn of 1781 broke the British will to continue, and hostilities ended on the mainland, but naval war continued in the Caribbean, with the sugar islands as the possible prize. Redcoats still held Savannah, Charles Town, and New York City, and the Americans had no means to dislodge them. In and around New York most civilians would have been happy with continued British rule. In Indian country people had no idea that they had been defeated. Vermont was effectively independent of New York, but it was scorned by Congress, and its leaders were flirting with the British commander in Montreal. During the mid-1780s the "State of Franklin" was trying to establish its own independence from North Carolina and Virginia.

One possible future was a broken political landscape, based on who controlled a given place when the shooting stopped. Such has been the outcome of many other great struggles, and the long-term result usually has been more war. America would not be spared such warfare, both as its white people encroached upon Indians' land and as Americans finally faced the problem that they were a house divided, half-slave and half-free. But at the end of the war Congress's diplomats in Paris obtained legal control over a far larger territory than the Continental Army had won. Following upon bringing Americans together to declare independence and organizing the successful war effort, this was Congress's third great achievement.

The embarrassments that American diplomats had suffered during the war in Paris, the Hague, and especially in Madrid had been very large, but they could be put behind. When Benjamin Franklin, John Adams, and John Jay assembled in Paris in 1782 to work out final terms of peace, they spoke on behalf of the whole United States, as a single sovereign power. Given the slowness of eighteenth-century communications, they enjoyed enormous discretion, and they used it to powerful effect.

Grateful to France and perhaps fearful of European intrigues, Congress directed the peacemakers to be guided by the Comte de Vergennes, the French foreign minister. But the three Americans were no novices at international negotiation and self-seeking. They realized that the foreign minister would put the needs of France first, and that France's needs did not necessarily include a strong or large United States. They seized the chance to negotiate on their own that the British envoy Richard Oswald offered.

Britain's military will was broken, but it was not in a lenient mood. The treaty deprived the United States of the trade benefits that the colonies had had under the old Navigation System, including access for American vessels to the West Indies and the right to fish in "British" waters off the Canadian coast. Congress was to "earnestly recommend" to the states that persecution of loyalists stop. Prewar debts had to be repaid, regardless of whatever politically popular and socially necessary steps the states were taking to protect the debtors among their citizens. In return, Oswald made a huge concession to the United States: There would be a complete British withdrawal south of Canada, north of Florida, and east of the Mississippi. A large proportion of the territory for which France and Britain had contested between 1700 and 1763 would now "belong" to the United States, as its legal sovereign if not as its actual owner. As international law dictated by that time, only a sovereign power could deal with people like Indians, particularly in terms of the Indians' "aboriginal" right to their land. The Articles of Confederation already asserted that Congress had that right, inherited from the British Crown; now it would be confirmed by treaty with the Crown. George Washington understood what he was saying when he congratulated his fellow Americans in 1784 on having become "lords of a great empire."

Four of the six Iroquois nations, the Mohawk, the Onondaga, the Cayuga, and the Seneca, had chosen to fight on the British side. They had to acknowledge defeat, a point that negotiators from Congress and from New York State made forcefully at Fort Stanwix (renamed Fort Schuyler) in 1784. New York City mayor James Duane, who speculated in western lands, told Governor George Clinton that the old customs of diplomacy simply should be abandoned. Traditionally negotiations had followed Indian etiquette, including in what order speeches were made, what signified a decision, and the giving of gifts. Abandoning those traditions would show the Indians who was in charge. Governor Clinton did follow the traditional customs the first time, perhaps enjoying the historic role in which he found himself cast. But after Fort Stanwix negotiations rapidly became mere business deals. Two Iroquois nations, the Oneida and the Tuscarora, had taken the American rather than the British side. They could not be treated as conquered peoples, and both Congress and the state assured them that their lands were secure. As of the Fort Stanwix meeting the Oneida's ancestral acreage stood at roughly five million. By 1846 the number of acres they still held within New York State had been reduced to a few hundred. In 1907, when the case arising from their situation first reached the Supreme Court, it stood at only thirty-two.

Indians farther west had not suffered defeat. Some, like the Choctaw, had never entered the war. Indians who did fight were outraged at Britain for abandoning them. They believed that at most Congress had stepped into the ambiguous "paternal" position formerly held by the British and French monarchs, but their land remained entirely their own, in their view, to be protected by warfare if necessary. Both in 1791 and in 1792 Ohio Valley Indians defeated American armies. Ohio did not become open for settlement until General Anthony Wayne's army defeated the Indians at Fallen Timbers in 1794. The final Indian "war" east of the Mississippi did not occur until 1832 in Illinois, when Black Hawk led his fellow Sauk and Fox in a futile attempt to reclaim prairie that had been theirs.

Nonetheless the Treaty of Paris opened the way to transform Indian country into a vast reserve whose owner as well as its sovereign was the American people, represented through their central government. After the envoys' great success in Paris, the next great achievement of the Revolution's leadership was to work out the terms on which both the sovereign people as a whole and separate American individuals would take and use that land.

The Revolution's victors wanted land. As soon as the war ended, New Englanders started crossing the Berkshires and the Hudson River/Lake Champlain Valley and pushing into Iroquois country. By 1830 their "belt of New England settlement" would spread as far as Illinois. Pittsburgh was changing from a frontier outpost to a commercial center whose farming hinterland stretched in all directions. Virginians and North Carolinians were crossing the Blue Ridge Mountains and the Cumberland Gap, taking land where they found it, and filing claims. After Kentucky became a separate state, it became clear that the grants within its own boundaries amounted to five times as much land as there actually was.

With Vermont's separation from New York and with the "State of Franklin" trying to conjure itself into existence in the Great Smokies, the new United States faced something like the problem that its own colonial beginnings had posed to Britain. New communities were forming, and they needed political institutions. If the new communities were truly self-created, a future of small, conflicting, weak, separate communities loomed, particularly given the difficulties of crossing the Appalachian mountain chain. Spain had acquired Louisiana from France in 1763, and Britain still held Canada. Should whatever lay between them prove disunited, that would virtually invite either or both of those powers to step in and try to dominate, much as Russia and Prussia dominated the weak, unhappy countries of the eastern Baltic.

Thomas Jefferson worked out a solution in the principles that underpinned the Northwest Ordinances, which Congress adopted in 1784, 1785, and 1787. The first and the third ordinances solved the political problem: There would be no more self-created Franklins and Vermonts; instead there would be "territories," organized under the authority of Congress and following a prescribed path toward eventual statehood. Jefferson wanted to call the initial new states Sylvania, Michigania, Cherronesus, Assenisipia, Metropotamia, Illinoia, Washington, Saratoga, Polypotamia, and Pelisipia. For once, Jefferson's facile pen had failed him completely, and the ungainly names were rapidly abandoned, but except for West Virginia, Kentucky, Tennessee, Texas, and California, every new state from Ohio to Hawaii has followed the path that he laid out.

Jefferson's other great idea, developed in the ordinance of 1785, was the land grid that spreads west from the Appalachians. Jefferson did not originate the idea of dividing land with straight lines and right angles. Egyptians and Romans had laid out gridded lands in the ancient Mediterranean; Spanish conquistadors did so in Mexico; there are gridded sections on Claude-Joseph Sauthier's map of New York as it appeared in 1775.

Much of Jefferson's grid covers territory so level that the endless lines running north and south, east and west make geographical sense. But the grid of six-mile-square "townships" and mile-square "sections" is wholly artificial. It was the intended product of an enlightened eighteenth-century mind determined to impose rationality and avoid unplanned conflicts. Instead of building upon the traces of centuries of experience, the grid buries them, whether the traces were made by Indians, Spaniards, the French, or the first white and black Americans.

The grid idea did solve the problem of chaotic, overlapping

grants that had tormented the colonial era. It also addressed two immediate needs of Congress: It provided the government with an income, by selling the land, and it provided a means to reward the Revolution's soldiers, in lieu of pay that most of them had never received. The grid and the terms of sale promised that there would be land both for large speculators and for independent farmers, and once the surveys were completed and registered, all of them could be sure of what actually was theirs.

Imposing the grid meant wiping out both Indians' and squatters' lines of property. Indians and squatters alike resisted, but the grid triumphed, as any glance from an airplane window over the Midwest today makes plain. What was rational and new would underpin modernity. Rationality and innovation were also qualities of the national leadership's final great achievement, the Constitution.

I I

We already have worked through how the Federalists of 1787 and 1788 came to a common understanding of the problems that America faced, how they turned their understanding into action, and how they achieved their goal by writing and ratifying the Constitution. And we have discussed individual Federalists. Let us now turn to the significance of the Federalists as a group, of what they achieved, and of other groups of people who also believed that they understood themselves, their situation, and their entitlement to pursue their own happiness.

To speak of the Revolution in terms of George Washington, Benjamin Franklin, John Adams, John Jay, and Thomas Jefferson is to understand it as the work of heroes. The premise of this book is that it was far more than that. Nonetheless, those five as well as James Madison and Alexander Hamilton did touch human greatness. All of them were ambitious. But save for Washington, who was widely known before independence for his blunder that ignited the Seven Years War, and for Franklin, who was celebrated for his scientific accomplishments, none could have expected to leap beyond local notability. As one after another started saving his correspondence during the independence crisis, they betrayed their growing realization that in history's eye they might amount to more than provincial lawyers, planters, and merchants. Fate had given them the chance for enduring fame.

These men were well off, even though some of them, such as West Indies–born Hamilton and former shoemaker Roger Sherman of Connecticut, had climbed to prosperity from obscure beginnings. Those ascents should be no surprise; no elite with any common sense has ever closed its ranks to talent from outside. Allowing for Washington, Franklin, and a few others, they were the Revolution's youth. They were heirs to the first great debates that had ripped open the rationale and the fabric of the British regime, rather than participants in that first round of arguments. Their work was to build, rather than destroy.

Even before the crisis some of them were transcending their local loyalties. Benjamin Franklin was the quintessential Philadelphian of his day, but that was somewhat like being a quintessential New Yorker now. Where he had been born did not count. He had migrated to Philadelphia from Boston, and he learned to be at home in London and Paris. George Washington left North America only once, on a youthful voyage to Barbados. As an adult he made Mount Vernon home, and the house expresses perfectly his sense of how a Chesapeake gentleman ought to display himself. But if tobacco measured a Virginia planter's worth, as historian T. H. Breen suggests, Washington started to pull away from his pure Virginia identity when he switched over to wheat just after the Seven Years War.

Beginning with the First Continental Congress in 1774, these men met and tested one another: in Congress itself; in the army as high-ranking field, staff, and supply officers; overseas as diplomats; and sometimes as businessmen. All of them learned to be impatient with the governments and needs and customs of the separate states. The economic crisis of 1778 and 1779, as we have seen, caused many to begin thinking not only in terms of the needs of a starving army but also in terms of the emergent national economy, with all that such an economy required. Unquestionably some would gain directly if that economy should prosper. Some proved to be nothing more than venal. But conscious, bottom-line, financial self-interest was not the only issue, or the main issue, on most of their minds.

These men were literate and sophisticated. Even before independence, they inhabited large mental worlds, through the college educations that many of them had received, through their long-distance correspondence on business and legal matters, through their travels, and through the books, magazines, and newspapers they read. Until the independence crisis they were intellectual provincials. Even thinkers as bold and insightful as John Dickinson, Benjamin Franklin, and John Adams worked in a framework of ideas that emanated from Britain. Read now, the early debates about internal taxation and external taxation, taxation and legislation, the power of the king, the power of Parliament, and the power of the local assemblies can seem as utterly remote as discussions about angels among medieval theologians.

Gordon Wood's account of how American political thought developed out of purely American conflicts between 1776 and 1788 shows the emergent national class finding its own mind and making that mind up. The debates that followed independence still can seem pertinent. Not provincial at all, they were about issues that continue to have places on the public agenda of American life. That is why the Founders' supposed "original intent" continues to be upheld by some legal thinkers as the standard against which legislation and public policy ought to be measured.

Whatever the fundamental understanding of these men about the cosmos and the destination of humankind, their main way of thinking was secular and political. All of them under-stood that the age of religious wars had passed, and they had no desire to see that kind of conflict return. The ardently Presbyte-rian John Jay addressed that point when he condemned the in-fluence of "wicked priests" on political life in New York State's constitution of 1777. The secular Thomas Jefferson addressed it equally strongly in Virginia's statute for religious freedom. Nei-ther Jay nor Jefferson proposed to destroy orthodox religion in the way that Jacobin France or Stalinist Russia would attempt to do, but both Jay and Jefferson understood that mixing religion with political life was very likely to bring nothing but unresolv-able conflict. They agreed that issues of politics and issues of faith and salvation needed to be worked out in different places.

III

The "balance" that the Constitution established among the three separate branches of the new government—representative, ex-ecutive, and judicial—often is celebrated in patriotic texts. In 1787 the idea of "balancing" political forces that all originated in one source, the sovereign people, rather than of "mixing" social elements because of the presumably unique qualities that each could bring to bear, was fundamentally new. The eighteenth-century British structure rested on the idea that the monarch, the lords, and the commons deserved their own separate places in the governmental structure. This was because of what each respectively was and what each respectively could contribute. The monarch would give energy, wisdom would emanate from the lords, and the commons would yield consent. The whole structure presumed not just differences, but fundamental in-equality among the one, the few, and the many.

The British structure also presumed deep respect for what the past had bequeathed, a point that Edmund Burke elaborated into the basis of modern conservative thought when he developed his *Reflections on the Revolution in France* in 1791. To Burke, the British Constitution's own long existence was proof enough that it ought to continue to exist roughly as it was. "Innovation" was (and still is) a suspect concept in British culture. As a member of Parliament, Burke had supported the colonial movement on the ground that it sought only to stave off unwise, unwanted change. But the American Constitution rejected most of the wisdom about institutions, authority, sovereignty, and society to which British experience presumably had led.

The very notion of "balancing" conflicting institutional forces rather than "mixing" separate social principles had its analogue in eighteenth-century physics, particularly but not exclusively the ideas of Sir Isaac Newton. Rather than asking *why* a given physical motion takes place and seeking the answer in the "essence" of whatever moved, Newtonian thought simply asked *how* movement happens and sought the answer in close description. It is not an accident that Benjamin Franklin, the foremost American scientific thinker, was a member of the Constitutional Convention. However great or small was Franklin's actual input, he and most of his fellows were thinking about the social and political world in the way that Newton and his like had thought about physics. How the polity operated was what counted, rather than any ultimate explanation of why it did so.

One reason they could think that way was that they radically simplified their understanding of what could make a political society work. Edmund S. Morgan has suggested that the Constitution was the end product of a long process of "inventing" the sovereign people. The very idea of "the People" is poetic. In any society larger than a village or a county, assembling the whole populace is a practical impossibility. The notion of a people being its own sovereign also distinguishes between any actual assembly of human beings and ultimate authority. Yet to call the idea poetic or mythic is not to call it false. Monarchical theory stumbled on the same problem of myth in relation to reality when it distinguished the fallible person who might be king or queen for a time from the Sovereign Who Can Do No Wrong.

Yet both the notion of a sovereign people and the idea of a sovereign king conform to Sir William Blackstone's dictum of 1765 that in all societies there must be an absolute, unquestionable power. The difference is where the power is to be found, among society's members or above them. In *ancien régime* France absolute power meant the king. In Britain it meant the King-in-Parliament, which in principle was just as absolute as any Bourbon monarch. The British sovereign could, and can, actually be seen in action, most especially when the monarch, the lords, and the commons assemble for the ceremonial state opening that marks each session of Parliament.

In America, however, sovereign authority would mean the People. Since it is amorphous, the sovereign American people cannot be seen. The closest Americans now come in practice to witnessing their sovereign authority is during the rare, drawn-out process that leads to an amendment to the Constitution. The Constitution's original device of securing ratification by winning the consent of special conventions in nine of the thirteen founding states amounted to a Newtonian solution to the problem of working sovereignty. The conventions and the elections that created them could only approximate the whole people. Nonetheless, the ratification process presented a completely rational substitute for the impossible task of assembling all Americans to give or withhold their consent. Its purpose was not to show why the Constitution should assume the condition of "supreme law of the land," but rather to show how it might do so in a convincing way.

This process cut through the remnants of earlier thinking about distinct social orders that had bedeviled the authors of the original state constitutions. Except for Pennsylvania and Vermont, whose revolutionary legislatures were unicameral, all the states had tried to sort out a "senatorial part of society," usually by some variation on the idea that the possession of more property marked some people as fundamentally different from others. It had proven to be a hopeless task.

The Framers themselves did believe they were different from most of their fellow Americans and that their difference made them uniquely fit to rule. But there are no formal statements about the politics of human difference in the Constitution. The task of sorting out "representatives [of] enlightened views and virtuous sentiments" was to be accomplished by the ongoing process of public life, not by prescription or prior social requirements. That did not contradict either the poetic truth about sovereignty embodied in the phrase "We the People . . . do ordain and establish this Constitution" or the earlier and still more poetic insight about the human condition that Jefferson summed up as "all men are created equal." How to find the people who ought to be in charge for a time, not determining what social qualities would mark them as a matter of birthright, was the concern.

The Constitution's rational, enlightened qualities are clearly illustrated by what it permits and by what it forbids. There is nothing in any of the state constitutions comparable to the powers that Article I bestows on Congress. Taken together with the actions that the same article forbids the states to undertake, the Constitution laid out a blueprint for a particular kind of American future. Some of the powers of Congress are simply continuations of the powers that the monarchy once had exercised, particularly in terms of foreign affairs. Others, however, set up the conditions of stability and predictability that were needed for a national economy to flourish. To the tasks posed by the Constitution itself—"to form a more perfect Union, establish Justice, insure domestic Tranquility, provide for the common defence, promote the general Welfare, and secure the Blessings of liberty to ourselves and our Posterity"—the Constitution offered a completely rational set of answers.

The Constitution was completely a product of the Enlightenment, with all its belief that rational deliberation could solve the most difficult human problems. Toning down the Constitution's own language, its goal was to create a system that would combine power in the world, republican consent and participation, economic prosperity, and institutional and legal stability. Taken together, the means has proven extremely effective.

IV

What the Federalists wrought has endured through enormous changes and stress. The United States is not a new country now. After Britain, it is the second-oldest continually existing polity on earth. In all that time it has yet to see Congress or the courts closed by executive order, an election put off, a president ejected by armed force, or the Constitution itself suspended. By global standards, which admittedly are dismal, that is no small achievement. Yet the Federalist achievement did not sum up the Revolution's changes. The settlement of 1787–88 fell short both of the Revolution's highest rhetoric and of the experiences that people lived through as the British Empire collapsed and the American Republic took shape. In another important way, the experience of the Federalists themselves spoke to how others would emulate, challenge, and seek to expand what they had achieved.

At the heart of the Revolution's language and ideology was the notion of liberty. Even Britons and loyalists agreed that liberty was an unqualifiedly good thing. As sociologist Orlando Patterson has suggested, the very notion of liberty, American or otherwise, always has been "chordal," the product of many voices, singing in different keys. The liberty whose "blessings" the Constitution proposed in 1787 to secure was the product of three decades of intense debate and struggle. It was very different from the traditional British "liberties" whose conflicting meanings had opened the chasm between Britain and the colonies. The liberty of 1787 also was different from the general, undifferentiated liberty of "all men" that Jefferson proclaimed in 1776. The Virginian had been at his most eloquent in the Declaration, which is why revolutionaries have since quoted and paraphrased it worldwide. But he also had been at his most woolly, since his language directly contradicted the large reality of American life. The debate about organizing the new order that followed opened up many of the possible meanings that American liberty might have.

One possible meaning in 1776 was civic liberty, the right of citizens to say "we," to act together in a political way. Jefferson certainly had this meaning in mind, even developing a plan to let each new generation remake the world as it chose when it came of age. The first right protected in most of the bills of rights that states adopted at independence was that of people to act together, even, if necessary, to overthrow their government. But whereas Jefferson wrote in terms of a still-misty "one people," the states had something smaller in mind. They meant their own people, as opposed to the larger but very amorphous body that was just beginning to be called and to think of itself as "American." Short of overturning the government, they meant their own people's liberty to protect themselves in difficult times, not just by military defense but also by the traditional practice of closing themselves off from the outside world during epidemic, economic downturn, or dearth of the goods needed for survival.

That is why five of the original state constitutions (South Carolina, North Carolina, Maryland, Pennsylvania, and Vermont) gave the new governments the right to impose embargoes and price controls if need should be, and why most of the northern states actually did so during the crisis of finance and supply of 1779. But the pronoun *we* could have an even narrower meaning, the right of a very small community to set its own norms and keep outsiders out or at least subordinate. Thomas Jefferson's Virginia and John Jay's New York separated state from church not only to protect individuals from coercion but also to allow groups to determine their own orthodoxy. In John Adams's Massachusetts, however, the state and the Congregational churches would remain joined until 1833, so that individual towns could set the terms on which their people would worship and support a minister who seemed to suit them. This was the notion of liberty—people in small communities acting together in a common interest—that underpinned traditional crowd action on both sides of the Atlantic. It did not vanish when the Constitution was adopted.

Neither in the Constitution nor in its Bill of Rights is there any protection of a liberty to overturn the government. The Constitution denied any state power to interfere in contract obligations, or in the conduct of foreign trade. That meant forbidding the price controls, embargoes, debtor relief, and state tariffs that had proven popular during the war and the postwar depression. The Constitution does protect people's freedom to assemble, both for secular and religious reasons, and to petition the government, but otherwise it is silent on collective liberties. By declaring itself and the laws and treaties made under its authority to be "the supreme law of the land," it effectively ended the legitimacy of the traditional customs, usages, traditions, and liberties whose defense had been so central both to the colonial movement of resistance and to the first steps in creating a new republican order.

Now liberty's official "blessings" would be different. The main body of the Constitution protects the liberty of individuals who are full members of the polity—"ourselves and our posterity"—to act publicly under a stable framework of republican institutions and to act privately under uniform law, primarily in the sphere of commerce. The Bill of Rights protects the liberty of individuals in relation to the central government, which may not interfere with their worship, their speech, the security of their homes against searches and seizures, or their trial by jury and may not force them to incriminate themselves. The "public good"—literally the *res publica*—of the new United States would have three major elements. First, there would be the essentially poetic belief that "the People" had created the Republic and that the same People constituted its own sovereign. The original right of revolution now would take the form of amending the Constitution or, if absolutely necessary, calling a new constitutional convention. Second, the large American entity would be a common market, organized around the best conditions for securing trade and exchanging ideas. Third, it would value innovation, as the provisions for patents and copyrights made clear.

In the broadest terms, the public good would represent the values and the needs of city people taking part in the large, impersonal, commercial world. That meant merchants, who needed predictability and trust across long distances, and professional lawyers, who could interpret a market society's rules and share their interpretations. But it also meant people whose economic world was becoming large rather than local. In a way, the Revolution came full circle. The original popular support for resisting British policies had taken shape among people in the port cities. Shoemakers, blacksmiths, bakers, brewers, shipwrights, printers, and ironworkers had known just as well as traders and lawyers that the taxes and regulations Britain tried to impose would affect them. Thinking of themselves originally as just Bostonians or New Yorkers, they developed their own strong consciousness and organizations by 1776.

Their self-awareness and willingness to act on their own were just as pronounced in their overwhelming support for the new Constitution. Most country people opposed it. They formed a large majority, and a fair plebiscite would have rejected it. But in every major town except Albany, the Constitution proved immensely popular. Three hundred and eighty Boston artisans convened in January 1788, to urge their state's convention to ratify. Paul Revere chaired the gathering. The meeting's goals included putting pressure on delegates Samuel Adams, who had his doubts, and John Hancock, who had been elected governor largely by rural, anti-Federalist voters. The artisans' intervention made a difference to the closely split convention. When the vote to ratify narrowly passed, the tradesmen celebrated both the Constitution and themselves, despite the cold of a Boston winter day.

Philadelphians celebrated the Constitution's ratification on July 4, 1788. The Boston parade had been near-spontaneous, but Philadelphia's whole day was carefully orchestrated, beginning at dawn with a peal of church bells and a salvo from a ship on the Delaware River. Ten other vessels rode along the waterfront, all decorated with pennants and banners. The parade that assembled at eight a.m. had so many units that the *Pennsylvania Gazette* needed three and a half pages to describe them. First came the Revolution's history: Independence, French Alliance, Treaty of Peace, "Washington, the Friend of His Country," the Convention, and the Constitution itself, borne by the justices of the state supreme court. A large float drawn by ten horses carried "The New Roof, or Grand Federal Edifice." Ten Corinthian columns held the roof aloft, with three more waiting to be raised, one for each of the states that had not yet ratified. Ten gentlemen rode on the float. They were "representatives of the citizens at large," emblems of an American people that simply had not existed fifteen years earlier, even in the most advanced political imagination.

"The New Roof" marked a transition in the parade from the history Americans had made to a display of what Americans could do. Immediately after it marched the members of the separate building trades: architects, house carpenters, saw makers, and file makers. "The Federal Ship Union" followed them, manned by twenty-five sailors, with pilots, boat builders, sail makers, ship carpenters, rope workers, and merchants in its metaphorical wake. The rest of the city's trades followed, some with their own floats and most with banners. Some of the floats were workshops on wheels. Cobblers made shoes on one. Blacksmiths beat swords into farm tools on another. Wheelwrights assembled a plow and a wagon wheel. Printers struck off copies of a federal ode. Bakers handed out bread.

The bricklayers' banner proclaimed that "Both Buildings and Rulers are the Work of our Hands." "Time rules all things," announced the clock and watch makers. "By Hammer and Hand, All Arts Do Stand," the smiths declared, with an emblem of arm and hammer that is now a familiar commercial trademark. "Let us encourage our own manufactures," said the whip and cane makers. "The Death of Anarchy and Confusion Shall Feed the Poor and Hungry" was the motto of the victualers. On the parade went, unit by unit: saddlers, stonecutters, and sugar refiners; gunsmiths, goldsmiths, and engravers; tanners, upholsterers, and brush makers; coopers and carvers; ribboners and stocking knitters; brewers and tobacconists. Finally came public officials, physicians, clergymen, students, and professors.

It seemed that all of Philadelphia was on display, proud, energetic, and confident of each group's place in the "New Era" that a single rider had represented near the parade's head. Warfare, republicanism, Benjamin Franklin's maxims, trade, manufactures, commerce, patriotism, revolutionary heroism, and the idea of equal citizenship all had their place in the parade's composition.

When the march was complete, the Scottish-born lawyer James Wilson mounted the float bearing the New Roof to deliver a patriotic oration. Angry militiamen had besieged Wilson's house during the economic crisis of 1779, and people who had taken part in the riot were in the crowd that Wilson addressed. The speaker himself went on to glory, as a legal thinker and a justice of the United States Supreme Court, and to humiliation, confined in a debtors' prison when he went bankrupt. He became a Federalist in the partisan sense of the 1790s, while at the same time many who heard him were becoming Democratic Republicans. Neither of those political groups existed in 1788. Without knowing so, the orator and his audience were presaging the system of national party politics. If the Constitution is the republic's bones, political parties have provided its tendons and its sinews. Completing that image, the printers in the parade represented its nerves transmitting information, the manufacturing artisans represented its muscles producing goods, and the merchants and seafarers represented its veins and its arteries.

Within the main body of the march, nobody enjoyed precedence. A royal procession in England would have begun with flower girls and culminated with "the king's most excellent majesty," but this republican parade bore a different message. The participants were supposedly equal citizens rather than subjects in their separate, unequal stations. The artisan groups' positions in the parade were drawn by lot rather than determined by precedence or social station. Each unit expressed the identity and interests and self-concept of the people taking part, come together now to celebrate the Constitution, but with the possibility that they might conflict in the future, as many of them had conflicted in the past.

The parade expressed the understanding of American society that Madison had presented in the tenth *Federalist*. There might be a sovereign people, but there was no single "public" or "commons." Instead there were many groups asserting themselves, so many that the prospect of any one group being able to oppress others seemed very remote. If heroes like Washington, public officials, and even college professors were different, the difference was not absolute. It stemmed from whatever such people had done with their own lives, not from what birth had destined them to be.

But save for a symbolic "Indian Chief" (who was no more a real Indian than the Bostonians dumping tea) smoking a calumet with "a Citizen," and for a few women working away at looms on the float of the Manufacturing Society, everybody in the parade was white and male. The *Gazette*'s long report presented no black Philadelphians at all in the celebration. When black people did try to join Philadelphia's July 4 party in 1805, a riot drove them away. Slavery's gradual abolition had been completed in Pennsylvania in 1799. Establishing equality among all the commonwealth's free people hardly had begun.

V

Republicanism that would endure; nationalism that could transcend the divisions of geographical section, social class, and state identity; pride in what an entire people had seemed to achieve; pride as well in what different kinds of people could do with their skills, muscles, and tools; a constitutional "machine that would go of itself," thanks to the dynamic balance that it created among functionally separate institutions; economic and geographic rationality that could wipe the shadows of a jumbled past off the very landscape—all these taken together seemed to form the Revolution's settlement as of 1788. No castles had been stormed by angry peasants; no archives had been burned; no one religious had been martyred by a relentless Antichrist. A king had been deposed and metaphorically executed, but the living George III still reigned in Britain. Royalty was abolished, but there would be no guillotines in American streets. It all seems bloodless, dispassionate, ordered, and purposeful, even, as it often is described, as "conservative" as a revolution can be.

It was not so. The settlement of 1787–88 resolved the problems about institutions, authority, legitimacy, sovereignty, and formal political society that the Revolution had raised. The settlement accomplished that task well enough that it has endured. But the political settlement only began to resolve the questions about identity, belonging, and society that people had raised. Philadelphia physician Benjamin Rush, who had signed the Declaration of Independence, got that point nicely when he observed that the war might be over, but the Revolution had only begun.

Consider first the "losers" of 1787–88, stuck as they were

with the negative description "Anti-Federalist." The Constitution's opponents formed a numerical majority, but they began without the organization that led to Federalist victory. They became the first people in American national history to be so badly wrong-footed in print that even the term that historically describes them has served them ill. In 1787 "Federalist" was a positive term, and it more accurately described the people who opposed the Constitution than the people who favored it. Within the Convention both Alexander Hamilton and James Madison were not federalists at all but complete centralists who wanted to reduce the states to near-nullities. Their project was to combine power in one set of institutions, not to distribute it among many. They did not get all they wanted, but the national government that they created possessed great potential ability to define and impose a single political will.

Anti-Federalists understood and feared that point. Federalists responded during the debates that if all power flowed from the People, the holders of the power never could be oppressive. That was just as much specious nonsense as were the British claims in 1765 that the colonials had been "virtually" represented in Parliament. The Constitution's effect was to create power that could operate directly against individuals. The foremost result of the Anti-Federalists' objections was the Bill of Rights, which at least in principle puts limits on that power, regardless of its being exercised in the sovereign people's name.

The Bill of Rights did not address the larger objection that Anti-Federalists posed. Their vision of good communities was hallowed by time and by almost all republican theory. Communities had to be small, coherent, and integrated. Their members had to share a genuine common interest. Anti-Federalists did not say so, but their ideas harked back to the heritage of uneven local liberties that had been the colonial version of British public culture. They also harked back to the idea that in time of stress and trouble each community might defend itself against a dangerous outside world on its own terms. That was precisely the heritage that had energized and rendered legitimate the crowd uprisings that had made Britain's policies impossible to enforce. It expressed a do-not-mess-with-me attitude and a readiness to act together that Americans still are likely to show.

But it has had another outcome as well. The American tradition of small communities defending themselves led to patrollers capturing and whipping escaped slaves in the Old South; to the informal committee of planters that hanged slave plotters outside Natchez, Mississippi, in 1861; to another informal committee hanging Union sympathizers in North Texas during the Civil War; to lynchings in the days of Jim Crow; and to the Ku Klux Klan. Outside the South it gave rise to mostly Irish immigrants turning on black New Yorkers during the draft riots of 1863; vigilantes assaulting both long-settled Spanish-speakers and would-be settler farmers in the Old West; respectable citizens destroying shantytowns; management goons attacking strikers in industrial cities and California farmlands; and self-styled militias preparing to stop a hostile takeover by a faceless enemy.

This ugly list may be a part of the Revolution's direct heritage. Of course, we cannot blame Stamp Act rioters for the Ku Klux Klan. Nor, even for a moment, can we suggest that American society would have been "better" if independence had not been achieved. The essentially Anti-Federalist tradition that underpinned the Slave South's supposed right to wage war against the United States when it learned in 1860 that it no longer could control presidential elections was also part of the Revolution's heritage. James Madison's ideas about the danger that a "majority" faction would crush "minority" rights does fit the white southern position in both the secession crisis and the civil rights era a century later, as long as one can blind oneself to the far greater denial of rights that black southerners long endured under both slavery and Jim Crow.

By 1788 many voices, including those of black Americans, were making themselves heard. People who found themselves defined as outsiders were posing the problem of their own existence during the revolutionary era. They used language of American liberty that no full, white, male, property-holding member of the sovereign people could fail to understand, if he should chance to read it.

As early as 1777 eight black Bostonians petitioned the government of Massachusetts to abolish slavery so that "the Inhabitanc of these States" could end "the inconsistancey of acting themselves the part which they condem and oppose in others." Their legal status is unclear, but they probably were free. Four were Freemasons and were led by Prince Hall, whose own enslavement had ended in 1770. Living in a port town where information circulated from distant places, the petitioners would have known about the widely publicized *Somerset's Case*, which had seemed to end slavery in England in 1771. They certainly would have known that Lord Dunmore had enraged white patriot Virginians in 1775 by proclaiming freedom for their slaves who rallied to the king's cause. They might have known that they were not alone among black people in raising the issue to the patriots. They marked only the beginning of a very long list of black Americans who have demanded that the republic live up to its own rhetoric. During the long history of human bondage, many slaves had won or been granted freedom. But these people were unique. Alone among former slaves, black Americans understood that they could use their exploiters' own rhetoric and procedures, and they were the first to begin a campaign against slavery itself.

Still, the obstacles they faced remained enormous. In 1797 North Carolina slaves tried to bring the same issue before Congress with a petition. They had the aid of the pioneering Philadelphia black minister Absalom Jones. James Madison himself advised the House of Representatives that the petition "had no claim on their attention"—despite his own authorship of the First Amendment's declaration that "Congress shall make no law . . . abridging . . . the right of the people . . . to petition the government for a redress of grievances." Madison did not like

slavery, but he participated in it all his life. To him both the enslaved Carolinians and the free Philadelphia minister were
among the American people's subjects, not part of the People in
their own right.

The Constitution never used the words *slave, slavery, black,*
or *Negro*. But until the amendments that followed the southern
war against the United States, the Constitution did considerably
more than presume the enslavement of black people in America.
By counting "all other persons" as three-fifths of free persons for
direct taxation and representation in the House of Representatives, it made slavery the only special social interest that the new
national order explicitly recognized. By 1787 slavery was on its
way to destruction in the northern states, turning it from a national fact of life into the South's "peculiar institution." Even in
the Chesapeake, where slavery would not be destroyed until almost eighty more years had passed, the number of free black
people was rising sharply.

Some blacks were voting, and a few even sought public office. During the wars of the French Revolution black seafarers
would be issued U.S. passports in order to protect them from
impressment into foreign navies. Yet in the epochal case of *Dred
Scott v. Sandford* (1857), the Supreme Court would hold that the
Constitution's original intent was to exclude all black people,
slave and free alike, from U.S. citizenship and the protection of
U.S. law. The Constitution was a "glorious liberty document,"
but in its protection of slavery and its denial of black people's
rights, it also was a bitter mockery.

Whether Chief Justice Roger B. Taney was historically correct in *Dred Scott* that the Framers intended to exclude free
black people from the American polity is an open question. But
though slavery's partial breakup and the emergence of a significant free black population were real outcomes of the Revolution, Taney was correct that the Constitution gave slavery
explicit protection. If one of the Constitution's large goals was to
even out the American economic terrain into an enormous free

market, slavery alone remained as an impediment on the free movement of people, ideas, capital, and goods. The holding of slaves remained as the only "liberty," in the old sense of a specific privilege "beyond the ordinary subject," that went with being a specific kind of person. Being enslaved meant being socially dead, bereft of honor, of legal family, of legal identity, and of rights. Slaves remained without protection from the law.

Beyond its special representation in Congress itself, the most obvious recognition of slavery in the Constitution were the clauses in Article I that permitted the African slave trade to continue for twenty years after ratification, and in Article IV requiring that "no Person held to Service or Labour in one state" could become free by virtue of another state's laws. By 1787 enlightened opinion among slaveowners regarded the African trade as an obscenity. The Convention successfully did its work without Rhode Island and North Carolina, but it yielded to South Carolina's and Georgia's threat to walk out if the African trade was banned immediately.

As legal historian Paul Finkleman has shown, many other provisions also gave slavery special protection. These included the preamble's general goal of ensuring domestic tranquillity, Congress's power to define and punish piracy at sea and suppress domestic insurrections, the guarantee "to every State . . . against domestic Violence," the prohibition of any capitation or direct tax except in accord with the three-fifths clause, and the prohibition of taxes or duties "on Articles exported from any state." None of these bore exclusively on slavery. But piracy could mean slaves taking over the vessel, domestic violence could mean a slave uprising, and economic pressure for political reasons had been one of the major means of American resistance to Britain. As the Constitution was understood, it guaranteed that slavery would be as firmly entrenched in the national polity as it was in the economy and society of the southern states.

To say now that white women raised their voices during the

Revolution is to repeat what has become commonplace. During the quarter-century since the pioneering scholarship of Mary Beth Norton and Linda Kerber, women have been recognized as major actors on the early American historical stage. Norton demonstrated that for the most part the basic patterns of women's lives remained unchanged between 1750 and 1800. But she also showed that patriot women's self-awareness changed markedly and that they were participants in the Revolution rather than witnesses. Kerber developed the notion of "republican motherhood" in order to understand women's attempts to resolve the tension between the restrictions that being a woman imposed and the promise of equal freedom that American rhetoric offered. More recently Cathy Davidson showed how the emerging genre of the novel offered a way to explore in the mind what law and custom denied in most women's actual lives.

Thomas Paine offhandedly summed up the old order's perspective on gender and politics in *Common Sense*. Attacking the whole idea of kingship as well as urging the need for independence, he wrote that "male and female are the distinctions of nature, good and bad the distinctions of heaven, but how a race of men came into the world so exalted about the rest . . . is worth enquiring into." Being female in a republic was not worth "enquiring" into. That changed quickly. A keyword search of a database that lists all titles published in America before 1800 shows 256 that included the word *ladies*. Of these, 215 appeared after 1776. A keyword search for *woman* shows ninety-seven entries, sixty-five published after 1776. There were nine separate publications during the 1790s by the British writer Mary Wollstonecraft, including three editions of her epochal *Vindication of the Rights of Woman*. Two of those appeared in 1792, the same year the book was first published in England. Judith Sargent Murray of Massachusetts made many of the same points as Wollstonecraft in *The Gleaner* (1798). She began developing her thoughts as early as 1779.

Agendas for public discussion are one thing; the basic structure of society is another. White women, black people, and Indians all found that whatever the Republic's rhetoric of individual freedom, its compelling structures locked them in. Replacing subjection with citizenship as the fundamental organizing social concept did mean replacing the idea of a hierarchy of conditions under a king with the idea of equality among the citizens. But at the Revolution's end being a full citizen meant a condition of mastery. It meant being an adult male who controlled his own body and will, and who probably also controlled property, skills, and the lives of other human beings. Mastering slaves and a plantation in South Carolina was similar to mastering a trade, a shop, apprentices, journeymen, a wife, and children in the south end of Boston. To be a master required that there be somebody beneath.

For a few adult white women, particularly in the cities, the personal liberty of being single did begin to prove "a better husband." But for most, the family formed society's basic structural unit, and the law of family life remained unchanged. The revolutionary settlement did absolutely nothing about the English common-law doctrine that decreed that when a woman married, she submerged her own personality in her husband's and surrendered her property to his control. Individual arrangements could be made through proceedings in equity, but the creation of married women's property laws lay far in the future. Young elite women found it possible to obtain demanding educations in ladies' academies, and many graduates of the academies did win fame in the nineteenth century, but higher education still remained beyond them. The learned professions remained closed, and male physicians were pushing midwives out of one place where women had traditionally ruled, the birthing room. Divorce did become more easily obtained in some states, but the probability remained very high that a woman who sought to end even an atrocious marriage would lose her children.

New state and federal land policies offered the promise of setting sons free from their fathers by obtaining public land rather than having to wait for inheritance. But not until the Homestead Act of 1862 would women become able to get public land on their own. The nineteenth-century women's rights leader Elizabeth Cady Stanton did attend one of the finest postindependence women's academies, Troy (New York) Female Seminary, now Emma Willard School. But she could not follow her brother to Union College. She was the Revolution's granddaughter, borrowing and adapting the Declaration of Independence in the Seneca Falls Declaration of Sentiments of 1848. But it took her own daughter Harriet Stanton Blatch, who was able to graduate from Vassar, most of her long lifetime to see woman suffrage become a national reality. Linda Kerber suggests that the heritage of English common law's notions about inequality between the sexes still is not fully resolved.

The Constitution's discussion of Indians is more limited. Article I, Section 8, gives Congress power "to regulate Commerce . . . with the Indian Tribes," and under the Trade and Intercourse Act of 1790 that power became exclusive. The only other direct reference is to "Indians not taxed" in Article I, Section 2, and that seems to exclude them, like slaves, from the polity, though not for exactly the same reason.

In 1778 the Continental Congress raised the idea that the Delaware Nation might become the nucleus of a new state whose people would be Indians. That idea died, but the guarantee in Article IV, Section 4, of a "Republican Form of Government" to every state did accord with the direction that some Indians took after the Revolution. The best-known example is the Cherokee, who adapted formal constitutional republicanism to their own purposes, only to see the State of Georgia crush their polity and expel them westward on the Trail of Tears. Seneca in New York State also changed from traditional tribal organization to explicit republicanism, and Catawba in South Carolina replaced the title *chief* with *general*, to the applause of their white neighbors.

To really incorporate Indians on a basis that maintained the

Indians' collective identities might have been possible. To incorporate them in terms that respected their hold on property in terms that suited themselves seems in retrospect to have been almost impossible. In one important regard, the material condition of both the American people as a whole and the Indian Nations west of the white zone was virtually the same in 1788: All possessed enormous holdings in common. But for the Revolution's victors, both the imperatives of republican theory and the demands of a market society required that the common holding be turned into freehold private property, which meant turning it into potential capital. Like the crops it would grow, the land would become an object in trade. Moreover, the republic's property in common included the exclusive right to acquire Indian land. That right had been inherited from the Crown, which had used it largely for the benefit of well-connected men in the colonies and Britain alike, and which had been hemmed by the Indians' real power to resist. Now it would be used first to create the national domain and then to turn that domain into private property, however large or small the private owner's holding might be.

That vast trove of western land proved to be one major underpinning of the enormous economic and social changes that were about to unfold at a dazzling pace. Nobody who debated the Constitution could foresee the Cotton Kingdom that would form after Eli Whitney of Connecticut showed how to gin short-staple cotton efficiently in 1793. But building a textile industry in the Northeast was on quite a few Americans' minds, including that of Alexander Hamilton. He backed a highly visible but unsuccessful venture at Paterson, New Jersey, just before Samuel Slater and Moses Brown opened the first successful American spinning mill at Pawtucket, Rhode Island, in 1791. That industry would prosper not on wool, the textile Slater had known in his native Derbyshire and that Brown expected to spin and weave, but on cotton, which slaves would grow.

Plantations where cotton was grown and factories where it

was spun required that southern public land be turned over to individuals. They would do with that land as they chose, proudly believing that they stood on their own land on their own terms, unbeholden to anybody else. But in practice that meant that they would do with their land as the large market for commercial goods required. Industrial cities would require food in enormous quantities that local hinterlands could not meet. That, too, required land. Feeding the cities also would require mechanized agriculture, mechanized transportation, and mechanized processing. None of this was compatible with most Indians' firm belief that they held and ought to keep holding their lands as whole peoples, for purposes that had nothing to do with either the republic's rising glory or its burgeoning market prosperity. Yet industrial entrepreneurs, a working class that was only starting to take shape, aspirant southern planters, slaves, would-be yeoman farmers, northern speculators, and Indians all were bound together in the republic's "rising glory."

History had happened to all these people, and they had also made that history. The American Revolution rewrote the rules that defined being human in America, and it did so thoroughly in two ways. One was the destruction of the British monarchy. The other was the creation of the republic on the particular terms that the Federalists of 1787–88 achieved, whether we call them Founders, Framers, or a would-be if short-lived ruling class. Whatever became of that ruling class, the institutions that it created proved much more effective at coping with the diverse, tangled people who made up the United States than the old institutions had proven with the equally but differently diverse and entangled people who had made up the colonial order.

The revolutionary settlement confirmed an observation made by that foremost nineteenth-century student of American ways, Alexis de Tocqueville. Pondering not the American events but rather the revolution that had transformed his own country between 1789 and 1814, the French thinker suggested that rather than tearing down an oppressive old order in the name of free-dom, a successful modern revolution builds a new centralized order in which the old order's uneven liberties lose their legiti-macy. The Founders were not outright Jacobins or Bolsheviks, concentrating all power in Paris or Moscow, but they did intend that "the blessings of Liberty" for themselves and their posterity should mean evenness and predictability under one "supreme law of the land," with strong institutions to enforce that law and with no naysaying on the part of localities and states.

The republic that the Founders created did not suit every-body's needs equally well, but its very structure permitted and encouraged people to define themselves and their interests and to seek to pursue those interests, even against the greatest odds and at the risk of their own lives, fortunes, and honor. That drama of self-assertion and claiming the blessings of supposedly equal American liberty was a direct consequence of the Revolu-tion itself. In a tepid, ritualized way, people in new territories would act out the drama each time they sought to advance to statehood. In a few instances, most especially Maine and Mis-souri in 1820, "bleeding Kansas" in 1854–56, and Utah in 1896, acquiring statehood meant confronting serious questions of social organization as well as creating a governorship, a legisla-ture, and state courts.

For the most part, the real drama of people finding them-selves, organizing themselves, and confronting the problem of being free in America has taken place in other dimensions than the making of new states. The urban artisans who celebrated the Constitution in 1788 found themselves opposing the Federalist Party by 1794. Black Americans who began emerging from slav-ery as early as 1775 did what no previous group of former slaves had done: organize themselves with the goal of bringing down slavery itself. Between the presidencies of George Washington and Andrew Jackson, the Cherokee Republic and the American Republic developed in parallel with each other. In 1848 the women of Seneca Falls paraphrased the Declaration of Independence. In each instance, and many others to the present day, the actors were giving honor by imitation to the example of the Congress members of 1776 and to the Convention members of 1787.

But they were following more than the example of an elite group. Without knowing Mary Hay Burn's name, they understood the importance of her insistence to her soldier husband in 1776 that American liberty had to mean something to her, in her own desperate situation, as she and their children faced the prospect of losing their house. That was virtually the same point that the black abolitionist Frederick Douglass would make with great power on July 5, 1851, when he asked, "What to the slave is your Fourth of July?" The answer, as Douglass certainly understood, was not really what the holiday did mean then and there, as he spoke in Rochester, New York. The solution lay in what people could make the holiday mean, even though that might take just as much outrage, insight, organization, struggle, danger, and creativity, and often as much loss, pain, and frustration, as the American Revolution itself.

Bibliographical Essay

The original version of this essay noted some of the high points in the study of the subject, suggested some approaches to the work of earlier historians, and discussed in some detail the studies produced in our own time. That version is reproduced here with a few silent cuts and with the addition of the important work that has appeared since 1985.

George Bancroft looms above all other nineteenth-century historians of the Revolution. His *History of the United States from the Discovery of the Continent—"The Author's Last Revision,"* 6 vols. (New York: D. Appleton, 1890), is a sweeping, vividly written account of the rise of American liberty. Like Bancroft, John Fiske wrote for a popular audience. In *The Critical Period of American History, 1783–1789* (Boston: Houghton Mifflin, 1888), he agreed with Bancroft's assertion that the Constitution marked liberty's final triumph. But from the beginning, other voices were also heard. The New York Anti-Federalist Abraham Yates wrote a history of the movement for the Constitution that was framed in very different terms, and the historian Staughton Lynd edited and published it in the *William and Mary Quarterly* [hereafter *WMQ*], 3rd ser. 20 (1963), 223–25.

The doubts that Yates first expressed lay behind the writing of the early-twentieth-century Progressive historians, all of whom quarreled with the notion that the Revolution was a simple, direct struggle for liberty. The work of Carl Becker, Charles A. Beard, J. Franklin Jameson, and Arthur Schlesinger, Sr., sums up their approach. Becker's *History of Political Parties in the Province of New York, 1760–1776* (Madison: University of Wisconsin Press, 1909) proposed that the Revolution "was the result of two general movements: the contest for home-rule and independence, and the democratization of American politics and society." His *The Declaration of Independence: A Study in the History of Political Ideas* (New York: Alfred A. Knopf, 1922) was for decades the major study of the Declaration. Beard's *An Economic Interpretation of the Constitution of the United States* (New York: Macmillan, 1913) argued that the Constitution marked the triumph not of abstract principles but rather of self-seeking speculators. It built on evidence first presented in Orin G. Libby, *The Geographical Distribution of the Vote of the Thirteen States on the Federal Constitution, 1787–88* (Madison: University of Wisconsin Press, 1894). Jameson's short book, *The American Revolution Considered as a Social Movement* (Princeton University Press, 1926), developed in broad terms the assertion that the Revolution had social roots and consequences; and Schlesinger's *The Colonial Merchants and the American Revolution, 1763–1776* (New York, 1918; reprinted New York: Atheneum, 1968) traced the experience of one group that was central to the Revolution's making. The Wisconsin historian Merrill Jensen kept their tradition alive in a scholarly career that stretched from *The Articles of Confederation* (Madison: University of Wisconsin Press, 1940) to *The American Revolution Within America* (New York: New York University Press, 1974).

The other major approach of early-twentieth-century historians was centered at Yale University and the figure of Charles McLean Andrews. His *Colonial Background of the American Revolution: Four Essays in American Colonial History* (New Haven: Yale University Press, 1924) summarized a position that he and his many graduate students adopted, maintaining that British imperial administrators were honest, fair-minded men concerned with running an empire, not with establishing tyranny. Lawrence Henry Gipson, in particular, developed that position. *The British Empire Before the American Revolution* (New York: Alfred A. Knopf, 1939–70) is a multivolume achievement in the spirit of Bancroft; and *The Coming of the Revolution, 1763–1775* (New York: Harper & Row, 1962) distills his argument.

In the mid-twentieth century a different approach appeared, critical of both Progressive and Imperial historians. Two books were central. Robert E. Brown's *Middle-Class Democracy and the Revolution in Massachusetts* (Ithaca: Cornell University Press, 1955) denied that the Revolution had internal causes and marked the beginning of a long attack by Brown on Carl Becker's professional reputation. Forrest McDonald's *We the People: The Economic Origins of the Constitution* (Chicago: University of Chicago Press, 1958) used Charles Beard's own methods to demolish Beard's argument. The work of both scholars was essentially critical, but the era brought positive achievements as well. Edmund S. Morgan and Helen M. Morgan argued in *The Stamp Act Crisis: Prologue to Revolution* (Chapel Hill: University of North Carolina Press, 1953) that political principles counted, and they showed how the colonials responded to the first stage of the imperial crisis. Jack P. Greene's *The Quest for Power: The Lower Houses of Assembly in the Southern Royal Colonies, 1689–1776* (Chapel Hill: University of North Carolina Press, 1963) explored the political matrix from which a large proportion of the revolutionary leadership emerged.

The work of these historians must stand for that of many others who addressed similar questions. Jack P. Greene discussed at length the historiography of the Revolution to 1968 in the introductory essay of his *The Reinterpretation of the American Revolution, 1763–1789* (New York: Harper & Row, 1968), which also includes the work of a wide range of writers. Among the essays reprinted are Stanley Elkins and Eric McKitrick's portrayal of the Founding Fathers as "Young Men of the Revolution" and John P. Roche's account of them as a "Reform Caucus in Action." That collection can be read in conjunction with the pre–World War II essays in Richard B. Morris, ed., *The Era of the American Revolution* (New York: Columbia University Press, 1939).

Since Greene surveyed the literature in 1968, an immense amount of writing has appeared. One way to approach it is through review essays, which consider major writing and discuss achievements, problems, and possibilities. A number of these have concerned themselves with the historiography of early New England. They include Richard R. Beeman, "The New Social History and the Search for 'Community' in Colonial America," *American Quarterly* [hereafter *AQ*] 29 (1977), 422–43; Richard S. Dunn, "The Social History of Early New England," *AQ* 24 (1972), 661–84; Rhys Isaac, "Order and Growth, Authority and Meaning in Colonial New England," *American Historical Review* [hereafter *AHR*] 76 (1971), 728–37; James A. Henretta, "The Morphology of New England Society in the Colonial Period," *Journal of Interdisciplinary History* 2 (1971–72), 379–98; and John M. Murrin, "Review Essay," *History and Theory* 11 (1972), 226–75. Douglas Greenberg surveyed writing on the middle colonies in "The Middle Colonies in Recent American Historiography," *WMQ* 36 (1979), 396–427. New studies of the South were considered in Edward Countryman, "Stability and Class, Theory and History: The South in the Eighteenth Century," *Journal of American Studies* [hereafter *JAS*] 17 (1983), 243–50. A number of review essays consider writing on the process and achievements of the Revolution. Among them are Edward Countryman, "The Problem of the Early American Crowd," *JAS* 7 (1973), 77–90; Pauline Maier, "Why Revolution? Why Democracy?" *Journal of Interdisciplinary History* 6 (1975–76), 711–32; Richard B. Morris, " 'We the People of the United States': The Bicentennial of a People's Revolution," *AHR* 82 (1977), 1–19; Robert E. Shalhope, "Toward a Republican Synthesis: The Emergence of an Understanding of Republicanism in American

Historiography," *WMQ* 29 (1972), 49–80, and "Republicanism and Early American Historiography," *WMQ* 39 (1982), 334–56; James H. Hutson, "Country, Court and the Constitution: Antifederalism and the Historians," *WMQ* 38 (1981), 337–68; and Michael Zuckerman, "The Irrelevant Revolution: 1776 and Since," *AQ* 30 (1978), 224–42. Daniel J. Rodgers brought one debate together in "Republicanism: The Career of a Concept," *JAH* 79 (1992), 11–38. The collection edited by Jack P. Greene and J. R. Pole, *Colonial British America: Essays in the New History of the Early Modern Era* (Baltimore: Johns Hopkins University Press, 1984), contains very thorough essays on practically every aspect of recent writing about early America.

The *William and Mary Quarterly* has carried several "forums" that have brought current debates about the Revolution into a single place. Among these are "The Creation of the American Republic, 1776–1787: A Symposium of Views and Reviews," 44 (1987), 549–640; "How Revolutionary was the Revolution: A Discussion of Gordon S. Wood's *The Radicalism of the American Revolution*," 51 (1994), 677–716; and "Rethinking the American Revolution," 53 (1996), 341–86. The same journal has published a number of special issues that bear on the Revolution. These include "The Constitution of the United States," 44 (1987), 411–657; "Law and Society in Early America," 50 (1993), 1–239; "Early American History: Its Past and Future," 50 (1993), 245–467; "Mid-Atlantic Perspectives," 51 (1994), 351–597; and "The Iroquois Influence, Con and Pro," 53 (1996), 587–636. The *Journal of American History* published "The Constitution and American Life: A Special Issue," 74 (1987), 656–1178, and "Discovering America: A Special Issue," 79 (1992), 828–1357, which includes an important essay by Carroll Smith-Rosenberg about the debate of 1787. "Symposium: The Republican Civic Tradition" appeared in *Yale Law Journal* 97 (1988).

During and since the bicentennial decade, many other anthologies appeared on the Revolution. In some cases they presented short statements of arguments that appear more fully elsewhere; in others the essays stand by themselves. Among the more noteworthy are Erich Angermann et al., eds., *New Wine in Old Skins: A Comparative View of Socio-Political Structures and Values Affecting the American Revolution* (Stuttgart: Klett, 1976); Bernard Bailyn and John B. Hench, eds., *The Press and the American Revolution* (Boston: Northeastern University Press, 1981); Richard Maxwell Brown and Don E. Fehrenbacher, eds., *Tradition, Conflict and Modernization: Perspectives on the American Revolution* (New York: Academic Press, 1977); W. Robert Higgins, ed., *The Revolutionary War in the South: Power, Conflict and Leadership: Essays in Honor of John Richard Alden* (Durham, N.C.: Duke University Press, 1979);

Jeffrey J. Crow and Larry E. Tise, eds., *The Southern Experience in the American Revolution* (Chapel Hill: University of North Carolina Press, 1978); Richard M. Jellison, ed., *Society, Freedom and Conscience: The American Revolution in Virginia, Massachusetts and New York* (New York: W.W. Norton, 1976); Stanley Nider Katz, ed., *Colonial America* (Boston: Little, Brown, 1971; revised editions, 1993, 2001); Stephen G. Kurtz and James H. Hutson, eds., *Essays on the American Revolution* (Chapel Hill: University of North Carolina Press, 1973); *The Development of a Revolutionary Mentality* (Washington, D.C.: Library of Congress, 1972); James Kirby Martin, ed., *The Human Dimensions of Nation Making: Essays on Colonial and Revolutionary America* (Madison: State Historical Society of Wisconsin, 1976); J.G.A. Pocock, ed., *Three British Revolutions: 1641, 1688, 1776* (Princeton University Press, 1980); Alfred F. Young, ed., *The American Revolution: Explorations in the History of American Radicalism* (De Kalb: Northern Illinois University Press, 1976) and *Beyond the American Revolution: Explorations in the History of American Radicalism* (De Kalb: Northern Illinois University Press, 1993); and Jack P. Greene, *The American Revolution: Its Character and Limits* (New York: New York University Press, 1987). Greene and J. R. Pole, eds., *A Companion to the American Revolution* (Oxford: Basil Blackwell, 2000) updates their *Blackwell Encyclopedia of the American Revolution* (Oxford: Basil Blackwell, 1991). Since the bicentennial of independence Ronald Hoffman and Peter J. Albert, in association with others, have edited many special collections on aspects of revolutionary America, all published by the University Press of Virginia. In alphabetical order these include: *Arms and Independence: The Military Character of the American Revolution* (1984); *The Bill of Rights: Government Proscribed* (1997); *Diplomacy and Revolution: The Franco-American Alliance of 1778* (1980); *The Economy of Early America: The Revolutionary Period, 1763–1790* (1988); *Launching the "Extended Republic": The Federalist Era* (1996); *Native Americans and the Early Republic* (1999); *Of Consuming Interests: The Style of Life in the Eighteenth Century* (1994); *Religion in a Revolutionary Age* (1994); *Slavery and Freedom in the Age of the American Revolution* (1983); *Sovereign States in an Age of Uncertainty* (1981); *The Transforming Hand of Revolution: Reconsidering the American Revolution as a Social Movement* (1996); *An Uncivil War: The Southern Back Country During the American Revolution* (1985); and *Women in the Age of the American Revolution* (1989). Also important are collections of essays that have honored recent major scholars. These include: James A. Henretta, Michael Kammen, and Stanley Nider Katz, eds., *The Transformation of Early American History: Society, Authority, and Ideology* (New York: Alfred A. Knopf, 1991), for Bernard Bailyn; David D. Hall, John M. Murrin, and Thad W. Tate, eds.,

Saints and Revolutionaries: Essays on Early American History (New York: W.W. Norton, 1984), for Edmund S. Morgan; and Carla Gardina Pestana and Sharon V. Salinger, eds., *Inequality in Early America* (Hanover, N.H.: University Press of New England, 1999), for Gary B. Nash.

During the bicentennial period historians paid relatively little attention to the link between Britain and the colonies, but some significant studies appeared. Cohn Bonwick's *English Radicals and the American Revolution* (Chapel Hill: University of North Carolina Press, 1977) is one of several discussions of the opposition within Britain to British government policies. John Brewer, *Party Ideology and Popular Politics at the Accession of George III* (New York: Cambridge University Press, 1976), is the most recent statement in a debate launched long ago by Sir Lewis Namier. John Brooke's *King George III* (New York: McGraw-Hill, 1972) is a fair-minded biography. J. M. Bumsted discusses the beginning of the idea of independence in "'Things in the Womb of Time': Ideas of American Independence, 1633 to 1763," *WMQ* 31 (1974), 533–64. More recently the subject has opened up. Theodore Draper, *A Struggle for Power: The American Revolution* (New York: Times Books, 1996), elaborates on Bumsted's argument. Both Linda Colley, *Britons: Forging the Nation, 1707–1837* (New Haven: Yale University Press, 1992), and Kevin Phillips, *The Cousins' Wars: Religion, Politics, and the Triumph of Anglo-America* (New York: Basic Books, 1999), stress the transatlantic dimension. In different ways so do James E. Bradley, *Popular Politics and the American Revolution in England* (Macon, Ga.: Mercer University Press, 1986); Eliga H. Gould, *The Persistence of Empire: British Political Culture in the Age of the American Revolution* (Chapel Hill: University of North Carolina Press, 2000); Ronald Hoffman with Sally D. Mason, *Princes of Ireland, Planters of Maryland: A Carroll Saga, 1500–1782* (Chapel Hill: University of North Carolina Press, 2000); K. R. Perry, *British Politics and the American Revolution* (New York: St. Martin's Press, 1990); and John Sainsbury, *Disaffected Patriots: London Supporters of Revolutionary America, 1769–1782* (Kingston, Ontario: McGill-Queen's University Press, 1987).

Paul G. E. Clemens, *The Atlantic Economy and Colonial Maryland's Eastern Shore: From Tobacco to Grain* (Ithaca: Cornell University Press, 1980), and Ralph Davis, *The Rise of the Atlantic Economies* (Ithaca: Cornell University Press, 1973), both consider the prerevolutionary Atlantic trading network. The same subject is discussed in Jacob M. Price, *France and the Chesapeake: A History of the French Tobacco Monopoly, 1674–1791* (Ann Arbor: University of Michigan Press, 1973).

A number of scholars have explored the political aspects of the transatlantic tie. Among the resulting studies are James A. Henretta, *"Salutary*

Neglect": Colonial Administration Under the Duke of Newcastle (Princeton University Press, 1972); Michael Kammen, *A Rope of Sand: The Colonial Agents, British Politics, and the American Revolution* (Ithaca: Cornell University Press, 1967), and *Empire and Interest: The American Colonies and the Politics of Mercantilism* (Philadelphia: J. B. Lippincott, 1970); Stanley Nider Katz, *Newcastle's New York: Anglo-American Politics, 1732–1753* (Cambridge, Mass.: Harvard University Press, 1968); Alison Gilbert Olson, *Anglo-American Politics, 1660–1775: The Relationship Between Parties in England and Colonial America* (New York: Oxford University Press, 1973), and "The London Mercantile Lobby and the Coming of the American Revolution," *Journal of American History* [hereafter *JAH*] 69 (1982), 21–41. Among recent studies of specific aspects of British policy are John L. Bullion, *A Great and Necessary Measure: George Grenville and the Genesis of the Stamp Act, 1763–1765* (Columbia: University of Missouri Press, 1983); Robert J. Chaffin, "The Townshend Acts of 1767," *WMQ* 27 (1970), 90–121; John Deny, *English Politics and the American Revolution* (New York: St. Martin's Press, 1976); Joseph Albert Ernst, *Money and Politics in America: A Study in the Currency Act of 1764 and the Political Economy of Revolution* (Chapel Hill: University of North Carolina Press, 1973); Philip Lawson, "George Grenville and America: The Years of Opposition, 1765–1770," *WMQ* 37 (1980), 561–76; and P.D.G. Thomas, *British Politics and the Stamp Act Crisis: The First Phase of the American Revolution, 1763–1767* (Oxford: Clarendon Press, 1975). The imperial problem is considered in wide terms in Ian R. Christie and Benjamin W. Labaree, *Empire or Independence, 1760–1776: A British-American Dialogue on the Coming of the American Revolution* (New York: W.W. Norton, 1976), and in Robert W. Tucker and David C. Hendrickson, *The Fall of the First British Empire: Origin of the War of American Independence* (Baltimore: Johns Hopkins University Press, 1982). In addition, two anthologies deal specifically with imperial relations: Peter Marshall and Glynn Williams, eds., *The British Empire Before the American Revolution* (London: Frank Cass, 1980), and Alison Gilbert Olson and Richard Maxwell Brown, eds., *Anglo-American Political Relations, 1765–1775* (New Brunswick, N.J.: Rutgers University Press, 1970). These studies provide a context for the ideas advanced in Thomas C. Barrow, "The American Revolution as a Colonial War for Independence," *WMQ* 25 (1968), 452–64, and in Richard B. Morris, *The Emerging Nations and the American Revolution* (New York: Harper & Row, 1970).

Jon Butler, *Becoming America: The Revolution Before 1776* (Cambridge, Mass.: Harvard University Press, 2000), and Alan Taylor, *American Colonies* (New York: Viking, 2001), are the two most recent attempts to make sense of

North America before independence. In addition see David Hackett Fischer, *Albion's Seed: Four British Folkways in America* (New York: Oxford University Press, 1989); Bernard Bailyn, *Voyagers to the West: A Passage in the Peopling of America on the Eve of the Revolution* (New York: Alfred A. Knopf, 1986) and *The Peopling of British North America: An Introduction* (New York: Alfred A. Knopf, 1986); and Edward Countryman, *Americans: A Collision of Histories* (New York: Hill and Wang, 1996). Geographer David W. Meinig presents a stimulating account of colonial and revolutionary-era American space in *The Shaping of America: A Geographical Perspective on 500 Years of History, Volume I, Atlantic America, 1492–1800* (New Haven: Yale University Press, 1986).

The study of early American social development has been extremely rich, both in terms of synthesis and overviews and in terms of narrowly focused monographs. Jack P. Greene, "The Social Origins of the American Revolution: An Evaluation and an Interpretation," *Political Science Quarterly* 88 (1973), 1–22, and Kenneth A. Lockridge, "Social Change and the Meaning of the American Revolution," *Journal of Social History* 6 (1972–73), 397–439, both consider the problem in wide terms. So do the essays by T. H. Breen collected as *Puritans and Adventurers: Change and Persistence in Early America* (New York: Oxford University Press, 1980). A number of studies have dealt with the demography of the revolutionary era. They include James A. Henretta, *The Evolution of American Society, 1700–1815: An Interdisciplinary Analysis* (Lexington, Mass.: D.C. Heath, 1973); Peter Charles Hoffer, *Revolution and Regeneration: Life Cycle and the Historical Vision of the Generation of 1776* (Athens: University of Georgia Press, 1982); Gary B. Nash, *Red, White and Black: The Peoples of Early America* (Englewood Cliffs, N.J.: Prentice-Hall, 1974); and Robert V. Wells, Jr., *The Population of the British Colonies in America Before 1776: A Survey of Census Data* (Princeton University Press, 1975). A multivolume series has provided histories of the thirteen colonies, beginning with Hugh T. Leffler and William S. Powell, *Colonial North Carolina: A History* (New York: Charles Scribner's Sons, 1973). There are volumes on New Jersey (by John E. Pomfret), New York (by Michael Kammen), Rhode Island (by Sydney V. James), Pennsylvania (by Joseph E. Illick), Georgia (by Kenneth Coleman), Massachusetts (by Benjamin Labaree), Delaware (by John A. Munroe), Connecticut (by Robert J. Taylor), New Hampshire (by Jere R. Daniell), Maryland (by Aubrey C. Land), and South Carolina (by Robert M. Weir). Since 1979, the series has been published by KTO Press, Millwood, N.Y.

A number of studies considered economic and social development in specific regions, provinces, and communities. Among the studies on New England are Kenneth A. Lockridge, "Land, Population and the Evolution of New England Society, 1630–1790," *Past & Present* 39 (April 1968), 62–81, and *A New England Town: The First One Hundred Years: Dedham, Massachusetts, 1636–1736* (New York: W.W. Norton, 1970); Michael Zuckerman, *Peaceable Kingdoms: New England Towns in the Eighteenth Century* (New York: Alfred A. Knopf, 1970); and Edward M. Cook, Jr., *The Fathers of the Towns: Leadership and Community Structure in Eighteenth-Century New England* (Baltimore: Johns Hopkins University Press, 1976), together with his "Social Behavior and Changing Values in Dedham, Massachusetts, 1700 to 1775," *WMQ* 27 (1970), 546–80. Among studies of rural Massachusetts are John L. Brooke, *The Heart of the Commonwealth: Society and Political Culture in Worcester County, Massachusetts, 1713–1861* (Cambridge, England: Cambridge University Press, 1989); Richard L. Bushman, "Massachusetts Farmers and the Revolution," in Jellison, *Society, Freedom and Conscience*, and *King and People in Provincial Massachusetts* (Chapel Hill: University of North Carolina Press, 1985); Philip J. Greven, Jr., *Four Generations: Population, Land and Family in Colonial Andover, Massachusetts* (Ithaca: Cornell University Press, 1970); Robert A. Gross, *The Minutemen and Their World* (New York: Hill & Wang, 1976); Gregory H. Nobles, *Divisions Throughout the Whole: Politics and Society in Hampshire County, Massachusetts, 1740–1775* (New York: Cambridge University Press, 1983); Bettye Hobbs Pruitt, "Self-Sufficiency and the Agricultural Economy of Eighteenth Century Massachusetts," *WMQ* 41 (1984), 333–64; and William Pencak, *War, Politics and Revolution in Provincial Massachusetts* (Boston: Northeastern University Press, 1981). For life in Maine when it still was part of Massachusetts, see Alan Taylor, *Liberty Men and Great Proprietors: The Revolutionary Settlement on the Maine Frontier, 1760–1820* (Chapel Hill: University of North Carolina Press, 1990). New Hampshire is considered in Jere R. Daniell, *Experiment in Republicanism: New Hampshire Politics and the American Revolution, 1741–1794* (Cambridge, Mass.: Harvard University Press, 1970), and in Lynn Warren Turner, *The Ninth State: New Hampshire's Formative Years* (Chapel Hill: University of North Carolina Press, 1983). Among studies of Connecticut are Richard Buel, Jr., *Dear Liberty: Connecticut's Mobilization for the Revolutionary War* (Middletown, Conn.: Wesleyan University Press, 1980); Richard L. Bushman, *From Puritan to Yankee: Character and the Social Order in Connecticut, 1690–1765* (Cambridge, Mass.: Harvard University Press, 1967); Christopher Collier, *Roger Sherman's Connecticut: Yankee Politics and the American Revolution* (Middletown, Conn.: Wesleyan University Press, 1971); and Bruce C. Daniels, *The Connecticut Town: Growth and Development 1635–1790* (Middletown, Conn.: Wesleyan University Press, 1979).

Modern debate on colonial urban development was launched by James A.

246 BIBLIOGRAPHICAL ESSAY

Henretta's article "Economic Development and Social Structure in Colonial Boston," *WMQ* 22 (1965), 75–92. Gary B. Nash develops Henretta's argument and its implications in *The Urban Crucible: Social Change, Political Consciousness, and the Origins of the American Revolution* (Cambridge, Mass.: Harvard University Press, 1979). G. B. Warden criticizes Henretta's conclusions in "Inequality and Instability in Eighteenth-Century Boston: A Reappraisal," *Journal of Interdisciplinary History* 6 (1975–76), 585–620. John K. Alexander discusses urban poverty before and after independence in *Render Them Submissive: Responses to Poverty in Philadelphia, 1760–1800* (Amherst: University of Massachusetts Press, 1980), as do Alan Kulikoff, "The Progress of Inequality in Revolutionary Boston," *WMQ* 28 (1971), 375–412, and Raymond A. Mohl, "Poverty in Early America, A Reappraisal: The Case of Eighteenth-Century New York City," *New York History* 50 (1969), 5–27. On Boston in particular, see David Hackett Fischer, *Paul Revere's Ride* (New York: Oxford University Press, 1994); Benjamin Woods Labaree, *The Boston Tea Party* (New York: Oxford University Press, 1964); and Alfred F. Young, *The Shoemaker and the Tea Party* (Boston: Beacon Press, 2000). On New York City, see Edwin G. Burrows and Mike Wallace, *Gotham: A History of New York City to 1808* (New York: Oxford University Press, 1999), and Joseph S. Tiedemann, *Reluctant Revolutionaries: New York City and the Road to Independence, 1763–1776* (Ithaca: Cornell University Press, 1997). Philadelphia is extremely well studied. In addition to Alexander, *Render Them Submissive*, see: Susan Branson, *Those Fiery Frenchified Dames: Women and Political Culture in Early National Philadelphia* (Philadelphia: University of Pennsylvania Press, 2001); Thomas M. Doerflinger, *A Vigorous Spirit of Enterprise: Merchants and Economic Development in Revolutionary Philadelphia* (Chapel Hill: University of North Carolina Press, 1986); Eric Foner, *Tom Paine and Revolutionary America* (New York: Oxford University Press, 1976); Gary B. Nash, *Forging Freedom: The Formation of Philadelphia's Black Community, 1720–1840* (Cambridge, Mass.: Harvard University Press, 1988); Steven Rosswurm, *Arms, Country, and Class: The Philadelphia Militia and the "Lower Sort" During the American Revolution, 1775–1783* (New Brunswick, N.J.: Rutgers University Press, 1987); Richard Alan Ryerson, *The Revolution Is Now Begun: The Radical Committees of Philadelphia, 1765–1776* (Philadelphia: University of Pennsylvania Press, 1978); Sharon V. Salinger, *"To Serve Well and Faithfully": Labor and Indentured Servants in Pennsylvania, 1682–1800* (Cambridge, England: Cambridge University Press, 1987); and Billy G. Smith, *The Lower Sort: Philadelphia's Laboring People, 1750–1800* (Ithaca: Cornell University Press, 1990).

A number of studies have considered the development of the interior of the middle colonies. Among studies of New York are Patricia U. Bonomi, *A Factious People: Politics and Society in Colonial New York* (New York: Columbia University Press, 1971); Edward Countryman, *A People in Revolution: The American Revolution and Political Society in New York, 1760–1790* (Baltimore: Johns Hopkins University Press, 1981); Sung Bok Kim, *Landlord and Tenant in Colonial New York: Manorial Society, 1664–1775* (Chapel Hill: University of North Carolina Press, 1978); Jessica Kross, *The Evolution of an American Town: Newtown, New York, 1642–1775* (Philadelphia: Temple University Press, 1983); and Thomas S. Wermuth, *Rip Van Winkle's Neighbors: The Transformation of Rural Society in the Hudson River Valley, 1720–1850* (Albany: State University of New York Press, 2001). Studies of New Jersey include Larry R. Gerlach, *Prelude to Independence: New Jersey in the Coming of the American Revolution* (New Brunswick, N.J.: Rutgers University Press, 1976); Dennis P. Ryan, "Landholding, Opportunity, and Mobility in Revolutionary New Jersey," *WMQ* 36 (1979), 571–92; and Donald Wallace White, *A Village at War: Chatham, New Jersey, and the American Revolution* (Rutherford, N.J.: Fairleigh Dickinson University Press, 1979). Pennsylvania society is the subject of James T. Lemon, *The Best Poor Man's Country: A Geographical Study of Early Southeastern Pennsylvania* (Baltimore: Johns Hopkins University Press, 1972), and of Stephanie Grauman Wolf, *Urban Village: Population, Community, and Family Structure in Germantown, Pennsylvania, 1683–1800* (Princeton University Press, 1977). In general terms, see Allan Kulikoff, *The Agrarian Origins of American Capitalism* (Charlottesville: University Press of Virginia, 1992) and *From British Peasants to Colonial American Farmers* (Chapel Hill: University of North Carolina Press, 2000).

A number of recent books and essays have dealt with the South in the revolutionary era. For collected essays, see Jeffrey J. Crow and Larry E. Tise, eds., *The Southern Experience in the American Revolution* (Chapel Hill: University of North Carolina Press, 1978), and Hoffman and Albert, eds., *An Uncivil War*. See also Ernest McNeill Eller, ed., *Chesapeake Bay in the American Revolution* (Centreville, Md.: Tidewater Publishers, 1981). Among essays that provide overviews are Allan Kulikoff, "The Colonial Chesapeake: Seedbed of Antebellum Southern Culture?" *Journal of Southern History* 45 (1979), 513–40, and Carville Earle and Ronald Hoffman, "Staple Crops and Urban Development in the Eighteenth-Century South," *Perspectives in American History* 10 (1976), 7–80. Development in Maryland is considered in Ronald Hoffman, *A Spirit of Dissension: Economics, Politics and the Revolution in Maryland* (Baltimore: Johns Hopkins University Press, 1974); Jean B. Lee, *The Price of Nationhood: The American Revolution in Charles County* (New York: W.W. Norton, 1994);

Allan Kulikoff, *Tobacco and Slaves: The Development of Southern Cultures in the Chesapeake, 1680–1800* (Chapel Hill: University of North Carolina Press, 1986); and Gregory A. Stiverson, *Poverty in a Land of Plenty: Tenancy in Eighteenth-Century Maryland* (Baltimore: Johns Hopkins University Press, 1978). Virginia society is studied in Richard R. Beeman, *The Evolution of the Southern Backcountry: A Case Study at Lunenburg County, Virginia, 1746–1832* (Philadelphia: University of Pennsylvania Press, 1984); T. H. Breen, *Tobacco Culture: The Mentality of the Great Tidewater Planters on the Eve of Revolution* (Princeton: Princeton University Press, 1985); Marc Egnal, "The Origins of the Revolution in Virginia: A Reinterpretation," *WMQ* 37 (1980), 401–28; Woody Holton, *Forced Founders: Indians, Debtors, Slaves, and the Making of the American Revolution in Virginia* (Chapel Hill: University of North Carolina Press, 1999); Rhys Isaac, *The Transformation of Virginia, 1740–1790* (Chapel Hill: University of North Carolina Press, 1982); Jan Lewis, *The Pursuit of Happiness: Family and Values in Jefferson's Virginia* (New York: Cambridge University Press, 1983); Edmund S. Morgan, *American Slavery, American Freedom: The Ordeal of Colonial Virginia* (New York: W.W. Norton, 1975); Charles S. Royster, *The Fabulous History of the Dismal Swamp Company: A Story of George Washington's Times* (New York: Alfred A. Knopf, 1999); and John E. Selby, *The Revolution in Virginia, 1775–1788* (Williamsburg, Va.: Colonial Williamsburg Foundation, 1988), among many others. The most recent accounts of North Carolina are A. Roger Ekirch, *"Poor Carolina": Politics and Society in Colonial North Carolina, 1729–1776* (Chapel Hill: University of North Carolina Press, 1981), and Marjoleine Kars, *Breaking Loose Together: The Regulator Rebellion in Pre-Revolutionary North Carolina* (Chapel Hill: University of North Carolina Press, 2002). On South Carolina, see Rachel N. Klein, *Unification of a Slave State: The Rise of the Planter Class in the South Carolina Backcountry, 1760–1808* (Chapel Hill: University of North Carolina Press, 1990); Jerome J. Nadelhaft, *The Disorders of War: The Revolution in South Carolina* (Orono: University of Maine Press, 1981). Also important for South Carolina is Robert M. Weir, " 'The Harmony We Were Famous For': An Interpretation of Pre-Revolutionary South Carolina Politics," *WMQ* 26 (1969), 473–501. South Carolina slavery is studied with great sophistication in Peter H. Wood, *Black Majority: Negroes in Colonial South Carolina from 1600 Through the Stono Rebellion* (New York: Alfred A. Knopf, 1975), which should be read in conjunction with Betty Wood, *Slavery in Colonial Georgia, 1730–1775* (Athens: University of Georgia Press, 1984). Florida, not one of the thirteen colonies that rebelled, is considered in J. Leitch Wright, Jr., *Florida in the American Revolution* (Gainesville: University Presses of Florida, 1975). Andrew Jackson O'Shaughnessy filled a long unmet need with *An Empire Divided: The American Revolution and the British Caribbean* (Philadelphia: University of Pennsylvania Press, 2000). John Hope Franklin discusses the large problem of regionalism in "The North, the South and the American Revolution," *JAH* 62 (1975–76), 5–23. Almost all these studies stand in debt to Jackson Turner Main, *The Social Structure of Revolutionary America* (Princeton University Press, 1965). All of them can be read in conjunction with the maps contained in Lester J. Cappon et al., eds., *Atlas of Early American History: The Revolutionary Era, 1760–1790* (Princeton University Press, 1976). Large interpretive frameworks for understanding rural development are also offered in James A. Henretta, "Families and Farms: Mentalité in Pre-Industrial America," *WMQ* 35 (1978), 3–32; in Michael Merrill, "Cash Is Good to Eat: Self Sufficiency and Exchange in the Rural Economy of the United States," *Radical History Review* 4 (1977), 42–71; and in Rowland Berthoff and John M. Murrin, "Freedom, Communalism and the Yeoman Freeholder: The American Revolution Considered as a Social Accident," in Kurtz and Hutson, eds., *Essays on the Revolution*.

In the first version of this essay only one entry covered "the frontier." One of the greatest gains that early American historians have made since then is the emergence of a very sophisticated body of scholarship on development away from the East Coast. These are some of the most important studies: Fred Anderson, *Crucible of War: The Seven Years War and the Fate of Empire in British North America, 1754–1766* (New York: Alfred A. Knopf, 2000); Colin Calloway, *The American Revolution in Indian Country: Crisis and Diversity in Native American Communities* (Cambridge, England: Cambridge University Press, 1995); Andrew R. L. Cayton and Fredrika J. Teute, *Contact Points: American Frontiers from the Mohawk Valley to the Mississippi, 1750–1830* (Chapel Hill: University of North Carolina Press, 1998); Barbara Graymont, *The Iroquois in the American Revolution* (Syracuse, N.Y.: Syracuse University Press, 1972); Francis Jennings, *The Ambiguous Iroquois Empire: The Covenant Chain Confederation of Indian Tribes with English Colonies from Its Beginnings to the Lancaster Treaty of 1744* (New York: W.W. Norton, 1983), *Empire of Fortune: Crowns, Colonies and Tribes in the Seven Years War in America* (New York: W.W. Norton, 1988), and *The Creation of America: Through Revolution to Empire* (Cambridge, England: Cambridge University Press, 2000); M. Thomas Hatley, *The Dividing Paths: Cherokees and South Carolinians Through the Era of Revolution* (Oxford: Oxford University Press, 1993); James H. Merrell, *The Indians' New World: Catawbas and Their Neighbors from European Contact Through the Era of Removal* (Chapel Hill: University of North Carolina Press, 1989) and *Into the American Woods: Negotiators on the Pennsylvania Frontier*

(New York: W.W. Norton, 1999); James H. O'Donnell, *Southern Indians and the American Revolution* (Knoxville: University of Tennessee Press, 1973); Daniel Richter, *Beyond the Covenant Chain: The Iroquois and Their Neighbors in Indian North America, 1600–1800* (Syracuse, N.Y.: Syracuse University Press, 1987), *The Ordeal of the Longhouse: The Peoples of the Iroquois League in the Era of European Colonization* (Chapel Hill: University of North Carolina Press, 1992), and *Looking East From Indian Country: A Native History of Early America* (Cambridge, Mass.: Harvard University Press, 2001); Daniel H. Usner, Jr., *Indians, Settlers, and Slaves in a Frontier Exchange Economy: The Lower Mississippi Valley Before 1783* (Chapel Hill: University of North Carolina Press, 1992) and *American Indians in the Lower Mississippi Valley: Social and Economic Histories* (Lincoln: University of Nebraska Press, 1998); Richard White, *The Middle Ground: Indians, Empires and Republics in the Great Lakes Region, 1650–1815* (Cambridge, England: Cambridge University Press, 1991); Anthony F. C. Wallace, *The Death and Rebirth of the Seneca* (New York: Alfred A. Knopf, 1970); and David J. Weber, *The Spanish Frontier in North America* (New Haven: Yale University Press, 1993).

Economic as opposed to social development has been the subject of a considerable amount of recent work. Marc Egnal offers a short overview in "The Economic Development of the Thirteen Continental Colonies, 1720–1775," *WMQ* 32 (1975), 191–222. Edwin J. Perkins presents a book-length discussion of the same subject in *The Economy of Colonial America* (New York: Columbia University Press, 1980). Jacob M. Price has written on the subject in a number of places, most recently in *Capital and Credit in British Overseas Trade: The View from the Chesapeake, 1700–1776* (Cambridge, Mass.: Harvard University Press, 1980). Also important are James F. Shepherd and Gary M. Walton, *Shipping, Maritime Trade and the Economic Development of Colonial North America* (Cambridge, Mass.: Harvard University Press, 1972) and *The Economic Rise of Early America* (Cambridge, England: Cambridge University Press, 1979). The difference between recent and earlier writing on the early American economy is considered in Gary M. Walton, "The New Economic History and the Burdens of the Navigation Acts," *Economic History Review*, 2nd ser., 24 (1971), 533–42. All students of the subject stand in debt to the monumental achievement of Alice Hanson Jones in *American Colonial Wealth: Documents and Methods* (New York: Arno Press, 1977) and *Wealth of a Nation to Be: The American Colonies on the Eve of the Revolution* (New York: Columbia University Press, 1980). Marc Egnal and Joseph Ernst offer suggestions about the links between economics and politics in "An Economic Interpretation of the American Revolution," *WMQ* 29 (1972), 3–32. Cathy D. Matson,

Merchants and Empire: Trading in Colonial New York (Baltimore: Johns Hopkins University Press, 1998), and Richard Buel, Jr., *In Irons: Britain's Naval Supremacy and the American Revolutionary Economy* (New Haven: Yale University Press, 1998), are recent studies. See also Cathy D. Matson and Peter S. Onuf, *A Union of Interests: Political and Economic Thought in Revolutionary America* (Lawrence: University Press of Kansas, 1990).

Recent study of the Revolution, as opposed to colonial development, has concentrated on two broad problems: the political culture of the era and the social and political experience of the revolutionary generation. It is silly, of course, to slot any author or work into one position or the other and confidently assert that one "knows" what he or she or it has to say. But most scholars who have dealt with political culture have concentrated on ideas and language that the revolutionary generation shared, while most scholars who have dealt with experience have been interested in what set different kinds of Americans apart.

The study of the language of the Revolution had its beginning in 1948, with Edmund S. Morgan's essay "Colonial Ideas of Parliamentary Power, 1764–1766," *WMQ* 3 (1948), 311–41. In the decade that followed, Clinton Rossiter expanded on Morgan's point in *Seedtime of the Republic* (New York: Harcourt, Brace & World, 1953); and Caroline Robbins developed their English background in *The Eighteenth Century Commonwealthman: Studies in the Transmission, Development and Circumstance of English Liberal Thought from the Restoration of Charles II Until the War with the Thirteen Colonies* (Cambridge, Mass.: Harvard University Press, 1959). H. Trevor Colbourn demonstrated in *The Lamp of Experience* (Chapel Hill: University of North Carolina Press, 1965) how the intellectuals of the revolutionary era read history and drew lessons from it. At the same time Douglass Adair and Cecilia Kenyon were publishing a number of important essays on the political ideas of the years following independence. Adair's were eventually collected as *Fame and the Founding Fathers* (New York: W.W. Norton, 1974). The central statement in this mode of understanding is Bernard Bailyn's *The Ideological Origins of the American Revolution* (Cambridge, Mass.: Harvard University Press, 1967), which appeared originally as the book-length introduction to his *Pamphlets of the American Revolution* (Cambridge, Mass.: Harvard University Press, 1965). Bailyn's *The Origins of American Politics* (New York: Alfred A. Knopf, 1968) supplements the argument made in *The Ideological Origins*.

Many have expanded on and argued with Bailyn's central contentions. Gordon S. Wood's "Rhetoric and Reality in the American Revolution," *WMQ* 23 (1966), and his enormous *The Creation of the American Republic, 1776–1787*

(Chapel Hill: University of North Carolina Press, 1969) are both important statements. J. R. Pole writes within much the same framework in *Political Representation in England and the Origins of the American Republic* (New York: St. Martin's Press, 1966), in *The Pursuit of Equality in American History* (Berkeley: University of California Press, 1978), and in *The Gift of Government: Political Responsibility from the English Restoration to American Independence* (Athens: University of Georgia Press, 1983). The French scholar Elise Marienstras takes a different approach in *Les Mythes fondateurs de la nation américaine: Essai sur le discours idéologique aux États-Unis à l'epoque de l'indépendance (1763–1800)* (Paris: François Maspero, 1977). Two German writers have also joined the discussion, and their works are available in English translation. The first is Gerald Stourzh, *Alexander Hamilton and the Idea of Republican Government* (Stanford, Calif.: Stanford University Press, 1970), and the second is Willi Paul Adams, *The First American Constitutions: Republican Ideology and the Making of the State Constitutions in the Revolutionary Era* (Chapel Hill: University of North Carolina Press, 1980). State constitutions are also considered in Ronald M. Peters, Jr., *The Massachusetts Constitution of 1780: A Social Compact* (Amherst: University of Massachusetts Press, 1978), and in Peter S. Onuf, "State Making in Revolutionary America: Independent Vermont as a Case Study," *JAH* 67 (1980–81), 797–815.

Several historians have tried to place the problem of American republicanism in a larger context. One is Jack P. Greene, who launched a debate with Bailyn in "Political Mimesis: Consideration of the Historical and Cultural Roots of Legislative Behavior in the British Colonies in the Eighteenth Century," *AHR* 75 (1969–70), 337–67. J.G.A. Pocock placed the subject within a larger explanation of the development of early modern thought, in a number of studies, most notably *The Machiavellian Moment: Florentine Political Thought and the Atlantic Republican Tradition* (Princeton University Press, 1975). Garry Wills looked to the influence of eighteenth-century Scottish thinkers in *Inventing America: Jefferson's Declaration of Independence* (New York: Doubleday, 1978). The current standard study of the Declaration is Pauline Maier, *American Scripture: Making the Declaration of Independence* (New York: Alfred A. Knopf, 1997). Edmund S. Morgan, *Inventing the People: The Rise of Popular Sovereignty in England and America* (New York: W.W. Norton, 1988), perhaps completes the cycle he began four decades earlier.

For Bailyn, political language, centered on the abstract notions of "liberty" and "power," was enough in itself to explain the Revolution. For Wood and Pocock, the key terms were "virtue" and "corruption," and for both, ideas took on importance as they interacted with social reality. "Corruption," for instance, was eighteenth-century shorthand for what we now call "capitalist" or "modern" society. By the mid-1970s a number of intellectual historians were turning to the link between political ideas and political economy. The lead was taken by Staughton Lynd in "Beard, Jefferson, and the Tree of Liberty," in his *Class Conflict: Slavery and the United States Constitution: Ten Essays* (Indianapolis: Bobbs-Merrill, 1967), and by William Appleman Williams in *The Contours of American History* (New York: New Viewpoint, 1973). Edwin G. Burrows and Michael Wallace showed the link between national liberation and the decline of patriarchal control in "The American Revolution: The Ideology and Psychology of National Liberation," *Perspectives in American History* 6 (1972), 167–306, and Jay Fliegelman has done something similar in *Prodigals and Pilgrims: The American Revolution Against Patriarchal Authority, 1750–1800* (New York: Cambridge University Press, 1982). J. E. Crowley set off in a different direction in *This Sheba, Self: The Conceptualization of Economic Life in Eighteenth-Century America* (Baltimore: Johns Hopkins University Press, 1974). At the same time Joyce Appleby was writing "Liberalism and the American Revolution," *New England Quarterly* 49 (1976), 3–26, and "The Social Origins of American Revolutionary Ideology," *JAH* 64 (1977–78), 935–58. More recently she has produced *Capitalism and a New Social Order: The Republican Vision of the 1790s* (New York: New York University Press, 1984) and collected her essays as *Liberalism and Republicanism in the Historical Imagination* (Cambridge, Mass.: Harvard University Press, 1992). Also noteworthy are Drew McCoy, *The Elusive Republic* (Chapel Hill: University of North Carolina Press, 1980), and Nathan O. Hatch, *The Sacred Cause of Liberty: Republican Thought and the Millennium in Revolutionary New England* (New Haven: Yale University Press, 1977), together with Lance Banning, "Republican Ideology and the Triumph of the Constitution, 1789 to 1793," *WMQ* 31 (1974), 167–88, and Steven M. Dworetz, *The Unvarnished Doctrine: Locke, Liberalism, and the American Revolution* (Durham, N.C.: Duke University Press, 1990).

The relationship between the Revolution and American law has been the subject of considerable recent study. Christopher L. Tomlins and Bruce H. Mann have assembled the most recent thinking in *The Many Legalities of Early America* (Chapel Hill: University of North Carolina Press, 2001). John Philip Reid discussed it in three books: *In a Defiant Stance: The Condition of Law in Massachusetts Bay, the Irish Comparison and the Coming of the American Revolution* (University Park: Pennsylvania State University Press, 1977), *In a Rebellious Spirit: The Argument of Facts, the Liberty Riot and the Coming of the American Revolution* (University Park: Pennsylvania State University Press, 1979), and *In Defiance of the Law: The Standing-Army Controversy, the Two*

Constitutions, and the Coming of the American Revolution (Chapel Hill: University of North Carolina Press, 1981). William E. Nelson explored *Americanization of the Common Law: The Impact of Legal Change on Massachusetts Society, 1760–1830* (Cambridge, Mass.: Harvard University Press, 1975); Morton J. Horwitz has developed a similar argument in *The Transformation of American Law, 1780–1860* (Cambridge, Mass.: Harvard University Press, 1977). See also: Hendrik Hartog, *Public Property and Private Power: The Corporation of the City of New York in American Law, 1730–1870* (Chapel Hill: University of North Carolina Press, 1983); Ellis Sandoz, *A Government of Laws: Political Theory, Religion, and the American Founding* (Baton Rouge: Louisiana State University Press, 1990); and Shannon C. Stimson, *The American Revolution in the Law* (London: Macmillan, 1990). James H. Kettner deals with the specific subject of citizenship law in *The Development of American Citizenship, 1608–1870* (Chapel Hill: University of North Carolina Press, 1978), as do Rogers Smith, *Civic Ideals: Conflicting Visions of Citizenship in U.S. History* (New Haven: Yale University Press, 1997), and Linda K. Kerber, *No Constitutional Right to Be Ladies: Women and the Obligations of Citizenship* (New York: Hill and Wang, 1998).

Republicanism was the central concept in the culture of the revolutionary era, and it found expression in other ways besides formal political discourse. Kenneth Silverman's *A Cultural History of the American Revolution* (New York: Thomas Y. Crowell, 1976) explores developments in painting, music, literature, and the theater. Michael Kammen's *A Season of Youth: The American Revolution and the Historical Imagination* (New York: Alfred A. Knopf, 1979) deals with similar material. The era produced several remarkable artists who have been the subject of recent biographies and critical assessments. See Irma B. Jaffe, *John Trumbull: Patriot-Artist of the American Revolution* (Boston: New York Graphic Society, 1975); Robert C. Alberts, *Benjamin West: A Biography* (Boston: Houghton Mifflin, 1978); and Jules David Prown, *John Singleton Copley*, 2 vols. (Cambridge, Mass.: Harvard University Press, 1966). Also informative are the catalogues of the many exhibitions that were mounted at the time of the bicentennial. One of the best is Charles F. Montgomery and Patricia F. Kane, eds., *American Art: 1750–1800, Towards Independence* (Boston: New York Graphic Society, 1976), produced for an exhibition mounted by Yale University and the Victoria and Albert Museum, London. Robert F. Dalzell and Lee Baldwin Dalzell, *George Washington's Mount Vernon: At Home in Revolutionary America* (New York: Oxford University Press, 1998), explores the complicated meanings of one building and its owner. Alfred F. Young and Terry J. Fife, *We the People: Voices and Images of the New Nation* (Philadelphia: Temple University Press, 1993), presents a rich display of objects and iconography.

Three other studies that speak in different ways to cultural development should also be noted. They are Jack P. Greene, "Search for Identity: An Interpretation of the Meaning of Selected Patterns of Social Response in Eighteenth-Century America," *Journal of Social History* 3 (1969–70), 189–221; Nathan O. Hatch, "The Christian Movement and the Demand for a Theology of the People," *JAH* 67 (1980–81), 545–67; and Stephen A. Marini, *Radical Sects of Revolutionary New England* (Cambridge, Mass.: Harvard University Press, 1982).

Study of experience, as opposed to consciousness and symbolic expression, has taken a number of directions. Some scholars have concentrated on familiar problems and major events, such as the independence crisis and the making and ratification of the Constitution. Among studies of the former are Benjamin Labaree, *The Boston Tea Party* (New York: Oxford University Press, 1964); David Ammerman, *In the Common Cause: American Response to the Coercive Acts of 1774* (Charlottesville: University Press of Virginia, 1974); Carl Bridenbaugh, *The Spirit of '76: The Growth of American Patriotism Before Independence* (New York: Oxford University Press, 1975); Thomas Flemming, *1776: Year of Illusion* (New York: W.W. Norton, 1975); Jack N. Rakove, "The Decision for American Independence: A Reconstruction," *Perspectives in American History* 10 (1976), 217–78; Maier, *American Scripture*; and Bushman, *King and People*. Among recent work on the latter, in addition to Wood, *Creation of the Republic*, and Pole, *Political Representation*, are Stephen R. Boyd, *The Politics of Opposition: Anti-Federalists and the Acceptance of the Constitution* (Millwood, N.Y.: KTO Press, 1979), and Linda Grant DePauw, *The Eleventh Pillar: New York State and the Federal Constitution* (Ithaca: Cornell University Press, 1966). Saul Cornell, *The Other Founders: Anti-Federalism and the Dissenting Tradition in America, 1788–1828* (Chapel Hill: University of North Carolina Press, 1999), supplants all previous studies.

Others have looked in different ways at the changing quality of political experience. For some, this has meant the study of the way in which ordinary people participated in the events of the Revolution, including crowds, revolutionary committees, political parties, and the military. For others, the emphasis is on the changing experience of different groups, such as artisans, farmers, black people, and women. Still others have created a remarkable collection of biographies of lesser leaders. Some studies have brought all these themes together.

Crowd action was a major topic of discussion in the late 1960s and the 1970s. Drawing on the work of European scholars such as George Rudé, E. P. Thompson, E. J. Hobsbawm, and Albert Soboul, a number of historians set out to place early American crowds in their eighteenth-century context and show how they became instruments of revolution. A debate was launched by Staughton Lynd in the essays now collected as *Class Conflict, Slavery and the Constitution* and by Jesse Lemisch in "The American Revolution Seen from the Bottom Up," in Barton J. Bernstein, ed., *Towards a New Past: Dissenting Essays in American History* (New York: Random House, 1968), together with Gordon S. Wood in "A Note on Mobs in the American Revolution," *WMQ* 23 (1966), 635–42. Pauline Maier made the first major statement in *From Resistance to Revolution: Colonial Radicals and the Development of American Opposition to Britain, 1765–1776* (New York: Alfred A. Knopf, 1972). By the time Dirk Hoerder published *Crowd Action in Revolutionary Massachusetts, 1765–1780* (New York: Academic Press, 1977), an extended literature had developed, of which Hoerder gives a full bibliography to that date (n. 19, pp. 5–7). The central debate has turned on whether crowds were means by which cohesive communities defended their established interests, which is the position of Maier and a number of other scholars, or whether they were the source of internal conflict. The state and community studies by Nash, Countryman, Ekirch, Bonomi, Holton, Kars, and Kim have all contributed to the debate. One major question has been the distinction between urban and rural crowds. The conflicting positions in the debate on country crowds are elaborated in Richard Maxwell Brown, "Back Country Rebellions and the Homestead Ethic in America, 1740–1799," in his anthology *Tradition, Conflict and Modernization*, and in Thomas L. Purvis, "Origins and Patterns of Agrarian Unrest in New Jersey, 1735 to 1754," *WMQ* 39 (1982), 600–27. Other significant pieces include James P. Whittenburg, "Planters, Merchants and Lawyers: Social Change and the Origins of the North Carolina Regulation," *WMQ* 34 (1977), 215–38; A. Roger Ekirch, "North Carolina Regulators on Liberty and Corruption, 1766–1771," *Perspectives in American History* 11 (1977–78), 199–258; and Edward Countryman, " 'Out of the Bounds of the Law': Northern Land Rioters in the Eighteenth Century," in Young, *The American Revolution*. More recent scholarship includes: Michael Bellesiles, *Revolutionary Outlaws: Ethan Allen and the Struggle for Independence on the Early American Frontier* (Charlottesville: University Press of Virginia, 1993); Paul A. Gilje, *The Road to Mobocracy: Popular Disorder in New York City, 1763–1834* (Chapel Hill: University of North Carolina Press, 1987); Robert A. Gross, ed., *In Debt to Shays: The Bicentennial of an Agrarian Rebellion* (Charlottesville: University Press of Virginia, 1993); Kars,

Breaking Loose Together; Brendan McConville, *Those Daring Disturbers of Peace: The Struggle for Property and Power in Early New Jersey* (Ithaca: Cornell University Press, 1999); Simon Newman and William Pencak, eds., *Riot and Revelry in Early America* (University Park: Pennsylvania State University Press, 2002); Barbara Clark Smith, "Food Rioters and the American Revolution," *WMQ* 51 (1994), 3–38; and Young, *The Shoemaker and the Tea Party*. For insights into the private worlds of ordinary people, see David W. Conroy, *In Public Houses: Drink and the Revolution of Authority in Colonial Massachusetts* (Chapel Hill: University of North Carolina Press, 1995), and Peter Thompson, *Rumpunch and Revolution: Tavern Going and Public Life in Eighteenth-Century Philadelphia* (Philadelphia: University of Pennsylvania Press, 1999).

Meanwhile historians were studying the popular committees of the independence crisis. Gordon Wood began the discussion in *The Creation of the American Republic*, and he was followed rapidly by Richard D. Brown in *Revolutionary Politics in Massachusetts: The Boston Committee of Correspondence and the Towns, 1772–1774* (Cambridge, Mass.: Harvard University Press, 1970). Richard Alan Ryerson provided an immensely detailed case study in *The Revolution Is Now Begun: The Radical Committees of Philadelphia, 1765–1776* (Philadelphia: University of Pennsylvania Press, 1978), and committees in New York constituted a central theme in Countryman's *A People in Revolution*.

A number of studies have focused on the development of political partisanship after independence. For colonial era precursors, see Alan Tully, *Forming American Politics: Ideals, Interests, and Institutions in Colonial New York and Pennsylvania* (Baltimore: Johns Hopkins University Press, 1994). For developments following independence, see Jackson Turner Main, *Political Parties Before the Constitution* (Chapel Hill: University of North Carolina Press, 1983), and H. James Henderson, *Political Parties in the Continental Congress* (New York: McGraw-Hill, 1974). Main's book should be read in conjunction with his *The Sovereign States, 1775–1783* (New York: New Viewpoints, 1973). Henderson's book should be balanced by Jack N. Rakove, *The Beginnings of National Politics: An Interpretive History of the Continental Congress* (New York: Alfred A. Knopf, 1979). Robert J. Dinkin contrasts the pre-independence and post-independence eras in two books: *Voting in Provincial America: A Study of Elections in the Thirteen Colonies, 1689–1776* (Westport, Conn.: Greenwood Press, 1977) and *Voting in Revolutionary America: A Study of Elections in the Original Thirteen States, 1776* (Westport, Conn.: Greenwood Press, 1982). Two books have explored the politics of taxation in the era: Dale W. Forsythe, *Taxation and Political Change in the Young Nation, 1781–1833* (New York: Columbia University Press, 1977), and Robert A. Becker, *Revolution, Reform and the Politics of American Taxation, 1763–1783* (Baton Rouge: Louisiana State University Press, 1980). For state-level partisan culture in one contentious place, see Robert Zemsky, *Merchants, Farmers and River Gods: An Essay on Eighteenth-Century American Politics* (Boston: Gambit, 1971); Ronald P. Formisano, *The Transformation of Political Culture: Massachusetts Parties, 1790s–1840s* (New York: Oxford University Press, 1983); Stephen E. Patterson, *Political Parties in Revolutionary Massachusetts* (Madison: University of Wisconsin Press, 1973); and Van Beck Hall, *Politics Without Parties: Massachusetts, 1780–1791* (Pittsburgh: University of Pittsburgh Press, 1972). Despite Linda Grant DePauw's assertion in *The Eleventh Pillar* that New York was consensual and nonpartisan at the time of the ratification struggle, it is clear that the state was deeply divided. See Alfred F. Young, *The Democratic-Republicans of New York: The Origins, 1763–1797* (Chapel Hill: University of North Carolina Press, 1967), and Countryman, *A People in Revolution*, chapters 7–10. There is an enormous debate on the struggle in Pennsylvania between Constitutionalists and Republicans. The most sophisticated statement is Richard Alan Ryerson, "Republican Theory and Partisan Reality in Revolutionary Pennsylvania: Toward a New View of the Constitutionalist Party," in Hoffman and Albert, eds., *Sovereign States in an Age of Uncertainty*. The emergence of partisanship farther south is the subject of Norman K. Risjord and Gordon Den Boer, "The Evolution of Political Parties in Virginia, 1782–1800," *JAH* 60 (1973–74), 961–84, and Norman K. Risjord, *Chesapeake Politics, 1781–1800* (New York: Columbia University Press, 1978), and is touched upon in such state studies as Hoffman, *A Spirit of Dissension*; Isaac, *The Transformation of Virginia*; and Nadelhaft, *The Disorders of War*.

Staughton Lynd and Alfred F. Young launched the contemporary study of working people in the revolutionary era with their paired works, published with a jointly written introduction as "After Carl Becker: The Mechanics and New York City Politics, 1774–1801," *Labor History* 5 (1964), 215–76. Among the books and essays that have appeared since then are: Roger Champagne, "Liberty Boys and Mechanics of New York City, 1764–1774," *Labor History* 8 (1967), 115–35; Philip S. Foner, *Labor and the American Revolution* (Westport, Conn.: Greenwood Press, 1977); James H. Hutson, "An Investigation of the Inarticulate: Philadelphia's White Oaks," *WMQ* 28 (1971), 3–25; Jesse Lemisch, "Jack Tar in the Streets: Merchant Seamen in the Politics of Revolutionary America," *WMQ* 25 (1968), 371–407; Charles S. Olton, *Artisans for Independence: Philadelphia Mechanics and the American Revolution* (Syracuse, N.Y.: Syracuse University Press, 1975); Sharon V. Salinger, "Artisans, Journeymen and the Transformation of Labor in Late Eighteenth Century Philadelphia," *WMQ* 40

(1983), 62–84, and "Colonial Labor in Transition: The Decline of Indentured Servitude in Late Eighteenth Century Philadelphia," *Labor History* 22 (1981), 165–91; and Billy G. Smith, "The Material Lives of Laboring Philadelphians, 1750 to 1800," *WMQ* 38 (1981), 163–202. See also Sean Wilentz, *Chants Democratic: New York City and the Rise of the American Working Class, 1788–1850* (New York: Oxford University Press, 1984). Richard Walsh, *Charleston's Sons of Liberty: A Study of the Artisans, 1763–1789* (Columbia: University of South Carolina Press, 1959), is an older work. Working people and their problems form a recurrent theme in Nash's *The Urban Crucible* and in Hoerder's *Crowd Action in Massachusetts*.

Working people provided most of the recruits for the revolutionary army and navy. The most stimulating recent study of the war experience is John Shy's *A People Numerous and Armed: Reflections on the Military Struggle for American Independence* (New York: Oxford University Press, 1976). Firsthand recollections of serving in the ranks are gathered in John C. Dann, *The Revolution Remembered: Eyewitness Accounts of the War for Independence* (Chicago: University of Chicago Press, 1980), and in Jesse Lemisch, "Listening to the 'Inarticulate': William Widger's Dream and the Loyalties of American Revolutionary Seamen in British Prisons," *Journal of Social History* 3 (1969–70), 1–29. The fullest account of the war is still Piers Mackesy, *The War for America, 1775–1783* (London: Longmans, 1964). Also significant are Robert Bray and Paul Bushnell, eds., *Diary of a Common Soldier in the American Revolution, 1775–1783* (De Kalb: Northern Illinois University Press, 1978); Dann, *The Revolution Remembered*; Sylvia Frey, *The British Soldier in America: A Social History of Military Life in the Revolutionary Period* (Austin: University of Texas Press, 1981); Sung Bok Kim, "Impact of Class Relations and Warfare in the American Revolution: The New York Experience," *JAH* 69 (1982), 326–46; Richard H. Kohn, *Eagle and Sword: The Federalists and the Creation of the Military Establishment in America, 1783–1802* (New York: Free Press, 1975); Don Higginbotham, *The War of American Independence: Military Attitudes, Policies and Practice, 1763–1789* (New York: Macmillan, 1971); Howard H. Peckham, *The Toll of Independence: Engagements and Battle Casualties of the Revolution* (Chicago: University of Chicago Press, 1974); Hugh F. Rankin, *The North Carolina Continentals* (Chapel Hill: University of North Carolina Press, 1971); James Kirby Martin, *Benedict Arnold, Revolutionary Hero: An American Warrior Reconsidered* (New York: New York University Press, 1997); and Charles Royster, *"A Revolutionary People at War": The Continental Army and American Character, 1775–1783* (Chapel Hill: University of North Carolina Press, 1979). E. Wayne Carp, *To Starve the Army at Pleasure: Continental Army Administra-*

tion and American Political Culture, 1775–1783 (Chapel Hill: University of North Carolina Press, 1984), deals with the problem of supplies.

Although we know a great deal about the social structure of revolutionary rural America, we have very few direct studies of the experience and consciousness of ordinary farmers. What we do have concentrates almost exclusively on the North, especially New England. The most sophisticated statement is Richard L. Bushman, "Massachusetts Farmers and the Revolution," in Jellison, ed., *Society, Freedom and Conscience*. The same group is the subject of David Szatmary's *Shays' Rebellion: The Making of an Agrarian Insurrection* (Amherst: University of Massachusetts Press, 1980) and of Barbara Karsky's "Agrarian Radicalism in the Late Revolutionary Period (1780–1795)," in Angermann et al., eds., *New Wine in Old Skins*. The best description of the day-to-day life of northern farmers is Karsky's "Le Paysan américain et la terre à la fin du XVIIIe siècle," *Annales: Économies, Sociétés, Civilisations* (Nov./Dec. 1983), 1369–91. The early chapters in Mary Ryan's *Cradle of the Middle Class: The Family in Oneida County, New York, 1790–1865* (New York: Cambridge University Press, 1981) trace the experience of one group of postrevolutionary New England migrants, and her work can be compared with Jonathan Prude, *The Coming of Industrial Order: Town and Factory Life in Rural Massachusetts, 1810–1860* (New York: Cambridge University Press, 1983), and with Gross, *The Minutemen and Their World*. More recent studies include: Bellesiles, *Revolutionary Outlaws*; Robert A. Gross, ed., *In Debt to Shays: The Bicentennial of an Agrarian Rebellion* (Charlottesville: University Press of Virginia, 1993); Ray Raphael, *The First American Revolution: Before Lexington and Concord* (New York: New Press, 2002); Alan Taylor, *Liberty Men* and *William Cooper's Town: Power and Persuasion on the Frontier of the Early American Republic* (New York: Alfred A. Knopf, 1995); and Wermuth, *Rip Van Winkle's Neighbors*.

Two excellent books began the discussion of the differences that the Revolution made for women: Mary Beth Norton, *Liberty's Daughters: The Revolutionary Experience of American Women, 1750–1800* (Boston: Little, Brown, 1980), and Linda K. Kerber, *Women of the Republic: Intellect and Ideology in Revolutionary America* (Chapel Hill: University of North Carolina Press, 1980). Important studies since then have included Branson, *Those Fiery, Frenchified Dames*; Joy Day Buel and Richard H. Buel, *The Way of Duty: A Woman and Her Family in Revolutionary America* (New York: W.W. Norton, 1984); Cathy N. Davidson, *Revolution and the Word: The Rise of the Novel in America* (New York: Oxford University Press, 1986); and Laurel Thatcher Ulrich, *A Midwife's Tale: The Life of Martha Ballard Based on Her Diary, 1785–1812* (New York: Alfred A. Knopf, 1990) and *The Age of Homespun: Objects and Stories in the Creation of an American Myth* (New York: Alfred A. Knopf, 2001), and Alfred F. Young's forthcoming study of the cross-dressing soldier Deborah Sampson/Robert Shurtleff, *Masquerade* (Boston: Beacon Press). On sexuality and gender in the era see Richard Godbeer, *Sexual Revolution in Early America* (Baltimore: Johns Hopkins University Press, 2002).

Study of the effect of the Revolution, and of slaves' effect on the Revolution, begins with Benjamin Quarels, *The Negro in the American Revolution* (Chapel Hill: University of North Carolina Press, 1961). The intellectual and cultural problems posed by slavery are explored in David Brion Davis, *The Problem of Slavery in the Age of Revolution, 1770–1823* (Ithaca: Cornell University Press, 1975), *Slavery and Human Progress* (New York: Oxford University Press, 1984), and *Revolutions: Reflections on American Equality and Foreign Liberations* (Cambridge, Mass.: Harvard University Press, 1990), which can be supplemented with Duncan MacLeod, *Slavery, Race and the American Revolution* (Cambridge, England: Cambridge University Press, 1974). Hoffman and Berlin, *Slavery and Freedom in the Age of the American Revolution*, pointed the way for work to come. Important books since then have included Sylvia Frey, *Water from the Rock: Black Resistance in a Revolutionary Age* (Princeton: Princeton University Press, 1991); Graham Russell Hodges, *Root and Branch: African-Americans in New York and East Jersey, 1613–1863* (Chapel Hill: University of North Carolina Press, 1999) and *Slavery and Freedom in the Rural North: African-Americans in Monmouth County, New Jersey, 1665–1865* (Madison, Wis.: Madison House, 1997); Sidney Kaplan and Emma Nogrady Kaplan, *The Black Presence in the Era of the American Revolution* (Amherst: University of Massachusetts Press, 1989); Nash, *Forging Freedom*; and Shane White, *Somewhat More Independent: The End of Slavery in New York City, 1770–1810* (Athens: University of Georgia Press, 1991).

Blacks who fled with the departing British constituted one sizable group of loyalists, and they are considered in James W. St. G. Walker, *The Black Loyalists: The Search for a Promised Land in Nova Scotia and Sierra Leone, 1783–1870* (New York: Holmes & Meier, 1976). Many other scholars have also written on loyalism. Their work includes studies of individuals, such as Bernard Bailyn, *The Ordeal of Thomas Hutchinson* (Cambridge, Mass.: Harvard University Press, 1974); Carol Berkin, *Jonathan Sewell: Odyssey of an American Loyalist* (New York: Columbia University Press, 1974); Isabel Thompson Kelsay, *Joseph Brant: Man of Two Worlds* (Syracuse, N.Y.: Syracuse University Press, 1984); William Pencak, *America's Burke: The Mind of Thomas Hutchinson* (Washington: University Press of America, 1982); and Anne Y. Zimmer, *Jonathan Boucher: Loyalist in Exile* (Detroit: Wayne State University Press, 1978). Janice

Potter explores the loyalist mind in *The Liberty We Seek: Loyalist Ideology in Colonial New York and Massachusetts* (Cambridge, Mass.: Harvard University Press, 1983). Robert McCluer Calhoon gives a synthesis in *The Loyalists in Revolutionary America, 1760–1781* (New York: Harcourt Brace Jovanovich, 1973), which is complemented by Mary Beth Norton, *The British-Americans: The Loyalist Exiles in England, 1774–1789* (Boston: Little, Brown, 1972). Ordinary loyalists figure prominently in Robert A. East and Jacob Judd, eds., *The Loyalist Americans: A Focus on Greater New York* (Tarrytown, N.Y.: Sleepy Hollow Restorations, 1975).

During the mid-twentieth century the major leaders of the Revolution were well served both by comprehensive collections of their papers and by multivolume biographies. Among the papers collected and published are those of Benjamin Franklin, ed. Leonard W. Labaree et al. (New Haven: Yale University Press, 1959); Alexander Hamilton, ed. Harold C. Syrett et al. (New York: Columbia University Press, 1961); Henry Laurens, ed. Philip Hamer et al. (Columbia: University of South Carolina Press, 1968); John Adams, ed. Lyman H. Butterfield et al. (Cambridge: Harvard University Press, 1962); Thomas Jefferson, ed. Julian T. Boyd et al. (Princeton: Princeton University Press, 1950); and James Madison, ed. William T. Hutchinson et al. (Chicago: University of Chicago Press, 1962). These collections are indispensable research tools, and carefully read, they tell about much else besides the life of the main subject. Among the major modern biographies are Irving Brant's of James Madison (Indianapolis: Bobbs-Merrill, 1941), with a one-volume synopsis; Dumas Malone's of Thomas Jefferson (Boston: Little, Brown, 1962); Douglas Southall Freeman's of George Washington (New York: Charles Scribner's Sons, 1948–57), with a one-volume abridgment by Richard Harwell (Scribner's, 1968); and Page Smith's of John Adams (New York: Doubleday, 1962–63).

The major gain in biographical work has been in the study of less prominent men and sometimes of very obscure men. Many books, theses, and essays have been produced; the following indicate the kind of work that is under way. Pauline Maier's account of *The Old Revolutionaries: Political Lives in the Age of Samuel Adams* (New York: Alfred A. Knopf, 1980) provides capsule studies of lesser-known radical leaders, such as Adams himself, Thomas Young, and Isaac Sears. Roger Champagne, *Alexander McDougall and the American Revolution in New York* (Schenectady, N.Y.: Union College Press, 1975); Stefan Bielinski, *Abraham Yates, Jr., and the New Political Order in Revolutionary New York* (Albany: New York State American Revolution Bicentennial Commission, 1975); and Ruth Bogin, *Abraham Clark and the Quest for Equality in the Revolutionary Era* (Rutherford, N.J.: Fairleigh Dickinson University Press, 1982), are excellent examples of illuminating studies of obscure leaders. Eric Foner, *Tom Paine and Revolutionary America*, is invaluable both for Paine himself and for the people among whom he lived. Perhaps most stimulating of all is Young, *The Shoemaker and the Tea Party*.

Finally come the studies of the Revolution's outcome and larger significance that have underpinned this rewriting. These include: David Waldstreicher, *In the Midst of Perpetual Fetes: the Making of American Nationalism, 1776–1820* (Chapel Hill: University of North Carolina Press, 1997); Simon P. Newton, *Parades and the Politics of the Street: Festive Culture in the Early American Republic* (Philadelphia: University of Pennsylvania Press, 1997); Loretta Valtz Mannucci, ed., *When the Shooting Is Over: The Order and the Memory* (Milan: Università degli Studii di Milano, 1996); Gordon S. Wood, *The Radicalism of the American Revolution* (New York: Alfred A. Knopf, 1992) and the 1994 *WMQ* forum that discussed it; and Young, *Beyond the American Revolution*. My speculations about Newtonian science and the Constitution are in debt to I. Bernard Cohen, *Science and the Founding Fathers: Science in the Political Thought of Jefferson, Franklin, Adams, and Madison* (New York: W.W. Norton, 1995). This edition's entire treatment expands on the ideas that I developed as "Indians, the Colonial Order, and the Social Significance of the American Revolution," and the criticisms by Michael Zuckerman, Sylvia Frey, and Philip Deloria that accompanied it in *WMQ* 53 (1996) and in my six-chapter contribution to Milton Klein, ed., *The Empire State: A History of New York State* (Ithaca: Cornell University Press, 2001).

Index

INDEX

267

Bushman, Richard, 25–26
Bute, Lord, 81, 104

Calhoun, John C., 157
Calhoun, Patrick, 157
Calvert family, 124
Cambridge University, 13, 30, 59
Canada, xvii, xx, 5, 31 43, 175, 208
Cannon, James, 123
Carnival, 28
Carroll, Charles, 125, 143, 146, 191
Carroll family, 26, 124
Carter family, 124
Catawba, 232
Catholics, 18, 23, 28, 30–31, 43, 110, ·124
"Cato," 56–57
Cayuga, 111, 207
charivari, 28
Charles I, King of England, 29, 95, 109
Charles II, King of England, 10
Charles Town (*later* Charleston), 156; commercial life in, 21–23; customs enforcement in, 52, 53; Sons of Liberty in, 94, 96; during war years, 205
chartered colonies, 9–10, 46, 172
Cherokee, xxi, 3, 16, 19, 153, 232; Republic of, 235
Chew, Captain Richard, 143
Cheyenne, 4
Chickasaw, 3
Chinese Revolution, xiv
Choctaw, 3, 207
Christianity, xxi, 53, 91–92, 129; evangelical, 114
Church, Benjamin, 101

cities: commercial life of, 21–25, 48; crowd actions in, 27–29, 69–72, 80–90; ethos of working people in, 27; refinement among elites in, 25–27; *see also specific cities*
civic liberty, 218
Civil War, 157, 226
Clinton, George, 11, 140, 144, 146, 163, 186, 193, 207
Clinton, Sir Henry, 153–55
Colden, Cadwallader, 16, 17, 82, 85–87, 96, 104
Columbia University, *see* King's College
Comanche, 4
Commission for Detecting and Defeating Conspiracies, 145
committee movement, 99, 107–9, 111, 113, 116, 138–42, 145–46, 160
Committee of Observation and Inspection, 142
Committee for Tarring and Feathering, 95, 138
common-law tradition, 55–56
Commons, John, 4, 117
Common Sense (Paine), 105–6, 122–23, 147, 230
composite monarchy, 12, 64
Concord, Battle of, 101–2, 133–36
Congregationalists, 78, 219
Congress, U.S., 167, 181, 194, 210, 216, 217; Indians and, 207; slavery and, 227; Vermont recognized by, 129; *see also* Continental Congress
Connecticut: boundaries of, 7, 172; colonial political authority in, 9, 51; creation of governmental institutions in, 152; and framing of Constitution, 179, 80; ratification